"An important contribution to understanding youth inequality in Europe, combining an ambitious, multi-dimensional theoretical framework, a critical discussion of EU policies, and concrete empirical knowledge from case studies of city neighbourhoods in ten countries. On the basis of experiences from the latter Stigendal also provides guidelines for local combats against inequality and exclusion."
Göran Therborn, author of The Killing Fields of Inequality, and of Cities of Power

"Mikael Stigendal makes a passionate plea to take young people serious in policies to combat inequality in European cities. After exposing the limits of policies that focus on problems and deficiencies, his potential-oriented approach offers rich empirical insights on initiatives and policies that empower young people in their cities and neighbourhoods."
Andreas Novy, Head of the Institute for Multi-Level Governance and Development, Vienna University of Economics and Busines

COMBATTING THE CAUSES OF INEQUALITY AFFECTING YOUNG PEOPLE ACROSS EUROPE

Inequality is one of the most burning issues of our time, affecting young people in particular. What causes inequality? And how can actors at the local level combat the causes, not only the symptoms? By seeking to answer these questions, the book will contribute to this growing and transdisciplinary subject area by using mainly qualitative research and a perspective that integrates theory in every phase of the analysis.

Drawing on cultural political economy, based on critical realism, the author claims that the most important causes of inequality are the ones inherent as potentials in capitalism and the capitalist type of state. Compared with the first post-war decades, these potential causes have been actualised differently since around 1980. They are also actualised differently across Europe. The book explores these differences concerning growth models and welfare regimes. In general, societies have developed into a new condition of social inclusion, which explains why many young people have become excluded. Societal borders have arisen in the cities, separating the winners and losers of inequality.

Positioning itself outside the box of what tends to be the majority of the publications in the field, the book proposes knowledge alliances between young people, policy-makers, civil society and researchers to combat the causes of inequality.

Mikael Stigendal is Professor in Sociology at Malmö University, Sweden. His doctoral thesis from 1994 dealt with the Swedish societal model, from a local perspective on Malmö. Thereafter, his research has highlighted the emergence of social exclusion in European cities, particularly regarding the situation for young people. In his explanations, he has explored how societies have developed into new conditions of social inclusion. Much of his research has been carried out interactively, in collaboration with municipal employees, voluntary workers and young people.

COMBATTING THE CAUSES OF INEQUALITY AFFECTING YOUNG PEOPLE ACROSS EUROPE

Mikael Stigendal

LONDON AND NEW YORK

First published 2018
by Routledge
2 Park Square, Milton Park, Abingdon, Oxon OX14 4RN

and by Routledge
711 Third Avenue, New York, NY 10017

Routledge is an imprint of the Taylor & Francis Group, an informa business

© 2018 Mikael Stigendal

The right of Mikael Stigendal to be identified as author of this work has been asserted in accordance with sections 77 and 78 of the Copyright, Designs and Patents Act 1988.

All rights reserved. No part of this book may be reprinted or reproduced or utilised in any form or by any electronic, mechanical, or other means, now known or hereafter invented, including photocopying and recording, or in any information storage or retrieval system, without permission in writing from the publishers.

Trademark notice: Product or corporate names may be trademarks or registered trademarks, and are used only for identification and explanation without intent to infringe.

British Library Cataloguing in Publication Data
A catalogue record for this book is available from the British Library

Library of Congress Cataloging in Publication Data
A catalogue record for this book has been requested.

ISBN: 978-0-415-78752-9 (hbk)
ISBN: 978-0-415-78753-6 (pbk)
ISBN: 978-1-315-22588-3 (ebk)

Typeset in Bembo
by Taylor & Francis Books

CONTENTS

List of figures   x
Preface   xi

1 Introduction   1

    1.1 The purpose of the book 2
    1.2 A broad and founded societal perspective 4
    1.3 Researching inequality 6
    1.4 Outline of the book 9

2 What is inequality?   12

    2.1 Income and exchange-value 14
    2.2 Labour power and use-value 17
    2.3 Housing and the value of it 20
    2.4 Unemployment – not taking part 23
    2.5 Working but unpaid 27
    2.6 Employed but on precarious conditions 28
    2.7 Conclusions: Inequalities – how many are there? 33

3 Why does inequality exist?   36

    3.1 Potential and actual causes 36
    3.2 Causes are inherent in social structures ... 39
    3.3 ... and also in contexts of meaning (cultures) 43
    3.4 Conclusions: So who and what causes inequality? 45

4 Systemic causes of inequality   47

   4.1 Causes inherent in capitalism 47
   4.2 Causes inherent in the state 58
   4.3 Conclusions: Five systemic causes of inequality 61

5 From decreasing to increasing inequality   63

   5.1 Those were the more equal days 63
   5.2 The neoliberal revolution 72
   5.3 But also other ways 78
   5.4 Conclusions: Neoliberal constraints but also new opportunities 80

6 Financialised economies   82

   6.1 Dependent financialisation in the south 83
   6.2 Superior export-orientation in the centre 87
   6.3 Dependent export-orientation and financialisation in the east 91
   6.4 Superior financialisation in the west 92
   6.5 Export-orientation and financialisation in the north 95
   6.6 Conclusions: Diverging economic contexts 97

7 Austerity and individualisation   99

   7.1 The conservatives and their "misérables" in the centre 100
   7.2 The liberals and their obstacles to economic growth in the west 102
   7.3 The constant transitions in the east 104
   7.4 The reliance on the family in the south 106
   7.5 The social democratic hesitancy in the north 110
   7.6 Conclusions: Converging welfare provisions 113

8 Inequalities in the cities   116

   8.1 The polarisation between exclusion and inclusion 116
   8.2 Societal causes of social exclusion 122
   8.3 New societal borders 128
   8.4 The making of the new societal borders 142
   8.5 Conclusions: The new societal borders belong to the neoliberal societal model 146

9 Combatting inequality   149

   9.1 Current EU policies 150
   9.2 The urgent need for societal transformations 151

9.3 Transformative social innovations 152
9.4 Conclusions: Five success criteria 161

10 Concluding summary   164

Bibliography   *167*
Index   *178*

LIST OF FIGURES

2.1	People at risk of poverty, 15–29 years and total population, 2013	14
2.2	Severe material deprivation of young people, 15–29 years	15
2.3	Early leavers from education and training, 18–24 years	18
2.4	Young people (20–24 years) having completed at least upper secondary education	19
2.5	Youth unemployment rate, 15–29 years	24
2.6	Youth unemployment ratio, 15–29 years	25
2.7	Youth unemployment rate and ratio, 15–29 years (2014)	25
2.8	The long-term unemployment rate, 15–29 years	26
2.9	Young temporary employees, 20–29 years	32
8.1	Young people (15–24 years) not in employment, education or training (NEET)	120

PREFACE

The idea to write this book was born out of the EU funded-project Citispyce, ("Combatting Inequalities through Innovative Social Practices of and for Young People in Cities across Europe"). This project was devised against the backdrop of research, which had shown the disproportionate impact of the global economic crisis on young people across Europe and received funding from the European Union's Seventh Framework Programme (FP7/2007–2013) under grant agreement n° 320359. Lasting for three years from January 2013 to December 2015, Citispyce was coordinated by Aston University in Birmingham UK and involved 13 partner organisations from 10 cities in just as many countries across the EU: Athens, Barcelona, Birmingham, Brno, Hamburg, Krakow, Malmö, Rotterdam, Sofia and Venice.

Many researchers and practitioners from all these cities participated in Citispyce. Those that I had the most to do with were Helen Higson, Jill Robinson and Ajmal Hussain at Aston University in Birmingham; Olga Jubany, Berta Güell and Malin Roiha at Universitat de Barcelona; Simon Güentner, Louis-Henri Seukwa and Anne-Marie Gehrke at Hamburg University of Applied Sciences (HAW); Jonas Alwall and Martin Grander at Malmö University; Pia Hellberg Lannerheim at the City of Malmö; Tomáš Sirovátka and Jana Valkova at Masaryk University in Brno; Michał Możdżeń at Crakow University of Economics; Henk Spies and Suzanne Tan at PlusConfidence in Rotterdam; Marko Hajdinjak and Maya Kosseva at International Centre for Minority Studies and Intercultural Relations (IMIR); Maria Pothoulaki and Pyrros Papadimitriou at Kendro Merimnas Oikoyenias Kai Pediou (KMOP) in Athens; and Francesca Campomori and Francesco Della Puppa at Università Ca' Foscari Venezia. Thanks to all of you for some great, rewarding and enjoyable years.

The Citispyce work at the local level in Malmö has also been very beneficial for the writing of this book. During the first year we cooperated with people associated with Sofielunds Folkets Hus, in particular Håkan Larsson, Göte Rudvall, Jessica Hultzén and Fredrik Björk. Many students from the course in Urban Integration at Malmö University produced case studies linked to Citispyce. Thereafter, we linked Citispyce to an ESF-funded project, where I worked together with Alexandra Fritzson, Mikael Sandgren, Lina Gustafsson and Alison Mendez from Rädda barnen (Save the Children); Elin Dagerbo and Ingemar Holm from Centrum för Publikt Entreprenörskap (Centre for Public Entrepreneurship), Maria Lagneby and Christoph Lukkerz from Nätverk Idéburen sektor Skåne, Mattias Larsson from Länsstyrelsen (now manager of Nätverket), Helena Thelander from Hållbar Utveckling Skåne (Sustainable Development Skåne), Eva Lidmark from PWC and Tom Roodro from the City of Malmö. Many thanks to all of you.

During the years with Citispyce, I also participated in other international initiatives which were beneficial for this book; one of them being EuroMemo Group; another one the FP7-funded project Improve; and also the work led by Ngai-Ling Sum and Bob Jessop to establish Cultural Political Economy as an emerging approach. I am particularly grateful to Bob Jessop for all the very important discussions we have had since the late 1980s.

Some colleagues have spent their precious time in reading draft versions of the book and provided me with important feedback. These include Martin Grander and Jonas Alwall, with both of whom I have worked in Citispyce on an almost daily basis for three years; Andreas Novy, whom I got to know almost ten years ago in the context of the FP7-funded project Social Polis and since then we have had an ongoing dialogue, intensified during the last years due to our involvement in two similar and parallel projects, he in Improve and me in Citispyce; and Helen Higson, who encouraged me to write this book. It also includes my dear old friend Göte Rudvall, one of the founding fathers in the 1950s of the Swedish comprehensive school, with whom I have worked on several projects, and who has supported me for so many years and, in his very wise way, so also in Citispyce and the writing of this book; and Jill Robinson, who with a tremendous generosity, kindness and patience has supported me until the very completion of the book. My sincere thanks to you all.

How could I go astray and make mistakes in such a favourable environment? Well, of course I could. Just as we all make our own history, so it then becomes imprinted by our shortcomings as well as our merits. Thus, for any shortcomings in the book, I alone am responsible.

Still, there are a few more people to mention: first of all, the one who I have discussed it all with, who has had to cope with all my ups and downs and that is my wife Kerstin, a big hug to you; and also to my two sons, Fredrik and Johan, who, both working as teachers, have shown a great deal of ingenuity in empowering young people, to my great pride; warmest hugs also to my two granddaughters, Sibelle and Elissa, who have their youth in front of them. What the future holds for them, obviously, I do not know, but the prospects worry me. It is my sincere hope, therefore, that the five criteria of transformative social innovations that I propose in the final chapter will be fulfilled also by this book and that it thereby will contribute to the societal transformation that is so much needed in Europe today.

Malmö in July 2017
Mikael Stigendal

1
INTRODUCTION

Inequality has vastly increased since the advent of the financial crisis in 2008. Young people have been highlighted as one of most affected categories. Because of this predicament, the European Council endorsed in 2009 a renewed framework for European cooperation in the youth field (2010–2018), also known as the *EU Youth Strategy*. The work has been divided into three-year cycles, each one ending with a European Union (EU) *Youth Report* drawn up by the Commission. The last report from 2015 shows some positive trends in the field of education during the last years, but the general picture continues to look gloomy as "many young Europeans are facing serious threats such as marginalisation in the labour market, deterioration of living conditions, and obstacles to social integration and political participation" (European Commission, 2016a: 158).

According to the report, employment has become more difficult for young people to find and also to retain, and, "when a job is secured, the risk of being overqualified is high for many young graduates. Unemployment, including long-term unemployment, has continued to rise amongst the young …" (European Commission, 2016a: 158). Furthermore, material deprivation rates have gone up and it has become increasingly difficult for many young people to meet their housing costs. As a consequence, overcrowding has risen in many EU Member States. The report contains a lot of interesting indicators on what seem to be the problems but not a trace of any causes; it restricts itself to the symptoms. Therefore, the youth policy presented in the first part of the report cannot deal with much more than symptoms. What else could it tackle due to the missing knowledge on the causes?

In contrast, this book sets out to identify the causes and one of them is inherent in precisely this limited approach to the symptoms. The *EU Youth Report* represents this latter approach, problem-oriented as I will call it, in contrast to the potential-oriented approach that this book represents, and as the *Youth Report* makes the reader look upon the symptoms as the main problems, it shows that not only the problems themselves but also how you perceive and define them can be problematic. If policymakers really want to solve the severe problems affecting many young people across Europe, the causes have to be combatted in the first place. To identify these causes and suggest how actors at the local level can combat them is the purpose of the book. Whilst I do not object to those who put the blame on neoliberalism in recent decades, I would claim that the causes are deeper than that. They are inherent in the way contemporary societies work.

I will start in this introduction by explaining the purpose of the book. It has a special relationship to the EU-project Citispyce, where I collaborated during 2013–16 with researchers and practitioners in ten European cities across the EU: Athens, Barcelona, Birmingham, Brno, Hamburg, Krakow, Malmö, Rotterdam, Sofia and Venice. Without Citispyce, it would not have been possible to write it. Furthermore, the book is based on more than thirty years work on a societal perspective, which in recent years I have been inspired to call Cultural Political Economy (CPE). This will be presented in the second section, but only briefly because it runs through the book and will be explained in more detail in many places.

The third section of this introduction dwells on the possibilities of undertaking this kind of research. It could run the risk of further stigmatising disadvantaged young people and neighbourhoods. I will explain, however, how that risk could be dealt with by adopting an approach to knowledge which recognises that even young people can be knowledgeable and, thus, should be treated as subjects in their own right. Such an approach to knowledge is inherent in my interpretation of Cultural Political Economy, founded as it is in critical realism. Finally, in the fourth section, I will present and explain the outline of the book.

1.1 The purpose of the book

During the course of the Citispyce project, every team produced reports on their cities and the situation of young people from national and local government perspectives together with those of NGOs and 'experts' working at the neighbourhood level as well as from disadvantaged young people themselves. All of these reports from across Europe display effects of the political project known as neoliberalism (see chapter 5.2), most obvious in the reports on Birmingham and the cities in Eastern as well as Southern Europe. Furthermore, neoliberalism appears in the far-reaching labour market reforms in Germany, driven by the principles of activation and workfare. It has put a decisive imprint on the transition of the Dutch welfare state. Neoliberalism shows itself clearly in the austerity measures pursued with the intention to "solve" the crisis, for example the excessive use of fixed-term contracts for young people. In the sense of being increasingly imprinted by neoliberalism, European societies have converged.

Neoliberalism has had an uneven impact but yet been very successful across Europe. A major reason for this success is that finance capital has become its main beneficiary. The political project of neoliberalism has made the European economies in general more financialised. The Euro has been crucial in the neoliberal project, urging the member states to strengthen competitiveness by increasing flexibility as well as promoting temporary and part-time work. All Eurozone countries have joined this race to the bottom and the race has been won by Germany. Because of that race, countries across Europe have diverged over the last years.

These patterns were clearly expressed in reports from Citispyce and identified as effects of different growth models in Europe. On that basis, we have seen how the growth model of dependent financialisation in the south of Europe has made young people with a job particularly vulnerable due to their employment in the most dependent sectors. We have seen some aspects of what is meant by the fact that labour markets with a low share of the type of organisation called discretionary learning do not tend to foster creative producers and demanding consumers. We have seen how labour markets with weak regulations make people unsecure. But we have also seen how highly regulated labour markets protect the ones included in them while making it difficult for young people without a formal education to get a job.

All the work in Citispyce – back and forth, up and down the levels of abstraction, and the turns between simplicity and complexity – has indeed reaffirmed the validity of the method known as retroduction, associated with critical realism, i.e. the philosophy of science which guides the book (see for example Sayer, 2000; Danermark, 2002; Jessop, 2015a: 240). What is required in research, as Moulaert et al. (2016: 179) put it, is a "reflexive spiral movement, which is typical of critical realist analysis, between meta-theoretical, theoretical, and empirical analysis, refining conceptual entry points in the light of substantive findings and deepening, widening, and modifying the empirical analysis in the light of the developing heuristic model in its articulation to specific middle-range theories." The purpose of this book is to take this very fruitful and rewarding spiral movement further.

Citispyce resulted in a rich material. In all the cities, two urban areas and the services provided for young people in them were studied in more detail. Many young people were interviewed on their life situation in more general terms. The Citispyce researchers in Venice (Della Puppa & Campomori, 2014: 7) give a beautiful glimpse into how such interviews could be carried out:

> As long as we interviewed him, trying to transform it in an informal chat, sitting in the cement and with a hexis corporelle as similar as possible to that of the respondents – they perceived us like figures close to the street educators which gave us their contacts and with whom they have a relationship of trust – some other guys approached us with curiosity, listening and sometimes speaking, sometimes standing in silence. Giovanni and Luca, they talked freewheeling solicited by our questions and, meanwhile, they were rolling joints and sharing with the others. However they appeared lucid and centred on the topic of the interview, but I started to ask myself how to preserve their confidence and their trust even in the case they would offer us to smoke. This did

not happen: they felt the need to respect the border of our positioning. The interview continued while, around us, the darkness was falling and the humidity of the evening rising.

Pilot projects and case studies were carried out in order to identify socially innovative practices. Parts of this rich empirical material have been used and analysed in a number of reports and articles. In this book, I intend to build further on all these efforts but its main purpose is to explain what actors at the local level can do not just to alleviate the symptoms of inequality, but to combat its causes.

1.2 A broad and founded societal perspective

This purpose has to be put in perspective and mine is a broad one. Once upon a time, broad societal perspectives belonged to the mainstream. Scholars like Adam Smith and David Ricardo called their science political economy. These classical political economists did not lock themselves into academic disciplines. In contrast, political economy was regarded by these and other polymaths "as the integrated study of economic organization and wealth creation, good government and good governance, and moral economy (including language, culture and ethical issues)" (Sum & Jessop, 2013: 16). Classical political economy took for granted the dependence of society and science on values. These political economists were driven by what C. Wright Mills called the sociological vision (1959). They did not treat method or theory as independent areas but as interrelated.

In contrast to such aspirations, a fragmentation of social science emerged in the latter part of the 19th century, much driven by the establishment of neoclassical economics, which I will address further in chapter 5.2. In recent decades, such a further fragmentation has made it increasingly difficult to understand social phenomena in their societal contexts.

An alternative to this fragmentation is the broad societal perspective called Cultural Political Economy (CPE), represented in particular by Ngai-Ling Sum and Bob Jessop (2013). It could be seen as a response to the so-called cultural turn in social science of the last few decades that was instigated in the 1980s, above all by Ernesto Laclau and Chantal Mouffe (1985). This cultural turn was in itself a response to the structuralism of the 1960s and 70s.

Another response to the crisis of structuralism was the philosophy of science developed around the same time, called critical realism, proposed in particular by Roy Bhaskar (Bhaskar, 1975, 1989; Sayer, 1992, 2000), and which underpins CPE philosophically. With the support of critical realism, we can distinguish between potential and actual causes of inequality as well as its forms of appearance. What appears to be happening constitutes only a part of reality, referred to as the empirical. Using an expression from Liedman (2006, 2015), who in his turn draws on Hegel, we could also refer to this as the surface forms of reality. The empirical – the surface forms – expresses a content which critical realism calls the actual, meaning that which actually happens. But what critical realism calls the real also includes the potentials.[1] To give but one example: young refugees may possess knowledge which thereby exists in its potential, but which cannot be actualised if society does not recognise it due to, for example, the grading system.

Similar philosophical ideas informed regulation theory, initiated by Michel Aglietta and others in the 1970s and 80s (Aglietta, 1987). Aglietta emphasised regulation theory as an alternative to the neoclassical theory of general equilibrium, a theory which was recently effectively shredded by Thomas Piketty (2014). Aglietta argued that the concepts of subject and condition should be replaced by relation and process as part of the bedrock of economics. Through critical realism, the foundation was laid for CPE. With regulation theory, the E was put in its place. On the same ground, the P has been developed, particularly by Bob Jessop's work on state theory, inspired, in turn, particularly by Gramsci and Poulanzas (Jessop, 2002; 2015b).

In recent years, the C in CPE has been put in place by the work of Ngai-Ling Sum and Bob Jessop (2013). Culture should not be seen as a separate part of a whole but as interacting and interwoven with social structures. CPE places culture and structures on an equal ontological footing. Reality is always more or less complex, and in order to be able to 'go on' – e.g. to be able to know what to do, what to decide, take the next step, how to act or to form an opinion – this complexity needs to be reduced. Two modes of reducing complexity exist: making sense and meaning of, as well as structuring, social relations. Basically, social science is about exploring how and in what forms actors simplify this natural and social complexity (Moulaert et al., 2016: 176).

The understanding of the first mode of complexity reduction is based on the theory of semiosis, because, in essence, it is a matter of signs (which according to Umberto Eco is "everything which can be taken as significantly substituting for something else" (quoted in Sum & Jessop, 2013: 24)). CPE highlights semiosis as an umbrella concept for many and diverse forms of sense- and meaning-making, one of them being culture. Yet, despite this subordination, the term culture has been used to label the CPE perspective. That is because the perspective has been developed in response to the cultural turn and the term culture seems easier to grasp and use than semiosis.

Both cultures and structures have to be made by actors. Otherwise they would not exist. I will return to what that means in chapter 3.1 but here only highlight actors and agency, as an essential concept, alongside structures and cultures (Brante, 2015: 249). Actors may make a difference due to their capacity for strategic calculation and action. There is always a discretion, by which I mean the scope that "exists for actions to overwhelm, circumvent, or subvert structural constraints" (Jessop, 2016: 55). The concept of discretion deals with the changing 'art of the possible'. I will explain this further in chapter 3.2.

1.3 Researching inequality

Researchers can be quite insensitive to how the choice of words, expressions, styles and modes of explanations may exclude those who are not initiated. That is certainly the risk with a highly theoretical perspective like CPE. It can easily give the impression of being a concern for just a small group of the highly educated. The use of such a mode of communication may become particularly detrimental in research on inequality. It may run the risk of actually aggravating inequality by further stigmatising the ones affected by it. That is also the case when the research focuses solely on this so-called losing-side of inequality. In contrast, this book pursues a relational definition of inequality, which treats it as a difference between two sides: winners and losers. The book deals with both sides.

Inequality might also be aggravated if the research treats the ones affected by inequality only as objects, as if they have nothing to contribute. In contrast, I have in many research projects worked together with the ones concerned by inequality, both those affected by it and those who try to manage the consequences of it, employed by the local council or volunteers in civil society. This book is imprinted by such an approach: potential-oriented as I call it.

It is my firm belief that young people have a lot of potential. The main problem of inequality is the inability of societies to take advantage of this potential. Young people have a lot of experience but also knowledge. Some of this knowledge has not been learnt in school but through interaction with peers, often by using social media and the internet. Sometimes this kind of knowledge is called informal, as it has not been graded and thus recognised formally. People who work with young people also have a lot of knowledge.

But can this really be called knowledge many would probably ask. The answer depends on how we view knowledge; what we mean by it. This is a profoundly important topic which a CPE perspective based on critical realism can have a lot to say about. Exploring this paves the way for an understanding of CPE as something more than a perspective and to call it an approach or a paradigm seems therefore more appropriate. The space in this book, however, is not sufficient for me to go into depth in these matters, so I shall make some crucial remarks in brief (see also Sayer, 1992: 13ff).

Firstly, knowledge should be seen as a context of meaning in which the terms take on meaning through their relationship to each other (Sayer, 1992: 56). It makes sense and meaning of something and that something can be called its referent object. By making sense and meaning of that referent object, knowledge constitutes a reference object. These two objects should not be confused, due to the insurmountable gap between them (Sayer, 1992: 47; Liedman, 2015: 41, 401). As a reference object, knowledge is always something other than what it concerns and refers to: its referent object.

Using inequality as an example, it intrudes on us empirically and provides us with referent objects in the shape, for example, of what we ourselves experience; stories we hear; reports we read; or pictures we see on the TV. We need to make sense of this complexity in order to express an opinion or perhaps do something about it. The sense we make of it, for example my attempt here in this book, is a reference object; i.e. something which refers to the referent objects (see also, for example Moulaert et al., 2016: 175).

Secondly, this sense-making is particularly demanding regarding knowledge which, therefore, should be seen as an act of production. Thus, knowledge does not exist by itself but has to be produced. Just as any other human activity, this production takes place in socio-spatial contexts, characterised by social relations and various forms of meaning. This concerns all knowledge on inequality, which, thus, has been produced, regardless of whether it appears in books, lectures, debates, politics or in the behaviour of council employees supporting young people facing inequality. Hence, it is imprinted by human incompleteness and is neither unquestionable nor final. Neither experience nor information is the same as knowledge although either one of them may become an important starting point for the production of knowledge. In order to become knowledge, experience and information have to be worked upon.

Thirdly, to make sense of this knowledge, we need to make it our own personal knowledge and that requires work as well. Therefore, learning cannot be achieved passively (see also Sayer, 1992: 52). It matters also in what context it takes place. If we succeed, knowledge becomes a reference object for us. We then understand what it is about, i.e. its referent object.

Fourthly, knowledge does not just take shape in the mind but also in the body. Such an approach appears in the *Swedish national Curriculum for the Compulsory School, Preschool Class and the Recreation Centre 2011*, which states that knowledge …

> … can be expressed in a variety of forms – as facts, understanding, skills, familiarity and accumulated experience – all of which presuppose and interact with each other. The work of the school must therefore focus on providing scope for expressing these different forms of knowledge, as well as creating a learning process where these forms are balanced to form a meaningful whole.
> (Skolverket, 2011: 12)

In Swedish, the name of each one of these four forms starts with an f and therefore they are called the four f's (fakta, förståelse, färdighet, förtrogenhet). To underline their character as knowledge they are all called knowledge in Swedish. To make the same point in English, they should perhaps be called factual, interpretative, skilled and tacit knowledge, respectively. I will return to these four 'fs' later when I claim that another approach to knowledge has become one of the major causes of inequality (see chapter 5.2).

The approach to knowledge represented in this book, however, inspired by critical realism and summarised in the four points above, enables us to understand that young people have a lot of experience, which in principle may be just as valid as, for example, statistics. Thus, researchers working together with young people, treating them as subjects, may get access to a wealth of experience, which is there to be processed into knowledge. Indeed, young people usually possess knowledge as well (potentials), in the form, for example, called tacit knowledge. For it to be shared, it first of all has to be actualised and made explicit, which could be done if young people and researchers had a chance to work together. Favourable social contexts and arenas need to be set up where researchers, young people and practitioners are allowed to take part and can be respected also on other grounds than their professional merits, for example owing to their consideration for others, sense of humour, values, etc.

The production of scientific knowledge requires a lot of creativity, which may be stimulated by other kinds of reference objects such as pictures and narratives. Another aspect of creativity is spurred on by questions from the outside. Indeed, as researchers we may benefit from being questioned by others and forced to explain ourselves using other means of expression than the typical ones in the scientific community. Such questions can make us aware of semiotic moments unconsciously incorporated in our scientific discourse. Involving practitioners in research could help, as Miciukiewicz et al., (2012: 1860) express it, the "sliding away towards idiosyncratic research attitudes".

The kind of research that this book represents and indeed builds on can be called interactive. Svensson et al. (2007) mention equal participation and shared learning as characteristics of interactive research. Moreover, the knowledge produced should "be of practical relevance and of a high scientific standard." (Svensson et al., 2007: 236) By interactive research, Svensson and co-authors mean a development of action research. The ambition to establish equal and mutually advantageous relationships between researchers and stakeholders is common to action research and interactive research, but "in action research these relations are based primarily on the researchers contributing to practical development and to a lesser degree on the participants contributing to the theoretical work" (2007: 239).

Equal and mutually advantageous relationships between researchers and non-researchers, good for both parties, is precisely what I have tried to develop over the years in many projects. I have done that by finding out what different groups could contribute to the research; what additional training they need to be able to help with that; how their participation can evoke a desire for continued learning. It then requires that researchers develop a special knowledge. As Svensson et al. (2007: 243) write about interactive research, "it demands a broad range of knowledge on the part of the researchers and is more work-intensive for both the researchers and the participants – in terms of data collection, dialogue, meetings, feedback, etc. – compared to traditional academic research".

This is the approach we took when working locally in Malmö with Citispyce and I will explain how in the final chapter where collaborations with young people and practitioners in so-called knowledge alliances will be presented as a criterion of success. Here I want to underline the importance of such collaborations in the achievements to make research not only relevant but also excellent. Excellence and relevance go hand in hand. Research is namely interference. No matter how you carry it out, you interfere in reality. You may pretend that you do not interfere, but simply by approaching people you make them think and react, perhaps with the effect that it becomes more difficult to access what you want to know. As a researcher, you often cannot get hold of what you want to know. And when you do get hold of it, you realise perhaps that this is not what you want to know. Thus, you may as well instead interfere deliberately, pay attention to what happens and try to be pleased with what you perceive; whatever this is, it has to be treated critically and interpreted. This is what we have done in Citispyce. We have stirred things up to see what comes down: how and in what shape. We have grabbed the opportunities to see how we could make use of them.

1.4 Outline of the book

The purpose of this book is to explain what actors at the local level can do, not just to alleviate the symptoms of inequality, but to combat its causes. To explain that, we need to know what a cause is but, before I go into details about that, I will in chapter 2 deal with the explanandum (the phenomenon that is to be explained), namely inequality: what should it mean and how does it appear? In chapter 3, I will explain the important distinction between potential and actual causes. According to critical realism, the concept of cause refers, first of all, to what an object is like and can do, regardless of whether it actually does it. I show how causes can be inherent in structures, cultures and actors, therefore also in societal systems.

Before we then can proceed to explain what has actually caused inequality, we need to know what has the potential to cause it. What in the main societal systems can cause inequality? This is the question that guides chapter 4, where I highlight five complex potential causes of inequality that are inherent in the capitalist economy and the capitalist type of state. For that reason, they should also be treated as systemic. These systemic causes have been part of western societies for a long time but they have been actualised differently. That explains the difference between "Les Trente Glorieuses" after the Second World War and the decades since around 1980. In the first period, inequality actually decreased, while it has been on the increase in most of the developed capitalist world since then. Chapter 5 explains why, but also what instigated the shift, namely the political project called neoliberalism. It can be defined with regard to three principles, but its strength also depends on the foundation in neoclassical economics. Those who use the concept of social capital contribute to reproducing it, I will claim.

In its first principle, neoliberalism urges extending competitive market forces by deregulations and privatisations. This has favoured finance capital and the financialisation of economies, which are covered in chapter 6. This chapter shows that financialisation has been actualised differently across Europe due to the existence of different growth models. In its second principle, neoliberalism urges consolidation of a market-friendly constitution by strengthening the surveillance, controlling and repressive functions of the state, while at the same time cutting down on welfare.

As its third principle, neoliberalism promotes individual freedom but on the basis of "economic man". These latter two principles have been actualised differently across Europe due to the existence of different welfare regimes as discussed in chapter 7.

The causes of inequality actualised by the financialisation of the economies, retrenchment of the welfare states and an outlook on people which 'blames the victims' have turned society into a condition of social inclusion. That explains the emergence of social exclusion. To the extent that this division between being included and being excluded coincides with segregation, societal borders exist in the cities. Chapter 8 explains what this means. It associates the causes of these borders with, firstly, processes of getting excluded and, secondly, the conditions for getting included. Such causes depend on how the particular society works. And it does work, but only to the extent that different actors reproduce it. That makes many actors contribute to inequality in their different roles, whether they know about it or not.

In order to show how this reproduction occurs, three societal models are identified on the basis of the previous chapters. The concepts of these models, carefully synthesising the outcome from previous chapters to avoid eclecticism (see also Moulaert et al., 2016: 173), deal with the potentials for a society to become quite stable and coherent. In two of these models, inequality belongs to the normal. That is not the case with the third model, the one which in many of its moments have been actualised in Sweden. By drawing on our research from Citispyce, I will show how Swedish society, as it exists in Malmö, is in a process of transformation towards another one of the societal models, the neoliberal. In our research, we have seen how different actors make that happen.

Finally, chapter 9 seeks to answer the book's question on what actors at the local level can do to combat the causes of inequality. Often, such efforts are being considered as directed towards the national or even the EU scale levels. That is of course very important, but if we want society to be transformed in a way which removes the causes of inequality, efforts made at the local level are also crucial. On the basis of all the case studies produced in Citispyce of local initiative, I propose five criteria which should characterise local initiatives with the intention not only to tackle the symptoms, but in the first place, to combat the causes of inequality.

All the examples and concrete sources of inspirations used in the book stem from the cities studied in the EU-project Citispyce: Athens, Barcelona, Birmingham, Brno, Hamburg, Krakow, Malmö, Rotterdam, Sofia and Venice. That covers the south and north as well as the east and west of Europe. All of them used to be major industrial cities that have then gone through difficult processes of transformation. All of them are either national or regional capital cities. In these senses, they are similar. My intention in this book is not to compare the cities per se and thus they will not be presented. The neighbourhoods that were selected in each city, however, will be presented but spread out in the book in places where they can provide illustrations or reasons for reflections. Likewise, the voices of young people from the ten cities will be heard in many places throughout the book.

Note

1 I have been told by native English-speaking persons that potential does not exist in the plural form in English. For that reason, I checked in Sum & Jessop (2013) to see if they used it in the plural form and they do, for example on page 9. Thus, the plural form might not be used in everyday language but it obviously exists in a scientific context.

2

WHAT IS INEQUALITY?

Inequality is "one of the most pressing issues of the day", Michael Burawoy, president of the International Sociological Association, said in his welcome address to the World Congress of Sociology in 2014 with the title "Facing an unequal world". The World Economic Forum, in its Global Risks Report 2017, ranks inequality first among the risks to the global economy and the underlying trends that will determine the shape of the world in the next decade.

As the OECD Secretary General Angel Gurria wrote in his editorial to the report *Divided we stand. Why inequality keeps rising* (OECD, 2011: 17), "inequality has become a universal concern, among both policy makers and societies at large". He then went on and mentioned the huge difference in incomes between the rich and poor. That is obviously an inequality, about which scholars like Anthony Atkinson, Branco Milanovic and Thomas Piketty (2014) have vastly expanded the empirical knowledge. Corresponding achievements have been made by epidemiologists like in particular Michael Marmot (2015) and Richard Wilkinson & Kate Picket (2009), focusing on inequality in terms of health (WHO, 2008). What have these inequalities in common? What makes them inequalities? What else is inequality? What should we mean by inequality?

First of all, inequality is a word; in itself it also has certain properties. Something exists which we have decided to call inequality and the name of it puts us on a certain track to an understanding of it. Similarly, the word poverty tends to direct us, but more narrowly, to focus on the poor. There is nothing inevitable in the word 'poverty' which makes us become interested in the rich. To be sure, our wider perspective may certainly motivate such an interest, but the single word poverty does not. You need to be thoughtful and as Tawney described it thoughtfully in the early 20th century "what thoughtful rich people call the problem of poverty, thoughtful poor people call with equal justice a problem of riches" (from Sayer, 2015: 29). Indeed, this lack of interest in the problem of riches is confirmed by the major part of research which has occupied itself solely with poverty and the poor. We could say that the word poverty has a potential, which, when we use and thus actualise it, tends to direct our attention towards the poor, although it does not constrain us to it.

The word inequality has another potential. It is not biased in directing us to either the poor or the rich. Instead, it could be said to highlight the relation between the two. This difference between poverty and inequality shows the non-neutral properties of words. They cannot be used for whatever purpose. Thus, we have to be careful about the choice of them. Yet this does not mean that the meaning of a word is fully predetermined. So far I have restricted myself to the properties of the words as signifiers. They signify something. For them to be able to do that, we have to fill them with meaning and thereby make them into concepts (Jessop, 2015a). In research, this means to define them, and that is very important.

In my definition of inequality, firstly, I want to stress this relational character; the one we cannot really escape from when we choose to use the word inequality. That accords with my wider perspective and understanding of society and the social world. This is also why I prefer to use the word inequality instead of poverty. For someone who wants to understand society as a multitude of social relations and not as consisting of independent individuals (see chapter 3.2), inequality seems to be a better word to use than poverty. The word inequality favours a relational understanding of society. To see it as a difference is important, because too often focus is put on only the latter of these poles; the losing side. Inequality is about both poles.[1]

For me, therefore, the word inequality signifies, first of all, a relation. That is part of the definition of it as a concept, i.e. the meaning of it and its content. Another word for that content is the signified. Inequality is, thus, both a signifier in the sense of a word and a signified in the sense of a concept. The signifier and the signified constitute together what I called in chapter 1.3 the reference object. In addition to these two, inequality is also that something which we refer to by using the word inequality (signifier) as a concept (signified): namely a referent object. These three aspects – the signifier, the signified and the referent – are characteristic of the philosophy of science, which this book builds on and to which I will return many times, called critical realism. There is something that may be referred to as inequality (referent object), but when we call it that, we have to make sure we define the word properly into a concept (reference object). That is what I intend to do in this chapter.

Thus, inequality is a relation, comprising at least two poles, like the one mentioned by OECD Secretary General Angel Gurria between the rich and poor. I subscribe to the general definition of inequality suggested by Amartya Sen (Therborn, 2013; Sayer, 2015: 344) as part of his 'capability approach'. On this basis, inequalities should be seen as differences, which violate the human rights of the disadvantaged (Therborn, 2013: 41). What differences can that be? This chapter answers the question by distinguishing between different types of inequality.

2.1 Income and exchange-value

When differences in incomes increase to the extent that they violate the human rights of the disadvantaged, it becomes an inequality. To be poor means that you do not have sufficient resources to participate in society (Therborn, 2013: 21). As Loïc Wacquant puts it in *Urban Outcasts* (2008: 30), it is a "curse of being poor in the midst of a rich society in which participation in the sphere of consumption has become a *sine qua non* of social dignity …". Such a difference can be understood as a particular form of inequality, called resource inequality. It expresses a relation between those who have and those who have not. The latter can for simplistic reasons be called the 'have-nots'.

How many young people are the have-nots in the ten Citispyce countries? What can we know about this? An indicator that measures the percentage of have-nots among young people is the at-risk-of-poverty rate. For this indicator, the population with income below a certain threshold is regarded as being at risk of poverty.[2] Yet the use of it for international comparisons can be misleading, as the European Commission (2016a: 211) states, "given the differences across countries in the average age when young people leave the parental household". It can be used, however, for comparisons with the total population in each country, as in Figure 2.1 below.

In all the countries except Bulgaria, the at-risk-of-poverty is higher for young people, aged 15–29, than for the population as a whole. In relative terms, the difference is particularly pronounced in the Netherlands and in Sweden. As mentioned above, however, the indicator does not lend itself particularly well to comparisons between countries as the poverty threshold varies.

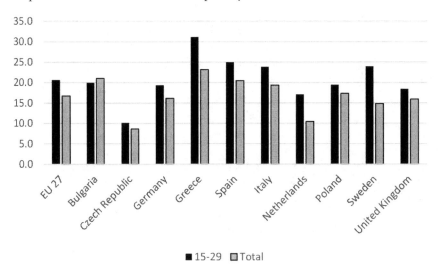

FIGURE 2.1 People at risk of poverty, 15–29 years and total population, 2013
Available at: http://ec.europa.eu/eurostat/web/youth/data/eu-dashboard (accessed 6 July 2017)

By contrast, the differences in living standards between countries can be captured by the indicator called the severe material deprivation rate. It is based on a single European threshold, defined as the percentage of the population that cannot afford at least three of nine pre-selected deprivation items.[3] Figure 2.2 shows extraordinarily high numbers in Bulgaria, where, before the European crisis, there were almost 60% of the young people living in severe material deprivation. Since then it has decreased substantially, although it remains at a high level.

Some of these young people in Bulgaria live in the neighbourhood called Fakulteta in Sofia. It constitutes a pole of poor people. It is a large neighbourhood with a population of around 35,000; widely known as a ghetto, it is the largest one in Sofia and almost exclusively inhabited by Roma. Most of the area is a "chaotic mishmash of narrow, winding streets with no names". Hajdinjak et al., (2014: 3) describe Fakulteta as a "hotbed of social problems, including devastating levels of unemployment, poverty, social exclusion, poor or non-existing infrastructure, and low quality of housing, education and health care."

A lot of children and young people grow up and live in Fakulteta. One of the expert interviewees estimates that between 30 and 40% of the inhabitants are less than 25 years old. "And they have their own children very young. It happens that people who are 20–22 already have 2–3, or 4 children – especially in the poorer parts." (Hajdinjak et al., 2014: 8). They have to manage without an official social infrastructure as Fakulteta is almost completely abandoned by the official (state and municipal) institutions. Apart from a municipal school, practically the only municipal service located in Fakulteta is a small police station. There is no municipal kindergarten and the nearest employment bureau is located in the neighbouring

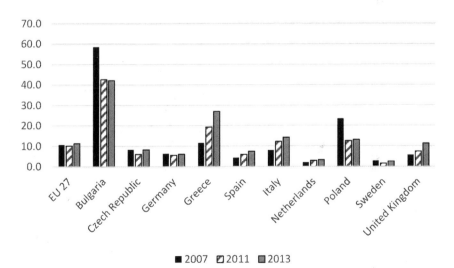

FIGURE 2.2 Severe material deprivation of young people, 15–29 years
Available at: http://ec.europa.eu/eurostat/web/youth/data/eu-dashboard (accessed 6 July 2017)

district. The bureau for social assistance in Fakulteta was closed down in the 1990s. The nearest office is located a few kilometres away. The authors describe the range of social inequalities in Fakulteta as shocking (Hajdinjak et al., 2014: 22):

> Compared to their peers in Sofia, the young people in the area have a poorer education, are more often without work or are employed in unattractive, low-paid jobs, have fewer opportunities to engage in leisure and culture activities, and live in worse housing conditions.

Relating again to Figure 2.2, the rate has increased in some countries, between 2007 and 2013, most of all in Greece, where 26.9% of young people suffered from severe material deprivation in 2013. That increase has its clear manifestations in the two neighbourhoods in Athens studied in Citispyce, Aghia Sophia and Elefsina. As the authors describe it, the current economic crisis has aggravated the already existing systemic inequalities and discriminations, although both of the areas have had prosperous pasts associated with the working class (Tryfona et al., 2014a: 3):

> During the past both of these areas, located in the wider Attica Region, were economically flourishing since they were centres of intense industrial and transport activity. This enabled the concentration of working class people and many immigrants, who benefited from high employment and low-cost housing opportunities. The gradual deindustrialisation of the country, however, the service-oriented economy and the recent recession due to the long-standing economic crisis were conducive to the economic stagnation of these areas, which led to deepening social inequalities and discrimination.

The increasing poverty has forced the authorities to react and, particularly in Elefsina, the municipality offers a number of services with the intention of alleviating the socio-economic problems. For example, the Municipal Social Grocery has been established which provides food and other basic commodities to citizens with low income, unemployed people, registered immigrants and people with disabilities. Another initiative is the Clothing Service which distributes clothes, blankets and household equipment to low-income or unemployed people and people with disabilities. The municipality has also launched a programme which enables direct distribution of agricultural products from producers to consumers and thereby excludes intermediaries from the purchasing process in order to reduce the price of products.

Aghia Sophia and Elefsina are interesting to compare due to the differences in municipal initiatives. In Elefsina, the municipality has initiated a lot of innovative services since the onset of the financial crisis in order to support its citizens, whereas Agia Sophia lacks such municipal initiatives, thus presenting a more apparent picture of decline. In Agia Sophia, "young unemployed people receive no official financial, psychological or social support from the local authorities and other public or private institutions. The absence of these services broadens the inequality in the job market and inside society" (Tryfona et al., 2014a). These differences show that societal systems do not fully predetermine action, but a space exists for, what I will call and emphasise throughout the book, discretion (see also chapter 3.2).

In a market society, poverty means a lack of money. This is a resource because it has a type of value called exchange-value. It functions as a claim on the labour, products and services of others (Sayer, 2015: 37). Without this claim, it would not have an exchange-value. Conversely, there has to be something to claim and with the same exchange-value. Hence, money is only in the trivial sense a thing. More substantially, it symbolises social relations between people, involving confidence and trust (Pettifor, 2017: 18).

A certain amount of money can be exchanged for, for example, a bottle of milk. Milk has such an exchange value as well, otherwise it would not be offered for sale, but in contrast to money, milk cannot be exchanged for any other commodity. For example, you can hardly buy a mobile phone with milk. Money has the potential of being an equivalent for all commodities. It can be used to buy anything and everything. In this sense, money has also another value, called use-value. Milk has such a value, too, but a rich and manifold use-value (taste, energy, etc), while you cannot use money to much more than purchase things. Except, of course, money equals power, and that is also a use-value, which is indeed very important.

Resources may thus be of two kinds (Marx, 1996; Sayer, 2015: 38). There are the ones which we ourselves make use of (for example our TV) and others (for example money) which we may exchange for something else. A use-value could be defined as the material content of a thing. It can take shape in machines, buildings or people, but also in culture and social networks. While the use-value depends on the relationship between the needs of the buyer and the material content of the commodity (Liedman, 2015: 231), the exchange-value depends on the relationship between different commodities. The use-value expresses a quality, often difficult to quantify, while the exchange-value is a quantity. Every commodity is a unity, although contradictory, of use-value and exchange-value. This is the definition of a commodity which I shall use in this book.

The concepts of use- and exchange-value, this classic distinction deriving from Aristotle (Liedman, 2015: 448), will be further used on many occasions in the book. They belong to its building-blocks and will turn up in the explanations of, among others, gentrification, the contradiction between wage-workers and capitalists, the distinction between economic and social policy, neoliberalism and civil society.

2.2 Labour power and use-value

Young people who belong to the have-nots could perhaps start their own business and produce something. That has indeed been a fashionable solution among policymakers for quite a while. It has turned out to be difficult, however, and most attempts do not survive for more than a short period. In the Netherlands, the report on the "Rotterdam-Buzinezzclub", which I will return to later, mentions

18 What is inequality?

figures which seem to indicate that more young people than ever are starting up their own business, but "the rate of failure of these attempts to run one's own business is also high" (Davelaar et al., 2015a: 24).

What then remains is to try to get a job. This means, in other words, that young people have to sell their labour power. That is also a commodity (Polanyi, 2001), and as such, it contains both use- and exchange-value. In this section, I will focus on the use-value of labour power, because its exchange value also depends on other things which I will deal with in subsequent chapters, for example the strength of trade unions and the existence of a labour market policy.

The use-value of our labour power consists of all that enables us to work and produce, to quote a researcher who wrote extensively on this, namely Marx (1996: 177), "the aggregate of those mental and physical capabilities existing in a human being, which he exercises whenever he produces a use-value of any description". These mental and physical capabilities are largely the result of work efforts, such as food and clothes, but also of services such as haircuts or health care; and not just of what we buy, but also, for example, parenting, cooking and family care; not only of what others do, but also, for example, our own study work. Our own labour power is produced by all this work.

Education has indeed become crucial for the production of our labour power. If you do not have an education, it may harm your possibilities of getting a job. One of the EU Youth Indicators covers this: i.e. early leavers from education and training who are defined as the percentage of the population aged 18–24 with the lowest level of secondary education and who are no longer in education or training.

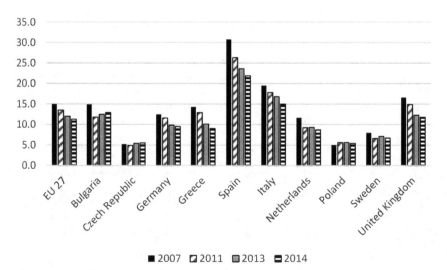

FIGURE 2.3 Early leavers from education and training, 18–24 years
Available at: http://ec.europa.eu/eurostat/web/youth/data/eu-dashboard (accessed 6 July 2017)

In general, the percentage of early leavers has decreased. Among the Citispyce countries, it is particularly low in the Czech Republic and in Poland. Spain stands out, although even there it has decreased, from 30.8% before the crisis to 21.9% in 2014. The extraordinary situation in Spain is confirmed by another indicator: the one which deals with the percentage of young people aged 20–24 having completed at least upper secondary education. Only 65.8% of the young people in Spain fulfilled that condition, far below the 82% in the EU 27 (see figure 2.4 below).

Do the statistics really prove that the early leavers and/or the young people who have not completed at least upper secondary education lack the labour power needed in the labour market or to function in society as a whole? Not necessarily. Grading is a meaning-making practice. By grading, the teacher assigns the students a meaning, which then becomes crucial for her/his future options. To the extent that they do not pass, they are considered lacking in the required knowledge, i.e. the use-value needed. The grades are meant to serve as a reference object for the knowledge of young people, with the latter constituting the referent object. But do they? It is usually taken for granted that they do. As a reference object, however, grades belong to a context of meaning (for example a curriculum and marking criteria), which means that the grades may reveal just as much about this context of meaning as the knowledge they seemingly refer to.

This lays the ground for two different types of inequality. Those who lack the labour-power (referent object) belong to the losing side of resource inequality. In

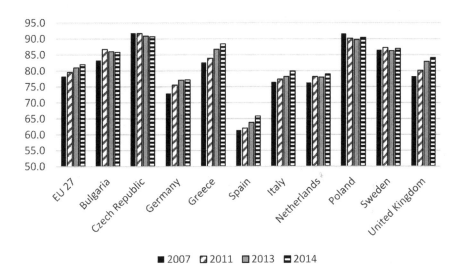

FIGURE 2.4 Young people (20–24 years) having completed at least upper secondary education
Available at: http://ec.europa.eu/eurostat/web/youth/data/eu-dashboard (accessed 6 July 2017)

contrast, those who belong to the losing side because of grading (reference object) suffer from a type of inequality which can be called cultural because it is inherent in contexts of meaning. Often these two forms of inequality are intertwined, mutually reinforcing each other, but for analytical reasons they should be kept separate. The distinction can, for example, help us to explain the situation of young people described by Tryfona et al. (2014b: 14) regarding Athens, the ones whose university degrees almost prohibit them from getting a job:

> "… I would never rely on my University degree to find a job. It's one thing to be a plumber and another to be a political scientist! If your faucet gets broken you will call the plumber but who will call me? There are so many political scientists who are nothing, just thin air"

The report mentions how most young people, especially University graduates "face the dilemma of either settling with jobs that are irrelevant to their field of studies and/or low status and no prospect jobs (e.g. waiter/waitress etc.), or remain unemployed" (Tryfona et al., 2014b: 15). I would say that the dilemma concerns what form of inequality you suffer from. Young people with degrees do not suffer from cultural inequality, but they may very well suffer from a resource inequality, as in the quote above, if they have acquired a labour power for which there is no need. Other young people may have the needed labour power, learnt informally in the contexts of friends or relatives, but if they lack the grades they perhaps still do not get the job. That makes them subject to a cultural inequality, a form of inequality inherent in the meaning-making of grading. It makes it seem that they lack the labour power as well, even if they do not.

2.3 Housing and the value of it

An important use-value resource in terms of inequality is housing. A place to stay in is fundamental. As we will see in later chapters, this differs due to welfare regimes. In general, however, it has become increasingly difficult due to the increased prices; the exchange-values. The character of housing as a commodity has been reinforced. Being a commodity means that it is both exchange-value and use-value. It is both a place to stay and an asset to trade. Rising exchange-values of housing favours the ones who can afford it and thus, causes inequality.

Such processes of rising exchange-values, usually known as gentrification, have taken place in the neighbourhood called El Raval in Barcelona. It is a densely populated neighbourhood with almost 50,000 inhabitants, located in the inner-city, close to the central tourist paths. Jubany et al. (2014a) describe it as the cradle of the industrial revolution in Barcelona and historically a working class neighbourhood. Following the industrial decline in the mid-20th century, it became a 'no-go' area associated with drugs and prostitution. A regeneration process started in the early 1990s, as part of the preparations for the Olympic Games in 1992.

An area of narrow streets was torn down to make way for the wider Rambla del Raval and in the upper parts, the Museum of Modern Art (MACBA) and the Centre for Contemporary Culture (CCCB) were constructed. This process has continued in the last decade with the construction of the Faculty of History and Geography of the University of Barcelona, and most recently, the new film archive (Filmoteca) (Jubany et al., 2014a: 3).

As Jubany et al. (2014a: 31) explain, this new "cultural infrastructure along the 'cultural axis' has not been designed for the people of the neighbourhood; it was a top-down initiative of the government without a process of political participation." That makes the gentrification very deliberate and, as I would add, power-based. In combination with the operation of a free market favouring the ones with monetary resources, it aimed at attracting other kinds of more affluent people to move into the neighbourhood. At the same time, young people who cannot afford it have been moved to the southern part of Raval and its concentrations of poverty.

But can prices of housing increase incessantly many young people ask. Is there a proper and just price of housing? Yes, there is, Adam Smith claimed in the 18th century. He introduced a new concept of value when he defined labour value as the amount of work that a commodity contains. The new concept means that labour not only produces use-values. Another type of value is the one dependent on the time that production takes, that is, the amount of work in terms of time. Money and goods, Smith said, "contain the value of a certain quantity of labour which we exchange for what is supposed at the time to contain the value of an equal quantity" (Smith, 2008: 36).

The labour value of a commodity is also called by Smith the natural price. That is nothing more than the labour value of the commodity expressed in money. The price on the market, called the commodity's market price, may be higher or lower depending on supply and demand, but the natural price is "the central price to which the prices of all commodities are continually gravitating." (Smith 2008: 56).

This does not mean that a slow worker creates a higher labour value than a fast one. It is not only the individual producer's labour time which determines the commodity's labour value, but it depends on the average working hours it takes by labour in society to produce it. When two independent commodity owners meet to exchange their commodities, it is this average labour of society which forms the basis for exchange and regulates the proportions in which the two commodities should be exchanged. If it then has taken the one individual less time to produce, it is to his/her advantage. Then he/she can make a profit on this difference. In contrast, if the commodity has taken longer to produce than the societal average it is to a corresponding disadvantage. Then, the one concerned should perhaps look for another job and do something else.

This has usually been called the labour theory of value. It was introduced by Smith and further developed by David Ricardo. Many of the Marxists in the 1960s and 1970s saw it as Marx pursuing this line of thought (Stigendal, 2010b). They regarded the theory of value in Marx as a direct evolution from Smith and

Ricardo. The purpose of the theory of value was considered, above all, to explain prices. From that point of view, one of the most famous Marxist economists, Maurice Dobb made a distinction between two types of theories. Prices are explained in the one type by production and in the second by market demand. Smith, Ricardo and Marx were considered as proponents of this first type, while the second group was made up of the neoclassical economists (Elson, 1979).

There are strong reasons to reject this interpretation by Dobb and others. It paved the way for much of the criticism directed against Marx. I agree with Therborn (2013: 57) that "the labour theory of value, at the root of Marxian economics, taken from Ricardo, is no longer held to be a tenable foundation for capitalist economics. This means that the prevalence and the amount of capitalist economic exploitation cannot be assessed empirically, nor can it be an axiom that all capital-wage labour relations are exploitative." There is another interpretation, however, namely one proposed already in the late 1970s by Diane Elson (1979). According to Elson, the theory of value in Marx is not aimed primarily at explaining prices. Marx does not pursue the labour theory of value in Smith and Ricardo but breaks in essential aspects with it.

> It is not a matter of seeking an explanation of why prices are what they are and finding it in labour. But rather of seeking an understanding of why labour takes the forms it does, and what the political consequences are.
> (Elson, 1979: 123)

Elson interprets the value theory of Marx in the first place as dealing with production, not with prices. Therefore, she claims that the labour theory of value in Smith and Ricardo instead becomes a value theory of labour in Marx. It is to explain what the labour value does with production that Marx develops his theories, not to highlight production as the sole determinant of labour value. This interpretation of the theory of value in Marx means that the labour value of a commodity is determined not only by production but also by the market. It is the competition in the market that puts the work of many individuals in relation with each other and equalises the differences, thus establishing the inherent value. Therefore, it is not only the labour value that determines the price, but the price also determines the labour value.

On the basis of such an interpretation, there is much to learn from heterodox and Keynesian economists like for example Amartya Sen, Paul Krugman, Thomas Piketty, Ann Pettifor and Joe Stiglitz on how markets operate. On the other hand, there are strong reasons to retain a value theory, however not as a labour theory of value but as a value theory of labour. The latter has much to contribute to the explanations on the causes of inequality, appearing, for example, in gentrification. What increases when urban neighbourhoods are renovated and revived by means of an influx of more affluent residents is the exchange-value of property, not necessarily its labour value. The labour value may just as well remain the same, indicated roughly by the cost for producing a new house. In fact, the labour value may even decrease due to more effective production methods.

Hence, gentrification means an exploitation of the difference between the exchange-value and labour value of property. It would not have been possible if the market was so-called "free" because then the exchange-value (market price) would correspond to the labour value (natural price) of property. The fact that market prices have risen high above their natural prices, reveals the power of the more affluent in society to influence markets to their advantage in a way which causes an increase in inequality. This is an example of how causes of inequality operate, namely as mechanisms which those that buy these properties actualise, whether they like it or not.

While gentrification concerns the one side of inequality, the other side tends to become characterised by "neglect, disinvestment, decay and closure," which "basically all case studies hold stories of", as Güntner et al. (2014c: 21), conclude in their analyses of the Citispyce reports on neighbourhoods:

> Abandoned places, when they lose their function, make space for uses that connote deviance, illegality and anomie. Vandalism, graffiti, gambling and drug abuse seem to be the rule in all case study areas, but they are only the more visible expressions that can occur at or in these respective places and give them a new meaning.

One such abandoned place is Hristo Botev in Sofia. As Hajdinjak et al. (2014: 4) describe it, the area is almost completely cut off from the rest of the city. The larger part of the area, however, does not differ much from other suburban neighbourhoods in Sofia. The population is mixed (Roma and ethnic Bulgarians), amounting to an estimated figure of between 8,000 and 10,000. Unlike Fakulteta (the other neighbourhood in Sofia studied in the Citispyce project), Hristo Botev was considered for a long time as a model example of coexistence between Roma and Bulgarians. This has changed dramatically, however, following the "closure of state-owned enterprises, which provided employment to most of the residents and the arrival of thousands of Roma from other parts of the country in the vain hope of finding a livelihood in Sofia which means that in recent years, Hristo Botev has started to resemble Fakulteta as far as the number and depth of social problems are concerned." (Hajdinjak et al., 2014: 4)

2.4 Unemployment – not taking part

In the previous chapter, I referred to Fakulteta neighbourhood in Sofia as a pole of resource inequality. However, it constitutes a pole of inequality also in at least two other senses. Besides lacking resources, the authors of the report estimate that close to 80% of residents are without legal employment. In other words, they suffer from not being able to participate in the social structures of society. That is a form of inequality which can be called structural inequality. It arises from a relation

24 What is inequality?

between those who do the right thing, i.e. labour, and those who do not. The latter can for simplistic reasons be called the do-nots.

The most often used indicator in this respect is the youth unemployment rate. It expresses the number of unemployed people in that age group as a percentage of the total labour force in the same age group. Figure 2.5 below shows the big differences across Europe. The youth unemployment rate increased from 2007–2013 in all the countries involved in Citispyce, except for Germany where it decreased from 11% to 7.3%. In contrast, the youth unemployment rate increased from 12.9% to 42.4% in Spain, and in Greece from 17.3% to 48.7%. This also shows the differences in the point of departure; Greece had the highest youth unemployment before the crisis set in. The youth unemployment rate was high also in Poland, 15.3%.

The percentages above are often used to claim that half of all the young people in Greece are unemployed. That is not the case. The youth unemployment rate measures unemployment in relation to the labour force. That comprises both employed and the registered unemployed, thus not students, for example, or, to use a broader term, the economically inactive. For that reason, another indicator called the youth unemployment ratio should be used to complement it. This measures the proportion of unemployed youth in relation to the total youth population (employed, unemployed and inactive). Figure 2.6 below shows how 24% of all the young people in Greece and Spain in 2013 were registered as unemployed.

Figure 2.7 below compares the two rates for one year, 2014. It shows the large difference. This does not mean that the rate indicator should be given up in favour

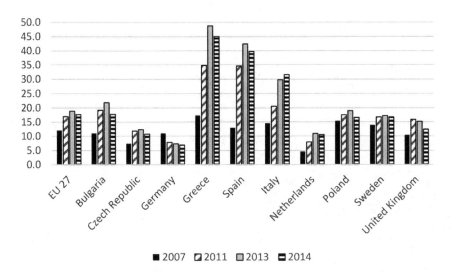

FIGURE 2.5 Youth unemployment rate, 15–29 years
Available at: http://ec.europa.eu/eurostat/web/youth/data/eu-dashboard (accessed 6 July 2017)

What is inequality? 25

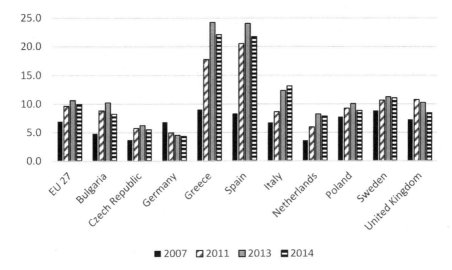

FIGURE 2.6 Youth unemployment ratio, 15–29 years
Available at: http://ec.europa.eu/eurostat/web/youth/data/eu-dashboard (accessed 6 July 2017)

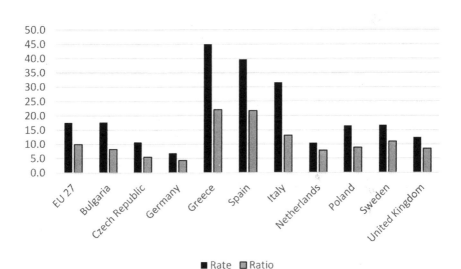

FIGURE 2.7 Youth unemployment rate and ratio, 15–29 years (2014)
Available at: http://ec.europa.eu/eurostat/web/youth/data/eu-dashboard (accessed 6 July 2017)

of the ratio indicator. As the *EU Youth Report* (European Commission, 2016a) states, high youth unemployment rates reflect the difficulties faced by young people in finding jobs. Furthermore, the ratio indicator has its limitations as well.

If the limitation with the rate indicator concerns its denominator, the ratio indicator has a similar limitation with its numerator. It covers only young people registered as unemployed and not the unemployed who have not even bothered to register themselves. The figures for Bulgaria reveal the effect of this limitation. In Bulgaria, only 27.2% of the young people, aged 15–24, were economically active in 2015, according to *Employment and social developments 2015* (European Commission, 2016b: 349). What do the other 72.8% do? Are they studying? That is highly doubtful. In Sweden, 55.4% of the young people belonged to the labour force (2016b: 449) and in the UK 57.9 (2016b: 453). The ratio indicator underestimates unemployment. It can be taken for granted that a higher percentage of young people are unemployed.

Does this also mean that they suffer from structural inequality in this sense? That depends on the difficulties they have in getting a job. An indicator for this is the long-term unemployment rate which covers the proportion of persons who have been unemployed for 12 months or more, related to the total number of unemployed persons in the labour market. Pay attention to the denominator. It comprises only the total number of unemployed persons. In Figure 2.8 below, it means that 7% of all the registered unemployed young people are long-term unemployed (2014). In relation to the labour force and in particular to the whole age group, it becomes quite a tiny proportion. This does not, however, take into consideration the economically inactive, which can be very many, as mentioned above, and 7%,

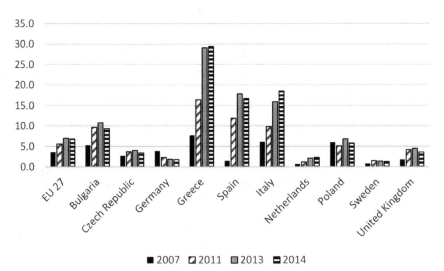

FIGURE 2.8 The long-term unemployment rate, 15–29 years
Available at: http://ec.europa.eu/eurostat/web/youth/data/eu-dashboard (accessed 6 July 2017)

thus, seems to be a gross underestimation of long-term unemployment among young people.

2.5 Working but unpaid

But what about other kinds of work? Unemployment does not necessarily mean that people lie in bed all the time. Yet, references to work nowadays, usually means paid work, i.e. labour. That was not the case in the 1700s and 1800s, when lively discussions were held among philosophers and scientists about how to define work (see, for example, Karlsson 2013). One of them was Marx, and for him, work was a central concept. He attached great importance to define it, such as in the following quotation:

> Labour is, in the first place, a process in which both man and Nature participate, and in which man of his own accord starts, regulates, and controls the material reactions between himself and Nature. He opposes himself to Nature as one of her own forces, setting in motion arms and legs, head and hands, the natural forces of his body, in order to appropriate Nature's productions in a form adapted to his own wants. By thus acting on the external world and changing it, he at the same time changes his own nature.
>
> *(Marx, 1996: 187)*

Work need not be the same as paid work. As Lars Ingelstam (2006: 57) has suggested, work can be, for example, the activities to assemble furniture that previously were paid for but which we now carry out ourselves (for example IKEA). It is also called do-it-yourself and is basically about a transformation of paid work to unpaid. If all of these do-it-yourself efforts were retransformed into paid work, the Gross Domestic Product (GDP) would probably increase significantly.

Another type of work is domestic work. It is part of a broader category that Statistics Sweden in their investigations of Swedish people's time use calls homework. "That includes most of all the chores that have to do with the maintenance and care of home and family. This includes housework (cooking, cleaning and laundry), maintenance (repair and maintenance of house, home, vehicle, gardening, and other), care for children and others, as well as purchases of goods and services." (SCB, 2003: 15 – my translation). In its definition of work, Statistics Sweden draws on the so-called third party criterion, which means that all that we do, but could pay someone else to do for us, is to be regarded as work (see also SCB, 2012: 33).

In the latest survey from 2010–2011 (SCB, 2012), it appears that women's total work consists of 46% unpaid homework, although it has decreased compared to 1990–1991 when the homework amounted to 55%. Men's unpaid domestic work accounts for 36% of their total work and it has increased slightly. Adding up paid work with unpaid homework shows that women and men aged 20–64 work just as much, namely an average of about 8 hours a day. The unpaid work, however, is not recognised as participation in the social structures of society. It is not counted in the employment rate and hardly in other statistics, either, except for the studies of time use made by Statistics Sweden. The unpaid homework does not serve as a basis for unemployment or sickness benefit and nor for pensions. Still, it can rightly be regarded as work. As Sayer (2015: 346) puts it, "… care work must be valued in itself, rather than as an inconvenient interruption to employment."

Structural inequality, thus, is not only about the difference between those who do the paid work and those who do not work at all. It is also about a difference between those who do the "right" work and those who do the "wrong" work; the latter being work not recognised as participation in the social structures of society. Therefore, it is a difference which violates the human rights of those who do the "wrong" but yet required work. It affects young people in particular when they have to do such unpaid work themselves because their parents are not managing, as described here by Gehrke et al. (2014b: 12) regarding the situation in Hamburg:

> Often, they had to handle contacts with authorities on behalf of their parents as well, alongside school. Many interviewees describe a childhood and youth where they had to translate official letters for their parents or accompany them to official appointments etc. In many occasions this was a humiliating experience after their parents were treated disrespectfully by officials.

The previous quote from Marx above helps us to understand structural inequality as also a matter of the quality of jobs. In the last sentence, Marx claims that while we are acting on the external world and changing it, we are at the same time changing our own nature. While we are working, we make ourselves the individuals we are. Thus, who we are and become depends on the kind of work we do, in what context, under what conditions etc. This is easy to understand when our work is making us sick but it has many more implications than that. That is also one of the reasons why we should be interested in class analysis, because we need to know who and how many make themselves who they are in different ways and in different senses, such as class. To that I will therefore turn now.

2.6 Employed but on precarious conditions

Should the relation between workers and employers be seen as a relation of inequality? Not necessarily, and at least not in the forms predominant in western countries during the first post-war decades. In that period, the human rights of an increasing number of workers were strengthened through collective agreements and the construction of the welfare state. During the last four decades, however, this development has gone into reverse and a new category of workers has arisen, characterised by having its human rights violated.

This new category has been called the precariat. A book about it that has attracted much attention in recent years is Guy Standing's *The precariat. The new dangerous class* (2011). The term precariat is said to have been coined by French sociologists in the 1980s (2011: 9), based on the word precarious and alluding to the proletariat. Standing speaks of the precariat as a new group of people in the world, not yet a class, but a class in the making (2011: vii). The emergence of the precariat is the result of the increasing flexibility of labour markets, which is, in turn, the result of the neoliberal agenda. This has transferred risks and uncertainty to workers and their families. But what does he mean by the precariat? Who is included in it and why?

Standing defines the precariat as one of seven groups. The first group, called the 'elite' consists of a small number of very rich. The next group he calls the 'salariat' and they are characterised by having permanent full-time jobs and pensions, paid holidays and service benefits. Besides the salariat, he identifies a third and smaller group called 'proficians', a term composed of the English terms professional and technician. All individuals with marketable specialist expertise belong to this group. Below these, he identifies a fourth group, which consists of a shrinking proportion of manual workers with permanent employment, which Standing calls the 'old working-class core'. The 'precariat' is to be found at the next level, which is the fifth group in order, and this group is described as flanked by the last two groups, which consist of an "army of unemployed" and "a detached group of socially ill misfits living off the dregs of society" (2011: 8).

Standing uses the concept of class with reference to Weber, "where class refers to social relations of production, and a person's position in the labour process" (2011: 8). Weber's class concept is, just as Marx', relational. It is in relation to each other as classes arise. For Weber, however, classes are distinguished in relation to what they have, not to what they do. A concept that is central to the Weberian class analysis is "opportunity hoarding" (Wright 2009: 104). Classes not just hoard opportunities, but they also make themselves distinctive by excluding others from accessing them (social closure). On that basis, Standing emphasises the division between wage-workers and officials. This is the key distinction, according to him, not that between wage labour and capital, i.e. the relationship between the selling and buying of labour power, which is central to a Marxist class analysis (see below).

According to Standing, however, the concept of class is not sufficient to define the precariat, and nor is it sufficient to refer to temporary workers and seasonal workers, in line with how the concept of precariat was used by French sociologists in the 1980s. Precarious forms of employment clearly have to be included in the definition, and Standing enumerates the absence of seven forms of work-related security characterising the precariat (2011: 22), but in addition he also includes the lack of a fixed identity based in an occupation (2011: 21). Obviously, Standing includes a lot in his definition: self-employed can be part of the precariat; call workers is another category and he mentions also trainees. In addition, the precariat is characterised by the existence of "anger, anomie, anxiety and alienation" (2011: 19).

Many are thus part of the precariat and it is characterised by many things. He gives the example of a teenager who hangs out in Internet cafes and lives from occasional odd jobs. This teenager has little in common with the immigrant who pushes him- or herself to the limit in order to survive. A completely different situation is the single mother who agonises over how she will get money for food.

Despite these large differences, they are still all seen as part of the precariat. Another example, this time from Citispyce, would be the case of Luca in Venice (Della Puppa & Campomori, 2014: 13), "that, given the sudden unemployment condition of both parents, had to combine three different work activities to meet the material needs of the family of which he suddenly became the sole breadwinner. It has obviously led to considerable repercussions on his educational trajectories, leading him to opt for an evening course – attended with fatigue and discontinuity":

> "I work in three different places: in two different transport companies in Venice and in a pizza place in Marghera and I study in an evening school course […] Should I go to school every evening, but, because of the work schedules and all things, it is impossible. At least, now with the work in the pizzeria, fortunately, everything is in order, I've got a regular contract and they give me a letter in which is written that I am on the workplace and not around to loiter and lose time and then, perhaps, the teachers try to help me in this regard: they know that those that use to go to the evening school course usually have to work, usually have family and, therefore, often we agree for homework, classwork … I try to be present for, at least, these moments and the rest of the hours I'm absent … let's see if it will be tolerated or not."

"However one defines it", says Standing, "the precariat is far from being homogeneous" (2011: 13). What is the use of such a concept? What does it help us to understand? What does such a concept say about the development of society when so many categories of people with such different characteristics are included? How can we use such terms to know something about where society is heading when it involves so many different processes? How large is the precariat? We can not know, because it is so unclear what it includes. Is the precariat growing or not? How large is it in different countries? You cannot find out on the basis of such an all-embracing concept.

The Marxist concept of class is more specific. It does not describe what people have in terms of status, resources and opportunities, although such descriptions are not belittled. For example, income inequality is very important to explore. The Marxian concept of class does not disclose what people have but what they do. As Therborn writes in his book about the class structure in Sweden (Therborn 1981: 13), the Marxian concept of class is tied to an analysis of the driving forces and dynamics of societal development. "It is precisely this that is the meaning of class analysis." (my translation)

In the Marxist sense, classes are defined as carriers of certain productive forces and relations of production. It is the similarities between us in these senses that allows us to be included in a particular class, and it does not depend on what we think and feel about it. What we ourselves think and feel can, however, very well be part of an identity, which is the second meaning that class can have, namely as a context of meaning. The one definition has to do with social structures and the other with meaning, that is, the two cornerstones of the reduction of complexity (see chapters 1.2 and 3.1). As a structural role, the concept of class aims to categorise the employed, and this categorisation does not take into account how you live, what interests you have or what you do in addition to paid work. Class roles, however, create the foundations of living conditions and interests, not only in terms of wages. The class we belong to can make us more receptive to one message than to another.

This distinction is not made by Standing. His concept of the precariat includes contexts of meaning, such as the lack of a fixed occupation-based identity. While this is of course important to comprehend, other concepts are also needed to do that. Another problem is that he does not use abstractions and distinguish between different levels. In contrast, abstractions are of crucial importance in a Marxian analysis (Liedman, 2015: 400). By abstractions, common to all critical realist research, one-sided components of a concrete object are singled out and analysed in their isolation (Sayer, 2000: 27). The aim is to determine the necessary and constitutive properties in different objects, those that determine the nature of them (Jessop, 2015: 243). From the highest abstractions, characterised by the simplest determinations, the scientific work should proceed by incorporating more determinations at lower levels of abstraction, moving from abstract-simple to concrete-complex analyses.

A Marxian class analysis distinguishes between at least four levels (see also Pijl, 1984). At the highest level of abstraction, capitalists and wage-workers are defined (see chapter 4.1). At a second level, the distinction between different spheres is introduced, making us understand the difference between, for example, industrialists and bankers. These distinctions will also be further dealt with in chapter 4.1. At a third level, a Marxist class analysis conceptualises the formation of the classes due to different growth models (Therborn, 1983: 43). This is where the precariat should be located. In my view, it belongs to the finance-driven growth model. An important advantage with the identification of it at this level of abstraction is that it can be counted, and I will return to that below. At a fourth level, other categories like gender, ethnicity and age should be incorporated.

A Marxian class analysis is not sufficient, however, to account for the situation of many young people in an era with high unemployment, "an army of unemployed" as Standing (2011: 8) calls his sixth group, which flank the precariat together with the seventh group, "a detached group of socially ill misfits". Eric Olin Wright (2009: 101) suggests a combination of Marxist and Weberian class analyses in a more comprehensive explanation:

> The inequalities generated by opportunity hoarding require power to be used in order to enforce exclusions; the inequalities connected to exploitation require supervision, monitoring of labour and sanctions to enforce discipline. In both cases, social struggles seeking to challenge these forms of power would potentially threaten the privileges of those in advantaged class positions.
>
> *(Wright, 2009: 109)*

32 What is inequality?

As I see it, the clarification of these two processes and its associated two forms of power helps to explain the combination of inequalities that comes to such clear expression in today's cities. It is a structural inequality that depends on exploitation but also a resource inequality depending on the hoarding of opportunities and social closure. It is a combination of inequalities that depends on both what you do (or do not) and what you have (or have not). This combination explains the emergence of the new societal borders which I will deal with in chapter 8.

Wright's suggestion makes it possible to analyse these processes in turn, instead of confusing them. If we add to that the need to analyse the structural role separately from the cultural/identity role, as well as the need to distinguish between different levels of abstraction, it seems reasonable to keep the original definition of the precariat and pay attention to, for example, temporary employment, also because such an indicator exists.

As the *Youth Report* (European Commission, 2016a: 194) states, "working patterns among young people in Europe have been directly affected by the crisis. As a consequence, more young Europeans might begin their employment career with a traineeship or by taking on part-time or temporary employment contracts interrupted by periods of unemployment or further education and training, thereby moving frequently in and out of the labour market." This is the situation particularly in Poland where 50% of the young people were temporary employees in 2013, as shown in Figure 2.9 below.

Some of these young Poles live in the neighbourhood Rzaka in Krakow, a peripheral residential complex with 4,351 residents, which, according to the authors of the report, "tends to be overlooked by city officials and does not enjoy a

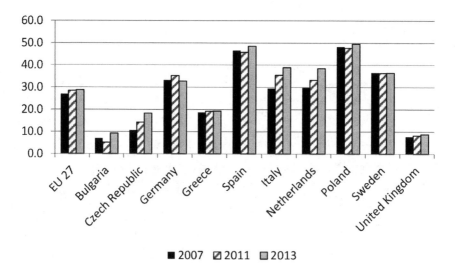

FIGURE 2.9 Young temporary employees, 20–29 years
Available at: http://ec.europa.eu/eurostat/web/youth/data/eu-dashboard (accessed 6 July 2017)

high status amongst the rest of the city population" (Chrabaszcz et al., 2014: 8). Rzaka is inhabited by a significantly larger and even increasing population of people aged 15–24 than the city as a whole. A higher percentage of them than in the city as a whole are unemployed.

As the *Youth Report* continues, "… relatively high rates of temporary employment among young people can also be seen as an indication of career insecurity. Where this is the case, young people may lack the stability needed to allow them to live independently. They can be trapped in a cycle of alternating periods of temporary employment and unemployment, which may adversely affect their status into their thirties and beyond" (European Commission, 2016a: 197). Precarious jobs can then also become a cause of health inequality, but not necessarily so. As I will explain in chapter 3.1, causes should first of all be seen as potentials. To have an effect, the potential cause has to be actualised and that always happens in a specific context, which means that actual causes emerge.

2.7 Conclusions: Inequalities – how many are there?

In this chapter, I have started to define inequality as a difference between a winning and a losing side, which violates the human rights of the latter. I will conclude this chapter by linking my findings to a distinction made by Göran Therborn in three types of inequality (2013). One of these types is resource inequality. The losing side in this relation of inequality is usually called the have-nots. One such subtype of resource inequality draws on income and money but I have also paid attention to labour power (or education, as others would perhaps call it) and housing.

In addition to resource inequality, Therborn mentions vital and existential inequality. The former refers to differences concerning life and death, while existential inequality means "the unequal recognition of human individuals as persons" (Therborn, 2006: 7). I will instead call it health inequality, in line with many other scholars (Marmot, 2015; World Health Organization, 2008), defined as systematic differences in health between socially determined groups of individuals on the basis of class, gender, ethnicity, age and residency. Health inequality should be seen as the most important form of inequality. As Amartya Sen (2013) has pointed out, health constitutes a human right that comes before other human rights since those rights can only be fully enjoyed if the individual first enjoys good health.

Regarding existential inequality, I want to take the distinction one step further and make a distinction between cultural and structural inequality, in line with Cultural Political Economy. This can be motivated by the ontological assumption of our social existence as being both cultural and structural. We become part of the social world by on the one hand making sense and meaning of it, and on the other hand structuring social relations.

Regarding structural inequality, I have suggested several subtypes. In the perhaps most obvious one, the unemployed belongs to the losing side. I have called this category the "do-nots" because they do not do what is required, namely wage-work. They might, however, do something else and even work, but unpaid. That calls attention to another subtype of structural inequality, one which often affects women, but also young people. They belong to the do-nots as well, not because they do not do anything but they do not do it for a wage and therefore not for the right thing. Another subtype of structural inequality is the one that depends on class and where the precariat can be regarded as the losing side. This category can also be seen as belonging to the do-nots as they do not do the right thing in terms of the quality of wage-work.

Regarding cultural inequality, it emerges when people representing and/or associated with another meaning than the prevailing one feel disadvantaged and limited in their life possibilities. For simplistic reasons, the losing side of this inequality can be called the mean-nots. For example, the population in the neighbourhood of Fakulteta in Sofia suffer from such a cultural inequality as they belong to the Roma community. Another example which I have highlighted is the stigma associated with a lack of or poor school grades. This is also an important subtype of cultural inequality as it makes these young people appear as less valuable and tends to violate their human rights.

As a final remark, I will emphasise the need for analysing the types separately and as abstractions, also at different levels. For a start, I defined inequality at a high level of abstraction. By introducing the four types, I have moved from abstract-simple to concrete-complex. In chapter 2.6, I located the distinction between capitalists and wage-workers at a high level of abstraction. Other determinants have then been brought in at lower levels of abstraction, rendering no more, in the words of Marx, "a chaotic conception of a whole, but a rich totality of many determinations and relations" (Marx, 1986: 37).

Similarly and as another example, housing at a high level of abstraction can be construed as both a use- and an exchange-value. Using that distinction, we can understand how the phenomenon known as gentrification, brought in at a lower level of abstraction, gives priority to the exchange-value side and the implications of it. Abstracting different types of inequality from their concrete contexts and analysing them at different levels of abstraction enables us to sharpen the object of explanation; i.e. what should be explained. This is particularly important in this book as its purpose is not only to describe inequality, but also to explain the causes of it. Therefore, we need to know what the causes are causes of. Having accomplished that and at the same time introduced several abstract concepts which will be used in subsequent chapters, I will now switch to the causes themselves.

Notes

1 Pole is used here in the sense of poles of a battery whereby there is a relationship between the two opposing poles. Thus, with regard to inequality, one group or neighbourhood is unequal in relation to another.
2 The threshold is defined at 60 % of the net median equivalised disposable income, which means the total income of a household, after tax and other deductions, which is available

for spending or saving, divided by the number of household members converted into equalised adults.
3 Definition: percentage of the population that cannot afford at least three of the following nine items: 1) to pay their rent, mortgage or utility bills; 2) to keep their home adequately warm; 3) to face unexpected expenses; 4) to eat meat or proteins regularly; 5) to go on holiday; or cannot afford to buy a: 6) TV, 7) Refrigerator, 8) Car, 9) Telephone; compared to total population. Source: Eurostat EU SILC.

3

WHY DOES INEQUALITY EXIST?

In the previous chapter I have shown the existence and extent of inequality by using descriptions, quotes and statistics. The question then arises of why inequality exists. What does it depend on? It must depend on something. Inequality is not inevitable but caused. In this chapter, I will explain what this means. What is a cause? The answer should not be seen as self-evident. In fact, it is this very self-evidence which has prevented a deeper understanding of why inequality exists.

3.1 Potential and actual causes

We see and hear about young people being affected by inequality or perhaps reacting against it. It might be the flames of discontent in Syntagma Square in Athens, the unemployed young people evicted in Barcelona, the large number of young people in Malmö lacking rental housing or refugees drowning in the Mediterranean. It is a reality that intrudes on us and that provides us with something to experience and refer to (referent objects). We respond by trying to make sense of it, using words and language but also particular concepts and understandings (reference objects) inherent in contexts of meaning: for example a certain theory, ideology, popular imaginary, etc. Such contexts of meaning cast light on some aspects of the experiences while other aspects remain in the dark. Hence, the contexts of meaning differ in what they cast light on, but also on what kind of light they cast. In other words, our understanding matters for what we experience and how we experience it. What context of meaning, then, do I represent and what kind of light does it cast?

In my understanding, influenced by critical realism, what we see and experience belong to a certain level of reality, called the empirical or the surface forms. We make sense of these experiences by understanding them as expressions of something else, i.e. by treating them as symptoms. As such, what we experience expresses a specific content – a unity of matter and depth forms (Liedman, 2015: 406) – which belongs, in turn, to another level of reality, called the actual. This level comprises the actualisation of potentials (Sum & Jessop, 2013: 9). The latter, i.e. the potentials, belong to the most basic level, which is called the real. The real comprises it all, i.e. not only what appears to be and what has been actualised, but also what an object can achieve by virtue of its nature, the impact it can generate or the liabilities and vulnerabilities it contains, whether it then actually generates effect or not (Sayer, 2000; Jessop, 2015a).

The division of reality in these three levels implies another view of causality than the one belonging to the philosophy of empiricism and associated with David Hume. In his view, only the empirical exists. Reality does not consist of anything more or less than what we can experience. In the mid-18th century, he established a law that identifies A as a cause of B if, first, A and B touch each other in time and space; second, B follows A in time, and, third, B only occurs because of A (Brante 1997: 317). What we see is what we get, so to speak. As Liedman (2006: 233) writes, there is therefore "no reason to imagine a substance that is the basis for what we can observe" (my translation).

In contrast, and according to the philosophy that I represent, critical realism (see for example Bhaskar, 1989; Danermark, 2002; Jessop, 2015a), the concept of cause refers first of all to a potential (Sayer, 2000). For example, we are able to talk and work, but we do not necessarily do it, at least not all the time. These real properties may, thus, very well remain latent, yet they still exist. We cannot take for granted when, where, why and how they are actualised. Nor can we take for granted what effects the actualisation of them will cause. This also depends on the context. Yet, we possess these so-called causal powers, or potentials, to do it and, for example, when we talk, someone may very well interrupt us and thus prevent that potential of ours being actualised and obtain an effect. The abilities to talk and work are examples of potentials that are inherent in individuals (Sayer, 1992). Such potentials to bring about changes and make a difference will here be called actorial or agential (see also Moulaert et al., 2016: 171, 173).

Potential can also be inherent in other single objects, for example a decision. Obviously, that is why decisions are taken, namely to cause effects. A highly relevant example of a cause in this sense is the decision taken by the Eurozone leadership on the night of 13 July 2015 to grant a third bailout to Greece on conditions of further austerity measures. As shown by work in the Citispyce project, the past years of austerity policy have already caused a lot of inequality, with consequences in particular for young people. As new austerity measures await, so probably do more inequalities. I want to underline "probably" because at the time that the decision was taken it had not yet been put into practice and thus we could not know if it would happen. However, the decision is an example of a potential cause, something that certainly exists and can be expected to have an effect, but which has not yet been fully actualised, apart of course from its existence in many people's minds where it surely gets actualised by causing worries and anxieties.

Whether the decision does cause more inequality depends, thus, on the actualisation of it. A potential cause has to be actualised to achieve an effect and this always happens in specific contexts where it enters into relations with other objects, including the ones which it is supposed to affect, and thus then becomes modified (Liedman, 2015: 398). The actual cause is, therefore, not the same as the potential cause, but an emergent effect of different potentials being actualised by entering into relation with each other, which for example happens when the players in a football team start to play. The actual cause of the team is not made up by a simple addition of each player's potential cause. Each coach strives to make the sum of eleven players more than eleven. The concept of emergence refers to such an effect, which cannot be derived from any of the interrelated objects (in this case the subjects). Life itself is an extraordinary example of emergence, arising as it has from complex organic combinations (Liedman, 2015: 538).

Furthermore, the actual cause of each player is not the same as their potential cause. What each player manages to achieve does not only depend on his/her potential, but also on the interdependent relations to the others in the specific context where the potential gets actualised. The actual cause of each player is, thus, in itself an effect, although not in the sense of what Hume prescribed. The potential cause should not be seen as a discrete object that can cause an effect, as A touches B which then follows A in time and only occurs because of A. The potential causes have to be actualised in a specific context to cause an effect, and that actualisation modifies it to an actual cause.

In explanations of why the one football team won, this is usually not attributed to one player solely. Instead, the explanation may also refer to how the players functioned together, the tactics, the efforts of the manager, to what extent the players were positioned in ways that enabled their individual potentials to be actualised in a flourishing way etc. That belongs to the actual causes of the win. Furthermore, the explanation probably includes something about the state of the other team and its players. Thus, that should also be seen as included in the actual cause. What a Humean notion of causality describes as an effect, the defeated team, belongs in certain aspects to the actual cause. Likewise, what a Humean notion of causality describes as a cause, the winning team, also includes effects, for example the exhaustion of players and that effect happens at the same time as the players cause the victory. Effects do not necessarily, thus, come after their causes in time but may emerge simultaneously as them. Cause and effect may be two sides of the same coin.

This means that one and the same football player can fail in one team and become successful in another. It also means that the team as a whole can be more or less successful, depending on what team they meet, the tactics of this team, the qualities of the ground, the audience, the weather, etc. The team as a whole has a potential, just as the individual players, but it matters how and where it gets actualised. What the potential of the team is inherent in cannot, however, be described as a single object. It is inherent in a more complex object, usually called a social structure and that is what I will turn to now.

3.2 Causes are inherent in social structures ...

It is one of the core messages of this book that inequality is not inevitable. It depends on the existence of potential causes but these have to be actualised to cause an effect. That requires people. Just like everything else in the social world, it takes people to exist. As Marx put it in a famous statement, "men make their own history, but they do not make it just as they please; they do not make it under circumstances chosen by themselves, but under circumstances directly encountered, given and transmitted from the past" (Marx & Engels, 1979/11: 103). This statement encapsulates the potential moments in an explanation of causes. As only people can make their own history and as inequality expresses a social relation, inequality has to be caused by somebody (the efficient cause, as Aristotle called it) with some kind of will to do it (the final cause, in Aristotelian terms). Furthermore, as history is made under circumstances directly encountered, given and transmitted from the past, causes of inequality can also be inherent in such circumstances, the forms of them as well as their materialities (the formal and the material cause in the Aristotelian typology) and the history behind them.

This Aristotelian typology is a good old idea which I think should be much more re-used (Pratten, 2009). It makes sense of a social structure as a kind of form. According to Aristotle, a form is that which makes something into what it is (Liedman, 2006: 15). That something is matter. A social structure and social phenomenon in general is, thus, made of matter (see also Sayer, 1992: 28). The form of it, however, makes it into something else other than just pure matter. Thus, the social structure cannot be reduced to the matter it is made of. To understand the potential of a social structure, we need to explore both the matter (the material cause) it is made of and its form (the formal cause). The unity of this form and matter can, with an inspiration from Hegel, be called content (Liedman, 2015: 406). This is also how I understand the actual, i.e. as the content which expresses itself in surface forms (the empirical).

As a form, a social structure can be defined as a pattern or composition of internally related objects, also called moments in the tradition from Hegel and onwards (Liedman, 2015: 235, 397; see also Moulaert et al., 2016: 169). The internal relations among these objects mean that they, as moments, become something else by being interrelated. For example, a house becomes rented property when it is owned by a landlord, i.e. somebody with the purpose of renting it out. Hence, these objects need to be understood in their interrelations, for example the football player in his/her relations to the others in the team and also to the opponents. Within a social structure there are particular positions associated with certain roles (Sayer, 1992: 92). Such a role in the example above is the landlord and another one is the tenant. In their roles they contribute to reproducing the structure. Other examples are the roles in a football team, like the goalkeeper.

Key to an understanding of structural causes is the relationship between structure and agency. The social structure would not continue to exist without the actors making it (efficient cause in Aristotelian terms) and their motivation to do it (final cause). When they reproduce the structure, for example the tenant paying the rent and the landlord taking care of maintenance work, they also experience the constraints and powers or lack of power associated with their particular role. That kind of power could be defined as structural, due to it being inscribed in the structure. Structures both constrain and enable, but what this means also depends on the actors making them and their potential: ideas, wills, interests, strategies, etc. There is always discretion. People can always make a difference, although it sometimes can be very difficult and hard to generate ideas about how. That is why a football club finally decides to sell a certain player. Although he/she may possess a lot of potential, he/she does not make the difference needed in the social structure of the particular team.

In contrast, individualism claims that we can make almost any difference at all. By individualism, I mean the tradition introduced by Hobbes and Locke in the 17th century, called liberal from the early 19th century and onwards, reinvigorated in recent decades by scholars like, for example, Gary Becker, and so strongly influencing current societal development (Liedman, 2015: 164). Individualism treats individuals as the origins of society. First of all, we are seen as individuals, basically driven by a predetermined 'human nature' to become social beings. Since the 19th century, selfishness has been seen as inherent in this human nature. What drives us, thus, is selfishness, regardless of who we are and where we live. In Sweden, this has been taught to several generations of students in economics by the most popular textbook for decades, where the author Klas Eklund claims that "the hypothesis of the utility-maximising humans survived as a cornerstone …" (Eklund, 2005: 44). According to Eklund "most economists accept … that people act rationally to maximise their utility. […] And this is also what is assumed in most of the theories presented in this book" (2005: 45 – my translations).

Contrary to this, and according to a tradition stemming from Aristotle, further developed by Hegel and then Marx, we are not basically individuals who become social beings, but it is as social beings, related to others, we become individuals (Liedman, 2015: 164). Therefore, the founding moment of the social world is not the individual but the social relation. As Sayer (2015: 21) expresses it in simple but yet beautiful terms, "dependence on others, particularly across generations, is part of being human …" To what extent we become individuals depends on how we develop in relation to others: power, resources, etc. As Gramsci (1971: 132) put it, "there is no 'human nature', fixed and immutable (a concept which certainly derives from religious and transcendentalist thought), but that human nature is the totality of historically determined social relations." Society, or in a more general sense the social world, thus, always has to be presupposed. Without society or some kind of a societal context, individuals would not exist. "People are living in structures which they take over from past generations and which their own activities help to change" (Liedman, 2015: 231 – my translation).

This tradition, however, turned into an impasse in the 1960s and 1970s when the theory of structuralism neglected the dependence on actors. Both constraints and opportunities were seen as fully pre-determined. Actors cannot do anything else than to reproduce it. A way out of this impasse was offered by Antony Giddens in the 1980s with the structuration theory. Giddens defined the relationship between structures and agency as a duality, i.e. as inextricably linked and two sides of the same phenomenon. This was criticised by Jessop at an early stage (for history, see Jessop, 2007). He rejected it as a dualism, as Giddens does not consider himself able to study the agency and structures in their relationship, but instead puts what he calls methodological brackets around one side of the duality to study the other. Then there will be no duality, says Jessop, but a dualism, however, masked as a duality (Jessop, 2005: 45).

Representatives of critical realism such as Roy Bhaskar and Margaret S. Archer have tried to build further on the structuration theory by advocating precisely a dualism (Healy, 1998). Thereby, they consider structure and agency as internally separated, albeit externally related. This approach is also represented by Danermark (2002) and called analytical dualism. Jessop is critical of this approach too, and the criticism has recently been reiterated (Sum & Jessop, 2013: 48):

> Much work on structure and agency brackets structure or agency to focus on the effects of its counterpart. But bracketing tends thereby to relate structure and agency in a rather mechanical fashion. It treats structure at any given time in isolation from action and so implies that a given structure is equally constraining and/or enabling for all actors and all actions. Similarly, action at any given time is isolated from structure, since actors are seen to choose a course of action more or less freely and skilfully within these rules and resources.

Instead, Jessop considers the relationship between structure and agency as a dialectical duality, which is part of the approach Jessop has called the strategic-relational (Jessop, 2007). Such an approach requires the ontological depth of critical realism. Due to the lack of such a depth, structuration theory fails to differ between the potential and the actual. It treats structure and agency at the level of the actual, rather than as potentials which have to be actualised (Jessop, 2005: 45) and when that happens something else emerges. It is one of the great merits of Bob Jessop to have pinpointed the problems of structuration theory and developed the strategic-relational approach on the basis of that criticism.

Instead of being seen as fully fixed and predetermined, the constraints and opportunities of a social structure – its potentials – should be understood in relation to the potentials of the actors that actualise them. Furthermore, the actualisation should be understood as a process. Thus, we need concepts that enable such an understanding and an important one is the concept of selectivities. Causes operate as selectivities: i.e. combinations of constraints and opportunities. A social structure promotes certain actions while limiting or even preventing others. The actual selectivity, however, is not only dependent on the inherent and potential properties of the structure but also on the strategic activities of the ones that reproduce the structure. The selectivity should thus be understood as strategic (Sum & Jessop, 2013: 214). Conversely, the actors must be analysed in relation to the structures they make and exist through, characterised by more or less structured social relations.

In contrast to structuralism and, thus, rather than structures being regarded as unambiguously constraining and enabling, they should be seen as containing variations, enabling different actors to pursue their roles in the structure more or less differently. This means that there is always a discretion, i.e. a scope for the 'art of the possible'. That could be a reason to involve researchers who on the basis of their research can say to actors, "I know that you've got good intentions and you may not be aware of it, but when you reproduce these structures, in your routines, you actually exclude other people. For that reason, couldn't we work together to try to change the structures or at least try to reproduce them differently?"

If we ask how a decision could be taken such as the one on the night of 13 July 2015 (see above) with the potential to increase inequality vastly, affecting young people in particular, some would probably blame an individual actor like the German finance minister Wolfgang Schäuble. Obviously, he has a lot of power, not only as an individual but also because he represents the collective actor of the German government. Two kinds of agency are articulated in him, collective and individual. Yet, the decision on further austerity measures cannot be reduced to him and his agency. The decision derives also from the interdependent relations within the social structure. It depends on how the structure works, or, with other words, how its mechanisms select some behaviour, actions and thinking while deselecting others.

Recent changes made in the neighbourhood called Bordesley Green in Birmingham show the implications of this. Bordesley Green is quite a large neighbourhood with 34,000 inhabitants, located in the inner city, not far from the city centre. As much as 86% of the population in this neighbourhood belongs to an ethnic minority and 51% see themselves as Pakistani. Many children live there, constituting a third of the population. The neighbourhood is one of the most deprived ones in the country, according to statistics (Hussain et al., 2014a).

In neighbourhoods such as Bordesley Green, "smaller, community-based or 'detached' youth services have been scaled back over the past few years in favour of larger, purpose built centres where broader based services for young people to socialise and organise have been consolidated at a district level" (Hussain et al., 2014a: 21). This is an illuminating example of the relationship between structures and actors, because the changes have rendered the expertise of the previous actors obsolete. In their previous roles, they catered for the needs of young people from certain ethnic groups or with a focus on certain activities. To reproduce these new structures and navigate in them, they need a new expertise.

> Some groups have complained of being obliged to abandon their expertise in engaging with certain groups (local communities) and in delivering interventions that they have a developed expertise in, in favour of adopting pathways prescribed centrally, which they see as not relevant to the needs of local people.
> *(Hussain et al., 2014a: 21)*

In the interview study made by Hussain et al. (2014a), "a number of agencies suggested that this is leading to disengagement among young people who choose not to take up services that do not resonate with their ambitions or which are unfeasible." Obviously, it increases inequality. But what causes this increased inequality? It would be easy to point to the policy makers of these structural changes. To be efficacious, however, they have to be actualised by actors and so they depend on how the social structures work. What discretion do these actor have? According to the report by Hussain et al. (2014a) not a lot.

3.3 ... and also in contexts of meaning (cultures)

The decision taken by the Eurozone on the night of July 13 is an example of how a structure may cause an external effect, in this case producing a potential cause of inequality affecting young people in Greece. But how come that the actors of the Eurozone have created such structures that cause devastating effects for young people in Greece? And how could it be that they, in addition, maintain and defend these structures, even though the negative consequences for young people become apparent?

This actualises another type of cause, namely that which can be called cultural. In the introduction, I made a brief presentation of the societal perspective which guides me in writing this book. A main characteristic of this perspective, Cultural Political Economy, is that it puts cultures (or semiosis, in a more generic and process-oriented sense) on an equal footing with structures (or structuration, for the same process-oriented reasons) by taking an ontological point of departure in the complexity of the world and the need to reduce this complexity to be able to go on (Sum & Jessop, 2013). This reduction of complexity is done in basically two ways, by structuration and by semiosis. That enables us to understand that not only structuration may cause effects but also semiosis.

To be sure, semiosis is about making sense and meaning, in line with what representatives of hermeneutics and phenomenology state, but in addition to making meaning, semiosis may also cause effects (Fairclough, 2003: 8). For example, I hope that this book will bring about changes, influencing readers in one direction rather than in another, enabling and reinforcing a certain kind of thinking while constraining another. Otherwise, I would not have written it. This hope is grounded in another view of causality than that which representatives of hermeneutics and phenomenology pursue. When they reject causality, it is a particular view of causality they reject: the one associated with empiricism and David Hume (Fairclough et al., 2002). In such a view, causality consists of relations between discrete and not interrelated objects (see also chapter 3.1). In contrast and from my point of view, a context of meaning is a form (formal cause), just like a social structure, made of matter (material cause) (see also Sayer, 1992: 33). It has to be produced as well as reproduced and that requires actors (efficient cause) with a certain motivation (final cause).

Accordingly, a cultural cause could be defined as a materialised form, reproduced by actors in a certain pattern of thoughts, speeches, choices, behaviour, clothes, etc. conveying a message (the signified). Just like social structures, a context of meaning cannot exist independently of actors (Sayer, 1992: 49). Vice versa, as social beings we cannot exist without reproducing contexts of meaning. As soon as you start to think or express yourself, you do that through a context of meaning – for example a language but also perhaps a certain culture, ideology or imaginary – and it does not belong only to yourself. It is profoundly social. Thereby, the constraints and opportunities of that context of meaning – the cultural causes – become effective and express themselves through us. Just as in the case of social structures, however, there is always discretion; i.e. scope for variations and the 'art of the possible'.

One of the case studies highlights implicitly such a cultural cause, namely the one inherent in norms. That is "Birmingham-Beatfreeks", a practice which according to the report "aims to give a voice to young people, develop life and transferable employability skills and create community leaders. It uses art forms such as dance, poetry, music and media as a tool to inspire, engage and empower young people." (Robinson & Commane, 2015: 2) One of the goals for its in-house apprentices and interns, as well as its sessional artists, is to improve their social competences by "opening their minds through challenging the norms which are derived from their personal history and culture". This confirms implicitly that such norms have been produced and that they consist of patterns which when they are reproduced, tend to reproduce certain behaviours and values of the individual that reproduces them. It is a good example of how norms can constitute causes. Similarly, but not mentioned in the report, societal actors reproduce norms. Such norms may very well constitute causes of inequality. To combat causes of inequality, such norms should be challenged.

Another case study which mentions cultural causes implicitly is the one called "Brno-Learning by working". According to the report (Sirovátka et al., 2015), it aims to improve the chances of a socially excluded group of Roma to get employment in the open labour market by increasing their competences and by offering opportunities. Later in the report (2015: 24), however, it is presented as one of the key innovations "to suppress discrimination in the labour market" and "improving the perception/image of Roma among the Czech public". This is said to address a "neglect of the target groups in the mainstream policy". I understand such neglect as a cultural cause of inequality.

Another example of a cultural cause is grading in schools (see chapter 7.4 for an example from Greece of how it works). In the previous chapter, I described grading as a meaning-making practice. The outcome of such a practice, the grades, constitute reference objects. They seemingly refer to the knowledge of young people, hence the referent object. They also, however, belong to a context of meaning with its own potential. As a part of that potential, the grades may make the ones with low grades appear as useless and that is how many feel about themselves. It becomes embodied and, thus, materialised in them. Even young people with incomplete grades certainly have potentials, but they do not get the chance to actualise them. The grades put a stop to that.

Imagine then if no other opportunities exist for these young people to actualise their potentials? That is largely how it is, because much of the work in society has become paid and any other work is not counted. Only through wage work is one considered to be involved and contributing to society, which is confirmed by all the rights that wage-work lays the foundation for. It is of course possible to actualise these potentials in other contexts, but as long as these efforts are not paid, they do not make you very involved in society. For those who are of working age, participation in society is mainly made through paid work.

Young people who do not get pass grades are thereby not only excluded from the labour market, but also in important respects from society. They are, so to speak, not allowed to take part in the making of society. They are not allowed to contribute to society, for this can only be done through work, and work has largely been synonymous with gainful employment; this is the kind of work from which young people with incomplete grades are excluded.

Contexts of meaning like norms or a scientific paradigm like Cultural Political Economy have to be produced and reproduced by actors. Otherwise they would not exist. To the extent that they do exist, they both constrain and enable, just like social structures. It might belong to the implicit view of a certain discourse to 'blame the victims'. If so, that is not a fallacy but a constituent part of the discourse which makes it hang together. If an individual adopts such a discourse he/she adopts that outlook on people as well. A self-sufficient and ambitious individual may just as well try to establish his/her own view, but we need to make sense of the world, not only in one of its aspects but in many. Moreover, these aspects also need to hang together, not contradict each other, at least not too much. Who has got the time and energy to make up their mind in all these respects? Not many, and, to some extent at least, all of us listen to others and cling to what is 'in the air'.

We may then very well contribute to the exclusion of other people, but perhaps, just as in the case of structures, unintentionally, because it belongs to the reproduction of this context of meaning to cause such an effect. Thus, even in this case it may be worthwhile to address these actors, saying "I know that you've got good intentions and you may not be aware of it, but in your routines you actually reproduce a meaning of life, including a view of people which excludes some. For that reason, couldn't we work together to try to change this meaning of life (culture) or at least use the possible discretion?"

3.4 Conclusions: So who and what causes inequality?

So why are the young people poor? Why are they unemployed? Why do they have to be satisfied with precarious working conditions? Why are they stigmatised by grading? In general, why are their human rights violated and in so many ways? This chapter puts us on track towards an answer by making the important distinction between potential and actual causes of inequality. Something must have the potential to cause inequality, but in order to do so it has to be actualised. This always happens in specific contexts where it enters into relations with other objects, including the ones which it is supposed to affect. Then it becomes modified into an actual cause, which is, therefore, not the same as the potential cause, but an emergent effect of different potentials being actualised by entering into relation with each other.

Each one of us may contribute to the actualisation of potential causes and thereby actually cause inequality, I have claimed, but what matters is if we do it intentionally or as actors reproducing a role in a social structure. In the latter case, causing inequality has more to do with how the social structures function and the cause can, thus, be called structural. This does not mean that our action is fully predetermined. There is always discretion, given how we construe our role, but if we use that discretion to exacerbate inequality, it has more to do with us as actors. So it is also when collective actors like an interest group push for an inequality which lies in their interest, for example by gentrification. Such causes can be called actorial or agential, whether pursued by individuals or collectives.

Perhaps we cause inequality because we believe such actions to be the right thing to do. That actualises another type of cause, called cultural, inherent in contexts of meaning, like for example norms or grading. Just as in the case of social structures, contexts of meaning have to be produced as well as reproduced by actors to exist. There is always discretion, however, to make a difference, perhaps by breaking with some aspects of the ruling norms from within them or putting more emphasis on one aspect than another in grading.

In abstract and also very simple terms, society can be understood as a combination of many social structures and contexts of meaning which many different actors take part in making, remaking, developing, reinventing, combatting, etc. If it were not for the actors, society would not exist, neither the social structures nor the contexts of meaning. To go on in the world, we need to structure social relations and make them, ourselves, others and what we do meaningful. When we do that, we also actualise the potentials of these social structures and contexts of meaning; i.e. the selective and filtering combinations of constraints and possibilities. We might then even contribute to causing inequality, perhaps unwittingly. Causes of inequality should, thus, not in the first place be seen as something external but internal to the way social structures and contexts of meaning operate.

4

SYSTEMIC CAUSES OF INEQUALITY

On the basis of the distinction in the previous chapter between potential and actual causes of inequality, this chapter will focus on the former. What has the potential to cause inequality? As we have seen in the previous chapter, a potential cause of inequality can be inherent in single objects like a decision. They can also be inherent in more complex objects like institutions. A variety of such institution-specific potential causes of inequality certainly exist across Europe due to the differences of institutions.

Here, I will restrict myself to potential causes of inequality which are inherent in the major societal systems and which therefore operate in all the ten countries, although actualised in different ways. Drawing on the approach by Marx to the crises of capitalism where he used abstractions to identify the potentials of such crisis in commodity circulation, further developed by Jessop (2015a: 259), I will identify five abstract potential causes of inequality. There may be many other causes of inequality affecting young people, but by singling out these five systemic ones, I will focus on those which I find most important and which also will allow comparisons between the life situations of young people in the ten cities involved in the Citispyce project. The next chapters will then show how they have been actualised differently.

4.1 Causes inherent in capitalism

To understand the potential of capitalism to cause inequality, we need to distinguish between capitalism and other modes of production. A distinction can be made with regard to growth. Not all production of goods and services grows. Nor should it. Why, for example, should the hairdresser in the square cut the hair of more customers if the current ones are sufficient for the business to operate? Then the hairdresser will soon have to employ someone else, but maybe she/he does not want that. She/he is only interested in providing for her/his own living.

The question arises why we need growth. Why not keep production constant and instead redistribute the enormous amount of wealth already in existence? The answer is that you cannot do this if you want to remain a capitalist. Capital must grow for it to remain capital. This growth imperative is inscribed in its mode of operation. By capital I mean assets and money but also labour power included in the profit-driven sector of the economy, i.e. the capitalist part of the economy. Growth is one of its basic characteristics. Capitalists are those who set the process in motion, driving the growth of capital (Harvey 2010: 40). They may be owners, managers or supervisors at various levels, but also, for example, speculators of all kinds. The need for growth does not basically inhere in them as individuals, but in the system. Those who fail to grow their business run the risk of losing it.

However, the growth imperative does not concern the entire market economy. There are small businesses, often privately owned, and also niche industries which can, as Richard Smith (2010: 33) explains, "carry on producing and marketing more or less the same level of output year-in year-out so long as they don't face immediate competition – because the owners of such businesses do not have to answer to other owners, to shareholders." Smith mentions regulated public utilities as another category of enterprises "that can also largely escape competitive pressures to grow because their sales, prices and profits are guaranteed and set in advance".

Many do not make this distinction between capitalism and the other parts of the market economy. Therefore, they also fail to highlight the specific properties of capitalism and, among them, its potential causes of inequality. One of them is Tim Jackson, author of one of the most popular books about growth a few years ago, *Prosperity without growth?* (2009). Jackson refers to the last decades as "the age of irresponsibility". Between 1990 and 2007 consumption increased to an extent that is unprecedented, due to a massive credit expansion and increased debt levels. The financial crisis in 2008 put the burden on the nation-states and, therefore, the taxpayers had to pay for it: i.e. bail the banks out. Already at the end of October 2008, governments around the world had paid more than the equivalent of three times as much as Britain's GDP to secure risky assets, guaranteeing threatened savings and recapitalise failing banks (2009: 20). Yet, Goldman Sachs at the end of the year paid bonuses equivalent to almost half of what the US government had used to support the banks. As Jackson writes, the bonuses were justified by the need to "attract and motivate" the best people.

> In short, the message from this chapter is that the 'age of irresponsibility' is not about casual oversight or individual greed. The economic crisis is not a consequence of isolated malpractice in selected parts of the banking sector. If there has been irresponsibility, it has been much more systemic, sanctioned from the top, and with one clear aim in mind: the continuation and protection of economic growth.
>
> *(Jackson, 2009: 26)*

Jackson emphasises the profit motive as the driving force. It is the possibility to make a profit that stimulates the continual striving for newer, better and cheaper products. This is not, however, sufficient for the wheels to spin. It also requires consumers who want and can buy what is produced: and indeed we do buy. It is closely associated with the symbolic significance which consumer goods have in our lives.

> … material artefacts constitute a powerful 'language of goods' that we use to communicate with each other – not just about status, but also about identity, social affiliation, and even – through giving and receiving gifts for example – about our feelings for each other, our hopes for our family, and our dreams of the good life.
>
> *(Jackson, 2009: 63)*

The consumer's restless desire is the perfect complement to the restless creativity of the entrepreneur. "Taken together these two self-reinforcing processes are exactly what is needed to drive growth forwards." (2009: 65) According to Jackson, it is this restlessness that must be broken. It includes government action because, as Jackson writes, "government also 'co-creates' the culture of consumption, shaping the structures and signals that influence people's behaviour" (2009: 11).

Jackson describes very well the spinning of the wheels and their different moments, but he does not get to the bottom of the question of where the drivers for growth originate. His book illustrates with many examples the unsustainability of continued growth. Nevertheless, growth continues to matter most of all. Why is it like that? What is it that drives this incessant demand for growth? Jackson emphasises the profit motive as the driving force. It is the possibility to make a profit that encourages capitalists to constantly strive for newer, better and cheaper products. That still does not explain, however, why they must constantly strive for more profits. Why can they not settle for what they have? The lack of an anwer from Jackson, as I see it, stems from his insufficient definition of capital. To be sure, Jackson himself mentions the problems with the definition:

> Oddly for a system which borrows its name from it, the term 'capital' is confusing in the sheer variety of meanings given to it within that system. Buildings and machinery are 'capital goods' sometimes called physical capital. Financial capital is used to refer to reserves of money (savings for instance), which of course can be used to invest in capital goods. And confusingly the term capital is also used to refer to the accumulation of wealth or assets – which include both financial and physical capital. In simple terms, capital simply means a stock of something.
>
> *(2009: 61, footnote iii)*

When Jackson is trying to find a common denominator in all these uses of the term capital, he characterises it as a stock of something. The same emphasis on assets is made by the commission appointed by the French president Sarkozy in 2008 and led by the Nobel laureate Joseph Stiglitz (Stiglitz et al., 2009: 29). Even Thomas Piketty in his much praised book *Capital in the twenty-first century* defines capital as an asset, "as the sum total of non-human assets that can be owned and exchanged on some market. Capital includes all forms of real property (including residential real estate) as well as financial and professional capital (plants, infrastructure, machinery, patents, and so on) used by firms and governance agencies" (2014: 46). A great merit of Piketty's book is the extensive empirical evidence of how inequality has increased. It is a very important statistic, that now no longer can be ignored.

Piketty has, however, been criticised for his lack of explanations as to why inequality has increased (Foster & Yates, 2014). Basically, as I see it, it is because he defines capital as an asset, or as he puts it, "all forms of wealth that individuals (or groups of individuals) can own and that can be transferred or traded through the market on a permanent basis". However, there is also another definition of capital.

4.1.1 The capitalist relation of exchange ...

Capital is defined as an asset by the scholars mentioned above. Not all assets are considered capital, however, but only those which are expected to make a profit. But what are these assets and why can they be expected to make a profit? From where does the profit stem? This is the question that the classical economists in the 1700s asked themselves and it received two basic answers. Both answers are present in the classical work by Adam Smith (2008) from 1776 *An Inquiry into the Nature and Causes of the Wealth of Nations*. According to the one answer, assets have an inherent ability to generate profits. This is precisely the definition of capital that Jackson as well as the Stiglitz Commission and Piketty represent. And it seems to be confirmed by experience, for example if we look at the last decades of continuous price increases in the housing market (Harvey 2012: 41).

Housing seems to have generated its own profit, that is as long as it is sold in time (Sayer, 2015: 99). When prices fall, it will become clear who the loser is and who will have to pay retrospectively for the earlier profit. The same goes for all other goods and services. You can make a profit on them if you manage to sell them dearer than their labour value. But that does still belong to the exceptions. In a fully competitive market, no one should be able to sell his or her goods and services at a price that is higher than the labour value. The invisible hand that Smith was talking about takes care of that. Profits, therefore, appear as exceptions. It does not seem to be possible to make a profit in the normal case, i.e. when the goods and services are sold at prices in accordance with their labour values.

There seem to have been grounds for a belief, strongly criticised by Marx, in the words of Jessop (2002: 13) "that economic value arises from the immanent, eternal qualities of things rather than from contingent, historically specific social relations". According to Marx, capital is essentially a social relation, namely the one that arises between the buyer and the seller of labour power. Even money, machinery, buildings and trucks may be capital but only when they convey this special social relation between persons (Liedman, 2015: 422). As Marx (1996: 753) puts it, "capital is not a thing, but a social relation between persons, established by the instrumentality of things". This requires that these things take part in a process, as Harvey (2010: 40) puts it, "in which money is perpetually sent in search of more money".

According to this definition, the normal profit in a capitalist economy derives from the relationship between the selling and buying of labour power. The capitalist pays for the use of the labour power for a certain time. The workers are paid for the value of their labour power, which is the cost to reproduce it. This includes the costs for food, housing, clothes and care but also entertainment and training. The value of labour power is determined socially by laws, norms, traditions and collective strength. What the workers produce, however, has in the normal case a higher labour value than the labour value of the labour power. The difference constitutes what Marx calls the surplus-value, which forms the basis of the profit. And it need not be unjust, as long as the workers are paid for the value of their labour power. It is a special advantage for the buyer of labour power, but really no wrong against the seller (Marx 1996: 204). At the same time, I will claim, it is a potential cause of resource inequality as it tends to amass societal resources in the hands of capitalists and their associates, at the cost of those that make up the losing side.

4.1.2 ... causing resource inequality

Resource inequality increases if the workers are paid less than the labour value of their labour power. That can happen when there is a lack of jobs. Many young people across Europe know what that pressure means, like one from Athens:

> "... You can see young people aged 26, 22, 28 years old standing in front of the telephone waiting for it to ring or sitting in front of the computer waiting for a job interview call. The situation of the people I know is truly frustrating. I am one of the few that are currently working, even if it is for these few hours. They are in constant search and as time goes by and they cannot find anything they become more and more disappointed and they lose faith in finding a job soon ..."
>
> *(Tryfona et al., 2014b: 13)*

They try to avoid the negative effects of unemployment, like poor income, the temptations of instead incurring personal debt, the lack of opportunity to leave the parental home and live independently, being bored, being stressed about the future and a feeling of standing still. Tan and Spies (2014b: 17) report from Rotterdam how a number of young people experience feelings of depression or hopelessness considering their future. "They're thankful for the benefits they receive or the support of their families (many young people have parents, an older brother or sister or an aunt that gives them some money) but it doesn't bring them any further."

> "Money isn't necessarily the problem as my parents help me. The future is the problem: I don't know where I am going".
>
> "You're bored. You go outside and sometimes fun things happen. But it is aimless and that doesn't give you a good feeling. Police keeps an eye on you as well, you don't feel good".

Unemployment and all its negative effects, make young people increasingly inclined to accept lower wages. What is worse, it tends to put a downward pressure on the labour value of labour power as well. It is, thus, not only about fluctuations of exchange-values but has deeper implications too. It implies an erosion of norms and expectations on what a reproduction of labour power requires. Hence, it runs counter to the political visions of a sustainable future because that would require a pattern of consumption with a higher quality based on an increased awareness and critically educated citizens.

The cause of this increasing resource inequality is the capitalist relation of exchange, driven as it is by the growth imperative; i.e. grow or die. The profits that feed growth derive basically from the relationship between wage labour and capital. Labour power is the sole source of new labour value and hence the surplus-value from which the profit derives (Sum & Jessop, 2013: 240). Only capital that includes living work and produces surplus-value can be called productive. That includes not only manfacturing but also transport, warehousing and retailing (see also Callinicos, 2010: 30). Furthermore, even services like schools may include productive capital as long as they are exposed to competition in the market and are driven primarily by the profit motive. The material form of the result is not crucial, but that a labour value is produced and that it exceeds the labour value of the labour power used.

Capital also appears in the form of money capital and commodity capital. And these forms of capital also generate profits if its representatives manage to sell them for more than what they have been bought for. In such situations, however, the one's gain only corresponds to the other's loss. That may require the one to be more powerful than the other. This is typical of money capital, usually also called finance capital (Lapavistas, 2013). Just as other types of capital, finance capital must accumulate to remain capital but how this occurs need not be through productive work, i.e. work that produces labour value. It may well be through, for example, differences between lending and deposit rates or by speculation (Sayer, 2015). The success of such extractions of wealth depends on power, for example the power relations between those that have and the have-nots, in precarious work organisations or in contexts of meaning which favour the wealthy by concealing their extractions.

A potential systemic cause of inequality, thus, inheres in capital, conceived as a social relation of exchange. This potential cause can occur in two basic forms. The first one arises when capitalists accumulate their wealth by paying for the labour value of labour power and get a higher labour value in return. The second one can be called accumulation by dispossession (Harvey, 2010: 48; Arrighi, 2007: 224) and I will return to that in chapter 6. In brief, it occurs when the existing labour value is extracted through either rent or interest, due to "power based on unequal ownership and control of key assets" (Sayer, 2015: 45).

4.1.3 The capitalist relation of production ...

In Marx's definition, capital is first of all a social relation and of two types (Aglietta, 1987: 46). It is a social relation of exchange and that was dealt with in the previous section. Here in this section, I will deal with the implications of the other type: namely capital as a social relation of production. The peculiarity of this social relation is that it provides the capitalist with the right to control the work of others and acquire the result of it, but also to ensure that the worker produces surplus-value which the capitalist furthermore has the right to acquire (Arthur, 2007: 3).

The formal exchange between workers and capitalists, thus turns into a substantial subordination as the living work of the former becomes incorporated in capital. It thus transforms substantially into an activity belonging to capital (Arthur 2007: 4). This does not happen due to each actor's own wishes but it is inherent in how the system functions. Marx wrote about how the division of labour and the introduction of all sorts of machines makes its mark in both body and soul, as "a labourer who all his life performs one and the same simple operation, converts his whole body into the automatic, specialised implement of that operation. Consequently, he takes less time in doing it, than the artificer who performs a whole series of operations in succession" (Marx, 1996: 344). The monotonous work "disturbs the intensity and flow of a man's animal spirits, which find recreation and delight in mere change of activity" (Marx, 1996: 346). The wage-worker turns into an increasingly smaller pawn in a greater game.

This was written by Marx 150 years ago, but is still just as valid. When the assembly line was introduced, it became especially clear that the wage worker does not use the means of production, but rather the means of production uses the wage worker. Many workers have been worn out because of it. It does not in the first place depend on the individual employer or single decisions, but on how the capitalist system works. It seems contradictory and it truly is. On the one hand, capitalism needs labour power and would not exist without it. On the other hand, it tends to wear it out. In their relation of production, the capitalists and the wage-workers have to deal with this contradiction between, at one and the same time, destroying and preserving labour power.

The contradiction is a fundamental characteristic of capitalism. It can at the same time be both good and bad (Gamble, 2016:104). It has been tremendously progressive in developing the forces of production. If it were not for capitalism, I would not have been able to write this book on a computer, taking advantage of the internet as well as a printer with the facility to print out even photos of a high quality. On the other hand, capitalism has also been tremendously destructive to which, for example, climate change and increasing inequality testify. The relation between these two sides of capitalism is obviously very contradictory. However, the contradiction is dialectic, which means that the two sides both presuppose and exclude each other. They are both inherent in the system and belong to how it works.

This is the contradiction that appears in the relation between those who buy and those who sell labour power: i.e. the capitalists and the wage-workers. It seems obvious that they have conflicting interests, but basically this does not concern the distribution of the newly produced labour value between the wage-worker and the capitalist because that is not the value for which the worker gets paid. He/she is paid for the labour value of his/her labour power. The conflicting interests do not concern quantities but the relationship between the use-value of the labour power and the exchange-value of the produced commodity. The workers must preserve the use-value of their labour power. It is the peculiarity of this use-value that it contains the ability to produce new labour value. The capitalist needs, however, to squeeze out as much surplus-value as possible; otherwise he/she will perhaps be thrown out of business as a capitalist. Yet, this endeavour to churn out surplus-value risks affecting the use-value of labour power. Capital cannot do without labour power, but it also tends to wear it out.

4.1.4 ... causing health inequality

This very special relation of production, including its dialectical contradiction, should be seen a potential cause of health inequality between the two kinds of labour that capitalism gives rise to: manual and intellectual labour. The potential cause inheres in the capitalist system, more precisely in its relation of production. It has a basis, however, in the commodity (see also Colletti, 1998). The commodity is a unit of use-value and exchange-value. It would not be sold without an exchange-value and not be bought if it lacked a use-value. As explained above, the relation between the two sides is a dialectical contradiction (Colletti, 1998; Jessop, 2002: 16).

Characteristic of capitalism is that even labour power constitutes a commodity, or more specifically that labour power is treated as if it were a commodity (Polanyi, 2001; see also for example Aglietta, 1987: 276). That is why the dialectical contradiction between use-value and exchange-value of the commodity is personalised also in the relationship between wage-workers and capitalists (see also Colletti 1998). The appearance of this dialectical contradiction is exactly what Hussain et al. (2014b: 12) refers to in the quote below. The employers need the young people but treat them in a way that tends to exhaust their use-value:

> Young people also complained that once they had served the two-year apprenticeship they would be left where they started; without a permanent job. These young people's experiences of apprenticeships were that they were more a tool to keep young people out of statistics on unemployment rather

than a meaningful way into sustainable employment, because employers disposed of them when their two-year subsidy to take on apprentices ended.

It is exactly what those belonging to the precariat experience. It does not in the first place depend on individuals or single decisions but on how the capitalist system works. It affects young people across Europe, which they tell us about in this quote from Athens.

> "You are subject to this kind of pressure, you have to like your job, you have to accept anything because there is so high demand from people who want to find employment and this builds up pressure. So, either you like it or not, you must submit to it and psychologically, that is the worst that can happen ..."
> *(Tryfona et al., 2014b: 14)*

The demand for surplus-value is materialised in the means of production, causing them to function as capital. It is built in to some extent as a coercion. So it is with the forms of organisation. They become aimed primarily at promoting the production of surplus-value and thus profits. That makes the wage-worker an object for this purpose. During the time when the wage-worker takes part in capital and in the places where this is happening, the labour power is not owned by her/him. It is owned right there and then by capital. During other times and in other places, the wage-worker remains outside not only capital but also its productive forces (i.e. equipment, facilities, technology, organisation, knowledge, etc.). That makes the wage-workers and indeed the entire society increasingly dependent on capital and the capitalists (Arrighi, 2007: 53). For some, work becomes increasingly intellectualised while the intellectual content disappears from the work of others, turning them into the losers of health inequality.

4.1.5 The capitalist rationalisation ...

In the course of time, capital evolves into an increasingly complex and societally productive force. This depends on the rationalisation of production, which enables a single capitalist company to produce more cheaply than its competitors and thus increase surplus-value relatively (Marx, 1996). Surplus-value can also be increased in absolute terms by forcing wage-workers to work longer without any wage increase. This happened all over Europe in previous times when workers had not organised themselves properly in trade unions. It still happens in many countries across the world, for example in an Ivanka Trump clothing factory which *The Guardian* reveals (13 June 2017), and also in Europe. In countries with stronger unions and labour legislation, however, capitalists have had to embark on increasing surplus-value relatively by introducing new machinery, reorganising and generally rationalising production.

When the competitors catch up, however, the societally average working time to produce the product (the labour value of it) drops. It removes also the relative surplus-value that the first capitalist managed to appropriate. This does perhaps not sound particularly remarkable. It is common knowledge that an individual company can make an additional profit from being more advanced than its competitors. A Marx-inspired theory, however, has more to say about it. It can explain how the drive of capital to invest in more competitive production leads to a change in the value composition of capital. Capital invested in machines (called constant capital) increases at the expense of the share of capital employing wage-workers (called variable capital). Marx refers to this development as the rising organic composition of capital (Marx, 1998). It means that there remain ever fewer workers to produce surplus-value. Hence, the rising organic composition of capital reduces the surplus-value in relation to the total capital, and this is usually called the tendential fall of the rate of profit, an idea launched by Adam Smith, then taken over by Marx (Arrighi, 2007: 45). It should be underlined that, just as any other potential, it works as a tendency, which means that it may not be actualised, due to the current conditions and existing counter tendencies like unemployment and bankruptcies (Callinicos, 2010: 45; Jessop, 2015a: 261).

By the rate of profit, Marx means the relationship between surplus-value and the labour value of the invested capital as a whole. As a result of rationalisation, therefore, capitalism tends to become less profitable. To counteract this reduction, greater investment is required. It also requires the production of new commodities, and to create new needs is certainly in the interest of capitalists (Liedman, 2015: 504). To remain profitable, capitalism needs to transform more unpaid work into paid labour. Privatisation of the public sector and acquisitions of small businesses are other options, which have proven succesful for capital.

> The more the socialization of the forces of production has expanded the share of past surplus-value in relation to the overall value of the labour-power producing surplus-value, the more capitalist relations of production demand that this expansion to be continued into the future.
>
> *(Aglietta, 1987: 58)*

4.1.6 ... causing structural inequality

The rising organic composition of capital, thus the peculiar rationalisation of production in accordance with a capitalist rationality, I would claim, is a potential cause of structural inequality between the losers and winners of capitalist rationality and rationalisations. On the one hand, it tends to make a lot of workers redundant, while, on the other hand, others get employed in exciting new branches where creativity may thrive, at least at the start, before the pressure sets in to rationalise according to capitalist conditions. Young people often belong to the losing side. Hindering this process of moving up the value chain is, however, not a solution. In an open and global capitalist economy, this affects young people even more, as a young person from Athens tells us about:

"... I think that these subsidized employment programmes have harmed the labour market. They benefit employers allocating them low-cost human resources ... On one hand it helps to have programmes from which companies can choose employees, but on the other hand it is an easy solution to achieve staff turnover ... It is always the businessmen who benefit ... More people remain unemployed and they are consumable. Every 6 months some people go back to unemployment and others take their place in order to keep the unemployment rates low ..."

(Tryfona et al., 2014b: 16)

As Tryfona et al. (2014b: 16) explain, "many companies take advantage of them in order to employ low-cost workforce, with limited employment rights. Basically, all that is achieved is high unemployed turnover among available job positions aiming at keeping low youth unemployment rates." These programmes are a disaster because they prevent the economy from becoming more competitive and thus pave the way for future unemployment when the state can no longer subsidise employment.

However, if moving up the value chain seems to be a solution, it only works in the short-term. In the long run, the rising organic composition of capital tends to cause structural inequality by making some workers redundant and others involved in new business sectors. To postpone such an outcome, this tendency has to be counteracted and thus modified by an active labour market policy. Yet, that does not prevent the organic composition of capital from rising but on the contrary, it makes capital develop into an increasingly societal productive force. In relation to this societal productive force, the individual workers stand there alone with their labour power and cannot do much else because they do not own any means of production, only their labour power. The worker is certainly included in the societal productive force, but only for a certain time and a certain place. And just at this time and in this place he/she does not own his/her own labour power, because that has been bought by capital. The wage-worker cannot contribute to the development of society other than as the property of capital.

Since capital owns the societal productive force, it appears also as a natural feature of it to press for surplus-value. Equally obvious it becomes necessary for the wage-worker to make his/her labour power a part of this societal productive force. How could he/she do anything else? The development of society's productive force becomes a part of capital while the wage-worker is shaped to be a part of this society's productive force and thus, in practice, becomes dependent on capital. As development progresses, it becomes increasingly difficult to produce in forms other than those included in capital. This makes unemployment an increasingly major problem. A young person in Athens is therefore spot on when saying that "unemployment is the root cause. Because we do not have a job, we do not have any money, our psychological well-being is poor, and we cannot do things." (Tryfona et al., 2014b: 13) It is also described by a young person in Rotterdam:

"When I am at the coffee shop, this means I have totally nothing to do. The night before I have been thinking: what am I going to do tomorrow? So it means I have no plans at all. So I stay home. At some point I go outside because I go insane. I really need a programme for the day because I go crazy!!"

(Tan & Spies, 2014b: 18).

As Marx predicted 150 years ago, people will become more socialised, interdependent and societalised, but on conditions set by capital and thus in forms that they do not themselves decide on. Those who decide on these forms are a small minority of the population which also tends to be smaller and smaller as capital buys up each other and gets more concentrated. Marx identifies this as a fundamental contradiction between the increasing societalisation of the productive forces and the increasing concentration of power over the means of production. All the fewer decide over ever more.

4.2 Causes inherent in the state

What does the state do about this? What is its function? It often appears as something clear and distinct; something that some people want to cut down on and others want to enlarge and strengthen. But the state is not a thing which can be used for whatever purpose. Furthermore, it is not so easy to establish exactly what institutions the state comprises of, and those that it definitely includes do not necessarily fit together. In addition, social forces try to develop the state in different directions. How, then, is it possible to get to grips with the state? How should it be understood?

My understanding is based on the definition suggested by Nicos Poulantzas (1980: 128) of the state as a social relation and, more specifically, a "material condensation of the relationship between social forces". Material condensation means the ensemble of institutions that the state unambiguously includes. As Liedman (1998: 518) puts it in his great book on the history of modernity, "institutions that normalise and codify various human relationships are inevitable in a society" (my translation). All social relationships take time to develop, Sennett (2007: 33) emphasises and "a life story in which individuals have a bearing on each other requires an institution that is retained for a generation". In an institution such life stories and ways of being with each other are maintained. "Indeed, it is thanks to our ability to rely on institutions that we have time to do anything new", as Sayer (2015: 141) puts it.

But what is an institution? Well, it is certainly not only those that belong to the state. Institutions can be anything from Christmas celebrations and funeral rituals to justice and schools. Moulaert et al. (2016: 169) defines it in abstract terms as "a relatively enduring ensemble of structural constraints and opportunities". Therefore, it is important to analyse this selectivity of institutions; i.e. what kind of ideas, activity and behaviour they select while others are filtered out. Given the strategic nature of selectivity, however, "there is always variable scope for agents to engage in institutional innovation, reinforcing, weakening, or overthrowing the dominant logic(s) of contemporary social formations" (2016: 178). In other words, there is always a discretion.

State institutions are particularly important to analyse. The power exercised by them depends also on the social forces (organisations, resources, strategies, etc.) created in other parts of society. Thus, not only the selectivity of these institutions has to be analysed but also "the historical and substantive organization and configuration of political forces in specific conjunctures and their strategies, including their capacity to reflect on and respond to the strategic selectivities inscribed in the state apparatus as a whole" (Jessop, 2011: 4). Furthermore, it requires an analysis of how these forces interact on this strategically-selective terrain. The state structures and contexts of meaning have a specific and disparate impact on these different social forces' ability to pursue their specific interests and strategies. State power can therefore be seen as an emergent actualisation of all these potentials and generative mechanisms (Jessop, 2007). A relevant theory of the state can thus only be created as part of a broader theory of society.

In this broader societal perspective, the state appears as one of several institutional contexts. Nevertheless, it is not an institutional context whatsoever, because it has the overall responsibility to hold society together (Aglietta, 1987: 383). For this purpose, its core can be defined as "a distinct ensemble of institutions and organizations whose socially accepted function is to define and enforce collectively binding decisions on a given population in the name of their 'common interest' or 'general will'." (Jessop, 2015b: 8). As implied by the quote, the developments and limits of the state do not only depend on the social structures. It also depends on the context of meaning through which the leading actors express a popular interest and acquire a popular support.

The state is thus responsible for holding together a larger context of which it is only a part. It means not only that the state puts its marks on this broader context, which we for simplistic reasons can call society. It also means that society leaves its mark on the state. Yet, a basic characteristic of the state in a society with a capitalist economy is its institutional delimitation from the circuit of capital. It is precisely this distinction and separation that allows the capitalist nature of the state to exercise a constitutional monopoly of violence (Jessop, 1990: 340). Thus it is not by being part of the circuit of capital that the state becomes capitalist. On the contrary, its institutions must keep their distance from the circuit and institutions of capital to remain a capitalist type of state. This separation, Poulantzas claims (1978: 49), "constitutes the organizing principle of the peculiar institutions of the capitalist State ...".

The necessary institutional separation from the circuit of capital and thereby also the boundary to the rest of society is always problematic and never becomes complete. That is because the state does not just consist of a core but also of institutions and organisations that temporarily and perhaps only partially are included (see Gramsci, 1971: 261). Furthermore, it is because the social forces that pursue their interests through the state and thus contribute to its power have a foothold in other parts of society. Other important features of the capitalist type of state are the hierarchical organisation, the role of bureaucracy as the principle of administrative cohesion/coherence, the territorial boundaries, its basis in the rule of law, taxation rights and dependence on money as a principle of regulation. This is combined, as Jessop puts it, "in its ideal-typical 'normal' form", with bourgeois democracy.

4.2.1 The outlook on people ...

As Poulantzas claims, all of this involves, "the atomization of the body-politic into what are called 'individuals' ..." (1978: 63). It makes the state oriented "to political subjects as individual citizens rather than as members of opposed classes and so disguises the objective reality of economic exploitation and class power" (Jessop, 2011: 2). Poulantzas describes it as a "political technology of the body" (1978: 66), supported by Foucault. In my understanding, it means that the state materialises a particular outlook on people, namely the liberal one, mentioned in chapter 3.2, which treats individuals as the origins of society.

This individualisation has on the one hand been a huge step forward as it allows the individual to decide about her/his life. On the other hand, however, it should also be seen as a potential cause of inequality because it tends to disfavour those who cannot assert themselves individually. As Liedman (2015: 165) puts it, drawing on Marx, "man is not already initially a full-fledged individual, as she *becomes* or rather, *can become* an individual" (my translation). To what extent she becomes an individual depends on the structures she takes part in, the opportunities she gets, role models, power etc. Later, I will mention individualisation as one of three characteristic principles of neoliberalism. What I want to highlight here, however, is that individualisation does not come with neoliberalism. It is inherent as a potential cause of cultural inequality in the capitalist type of state. What neoliberalism does is to provide a context of meaning which reinforces it.

4.2.2 ... and approach to knowledge ...

Poulantzas mentions yet another such potential cause of inequality, although he does not describe it as such. In all its apparatuses, Poulantzas claims (1980: 55), "the State incarnates intellectual labour as separated from manual labour ...". That materialises in the state apparatuses a special relationship between knowledge and power. Amongst others this relationship finds expression in particular techniques of the exercise of power: "These comprise a series of rituals and style of speech, as well as structural modes of formulating and tackling problems that monopolizes knowledge in such a way that the popular masses (here equivalent to manual labour) are effectively excluded" (Poulantzas, 1980: 60).

I would like to take this further and say that it also materialises a special approach to knowledge, namely one which associates knowledge with the mind at the expense of the body. More specifically, it is an approach which associates knowledge with writing, more than the spoken word. As Poulantzas puts it (1980: 59), "nothing exists for the capitalist State unless it is written down …" This approach to knowledge, I suggest, should be seen as a potential cause of inequality. Young people may be 'street-smart' which most bureaucrats are not. Indeed, many young people are very skilled in navigating across multicultural boundaries, intercultural competence as it is called; this is something which most bureaucrats could at best only dream about. However, this knowledge possessed by young people is not recognised, simply because that would require another approach to knowledge than the ruling one.

4.2.3 … causing cultural inequality

As the quotes from Poulantzas make clear, the ruling approach to knowledge filters out those whose knowledge does not sit primarily in the mind but perhaps more in the rest of the body: those that have problems with writing and those who are not familiar with the required "rituals and style of speech, as well as structural modes of formulating and tackling problems". All this selectivity certainly disfavours a lot of young people, however street-smart and interculturally competent they may be. In particular, it disfavours immigrants, as mentioned here by a young person in Hamburg:

> "Those were two years that were really pretty bad for me because the school was hard and I had problems with my German skills. And I just didn't know a lot of basics. And therefore my grades were also bad and I was always the poor student and I somehow felt treated like that, too."
>
> (Gehrke et al., 2014b)

In the report, Gehrke et al. (2014b) attribute it to discrimination. That may be so, but I also want to treat it as an effect of the ruling approach to knowledge. I will return to this potential cause of cultural inequality but here just underline that basically it inheres in the capitalist type of state and so does the individualising outlook on people. The losing side of the cultural inequality consists of those assigned to mean less, either because of the individualising outlook on people or of the intellectualising approach to knowledge.

4.3 Conclusions: Five systemic causes of inequality

In this chapter, I have shown how causes of inequality are inherent in societal systems. The most important societal system in contemporary societies is capitalism. In the definition pursued throughout this book, capital is basically a social relation, both one of exchange and one of production.

The first such systemic cause of inequality, hence, is the one associated with the capitalist exchange relation. Due to the growth imperative, capitalists have to make a profit and accumulate their capital; otherwise they will not remain capitalists. This can be achieved by the production of labour value through employing workers who produce a higher labour value than the labour value of their labour power, which the capitalist pays for. That can also be achieved through accumulation by dispossession. In both these forms, the capitalist exchange relation tends to cause a resource inequality.

Secondly, capital should also be defined as a relation of production. As such, it tends to divide the workforce between intellectual and manual labour, where the latter constitutes the losing side. I have treated this as a potential cause of health inequality between the ones who get the more intellectual job opportunities and the ones who get increasingly worn out through manual labour.

Thirdly, capital contains a potential cause of structural inequality, which is inherent in the tendency of the organic composition of capital to rise. That occurs when constant capital (machinery, etc.) increases at the expense of the variable capital (living work) due to the rationalisation of production. That forces capital to expand, create new needs and launch new products in order to remain profitable. This is a potential cause of structural inequality as it tends to make some workers redundant and create new jobs for others, in particular due to the inventions of new techniques.

Fourthly, the capitalist type of state materialises a liberal outlook on people which treats the individual as the origin of society. The state makes this outlook on people appear as normal. This is, however, a systemic cause of cultural inequality as it favours the ones who are strong individually due to their class position while it disguises the objective reality of economic exploitation and class power.

Fifthly, as the capitalist type of state incarnates intellectual labour in its division from manual labour it favours a special approach to knowledge, namely one which associates knowledge with the mind and writing at the expense of the body and speaking. This intellectualisation of knowledge should be seen as a potential cause of cultural inequality, actualised and thus reproduced by state officials in their daily work.

5
FROM DECREASING TO INCREASING INEQUALITY

Inequality has not always increased. During the first post-war decades until about 1980, virtually the whole developed capitalist world went through "egalitarian advances of existential rights and respect and a general equalisation of health and life expectancy, as well as major national equalisations of resources of income and education" (Therborn, 2013: 155). Gamble (2016: 21) describes it as a "a time of falling inequality, rising social mobility, and high levels of political participation, as well as high employment, low inflation, and rapid increases in productivity, output, and wages." To understand why inequality has increased in recent decades, it is important to explain why it decreased before this.

5.1 Those were the more equal days

"Those were the days, my friend", Mary Hopkin sang in a song with the same name, produced by Paul McCartney, which became a number one hit in the UK Singles Chart in 1968; it was very popular also in Sweden and I guess in many other countries. The song recalls the memory of a tavern, "where we used to raise a glass or two", "laughed away the hours", and "dreamed of all the great things we would do".

And dreamed young people certainly did during those days, particularly during that year, 1968: the year of the youth revolt. The song could just as well have been sung now, in remembrance of those days in the 1960s when equality increased. As the lyrics go, "we thought they'd never end", because at that time equality had been increasing for decades (and people had got used to it), indicated by a rapid expansion of social services and transfer payments.

Those days did end, however, a little more than ten years after the success of the song, around 1980. Since then, an increasing inequality has become the new normal. Before I go into depth about the causes of inequality during the last decades, I will explain briefly why it became more equal during the first post-war decades. That will then serve as an important background to the understanding of the increasing inequality which started around 1980.

5.1.1 The emergence of welfare

A lot of working class struggle lay behind the times of decreasing inequality but also a growing insight among industrial capitalists on how to increase relative surplus-value by cooperating with trade union representatives of workers. As Aglietta (1987: 71) has conceptualised it, capitalism went from an extensive to an intensive regime of accumulation. In the former, surplus-value is produced by the prolongation of the working day and the deterioration of working conditions. It can also be called sweat-shop growth. In such a growth model, the capitalists do not care much about the wage-workers, simply because they have no interest in their demand. Their wages do not generate the demand required for the wheels to spin.

Due first of all to an intensified class struggle, the industrial capitalists turned instead to rationalising production in line with an intensive regime of accumulation (Aglietta, 1987: 71). It is associated with an increase in the relative surplus-value. Such a focus led to a whole new way of life for the working classes, because a continued spinning of the wheels was made dependent on ordinary people's demand. It is in this transition from an extensive to an intensive regime of accumulation that welfare has its origins. A new time alongside wage-working arose called 'leisure' and it developed into a new societal sphere, subsequently increasingly marked by consumption (Aglietta, 1987: 25). The intensive regime of accumulation created much more favourable conditions for a mutual understanding between the parties in the labour market. Thanks to a joint effort for higher productivity, wages as well as profits could rise.

This new era took shape in space by the building of new housing neighbourhoods. Some still exist, for example Dulsberg in Hamburg. Gehrke et al. (2014a) describe it as an old working class neighbourhood, built in the 1920s and 1930s for the accommodation of workers' families. It still looks almost the same, characterised by dense architecture of red brick houses with 2–2.5 room apartments. Nowadays, the apartments have become too small relative to the size of families and current ideals. Overcrowding is, thus, one of the problems in this neighbourhood with its 17,300 inhabitants. In addition, Gehrke et al. (2014a) highlight poverty and low levels of education. Furthermore, the neighbourhood has not very much to offer young people, except for the local youth centre, which was established 40 years ago when gang violence tormented the neighbourhood. The centre is still there and has great significance. Besides this, however, there are no bars, cafes or clubs. Interviewees report on loneliness, substance abuse and boredom among young people in Dulsberg.

Yet, youth unemployment is lower than in Hamburg as a whole. Criminality is not prevalent and the media has not contributed to stigmatising the neighbourhood. Although the neighbourhood has become multicultural, it is noticeable, as one of the interviewees says, "that there is no open xenophobia and not a lot of tension between ethnicities. This might be influenced by the long social democratic working class history of the neighbourhood". Obviously, Dulsberg shows how history can put its imprint on a place and endow it with a certain potential. It materialises the memory of a previous collective empowerment and passes it on. To be fully understandable, however, this memory must be set in its historical context and it was a time of a strong working class demanding a fairer society (see also Goss, 1988).

Fundamentally important for the start of the new era with its ever-faster spinning wheels, however, were changes in production. At the end of 1920, the Italian Marxist Antonio Gramsci asked himself if the changes that took place within the capitalist production process marked the beginning of a new era (Gramsci, 1971). Gramsci was referring to the changes that Henry Ford initiated when, in 1914 at his plant in Michigan, he increased salaries and reduced the working day to 8 hours in exchange for the introduction of mass production on assembly lines. As David Harvey remarks, Ford differed from earlier visionaries, including Taylor, through the "explicit recognition that mass production meant mass consumption, a new system of the reproduction of labour power, a new politics of labour control and management, a new aesthetics, and a new psychology, in short, a new kind of rationalised, modernist, and populist democratic society" (Harvey, 1992: 125).

Ford tried to create a new human being whose morality, family life and consumer habits were suited for mass production and mass consumption. In his endeavour, he even engaged social workers who were sent into the homes of the workers (Harvey, 1992: 126). With his belief in the possibilities of regulation of the capitalist economy, he preceded Keynes and raised wages in the initial stages of the Great Depression in order to increase demand and revitalise the market economy. Ford, however, encountered great difficulties for his groundbreaking ambitions. Almost all workers in his factory were immigrants as domestic workers refused to give up their professional skills. Ford's plants were characterised in general by a high turnover of workers. In addition, he was opposed by the state, which at that point lacked the means of regulation suitable for Fordist production and whose competition laws instead forced him to cut wages.

What Ford carried out in practice, Gramsci tried to conceive the principles of. Gramsci characterised Fordism as "the biggest collective effort to date to create, with unprecedented speed, and with a consciousness of purpose unmatched in history, a new type of worker and a new type of man" (Harvey, 1992: 126). He linked the introduction of new working methods to questions of lifestyle, emotions, consumption, thinking, form of the family, sexuality, morality and form of the state. Subsequently, Fordism became an important concept in the understanding of the golden decades after the Second World War. It has been used by the regulation theory to explain the stability and coherence that, in contrast to the beliefs of neo-classical economics, never can be taken for granted in societies dominated by capitalism.

5.1.2 Prospects of stability and coherence

One of the most discussed books on inequality in recent years, mentioned also in a previous chapter, is the one by Thomas Piketty. The book has great merits, but contains also major limitations and shortcomings, both related to the author's theoretical perspective. Piketty represents on the one hand neoclassical economics, the perspective which emerged in the 1870s and has since been predominant. On the other hand, his book contains a critique that points away from the neoclassical paradigm; yet, Piketty does not abandon it (Foster & Yates, 2014).

The neoclassical paradigm rests heavily on the law associated with Jean-Baptiste Say, introduced by him in the early 1800s. The law implies that there arises an equilibrium between supply and demand if the market forces are allowed to operate freely. This equilibrium includes full employment. How has it worked? Poorly, to say the least. Despite all deregulations, privatisations and liberated market forces over the past decades, no equilibrium with full employment has appeared. On the contrary, unemployment has remained high in many countries, in particular with regard to young people.

High unemployment was a major feature of the economic recession in the 1930s and that led Keynes to reject Say's law. Keynes argued in his book from 1936, *The General Theory of Employment, Interest and Money*, that the capitalist economy instead leads to stagnation. And stagnation is precisely what has characterised the last decades of low growth, high unemployment and unused production capacity. It has been like this for almost 40 years, but that is what the neoclassical economists have not admitted. That is what Piketty does: according to him there is nothing in the capitalist economy that ensures stability and prevents the worsening of inequality. Thereby, he rejects Say's law, just as Keynes, but he also rejects another cornerstone of the neoclassical paradigm, namely Kuznets famous curve of how inequality would decrease (see also Therborn, 2013: 137). Thanks to Piketty's book, this rejection of Kuznets curve has now been acknowledged by leading representatives of the neoclassical establishment. It is one of his greatest merits. The theory has, so to say, in this respect caught up with reality.

What the book lacks, however, are explanations of why the capitalist economy tends to cause instability and inequality. To achieve such an explanation, one needs to reject the neoclassical paradigm and instead define capital as a social relation. Such an explanation, called regulation theory, was introduced in the 1970s and 1980s, with Michel Aglietta, Robert Boyer and Alain Lipietz as the leading representatives. In his seminal book *A theory of capitalist regulation: The US experience* from 1987, Aglietta turned against neoclassical economics and its belief in Say's law of an economy that regulates and stabilises itself. Its hypothesis of the utility maximising man was also rejected. Aglietta presented regulation theory as a complete alternative to the neoclassical theory of general equilibrium. He argued that the concepts of subject and state must be replaced by relation and process in the foundation of economic theory (1987: 13), fully in line with the aim of Marx to develop a theory which captures the motion in capitalism (Liedman, 2015: 508).

Capitalism cannot work without being regulated, regulation theory contends. It is not a self-playing piano, but regulations belong to the normal. One of the main reasons why capital needs to be regulated is the inherent contradictions. In chapter 4.1.3, I explained how the contradiction between capitalists and wage-workers have a basis in the commodity between its use-value and exchange-value.

This contradiction is also reflected in the wage relation. On the one hand, the wage is a cost of production, but it corresponds, on the other hand, to the use-values that the wage-workers need to buy to reproduce their labour power. The wage is thus contradictory: it is in the interest of capital, on the one hand, to keep wages down, thus enabling high profits, but, on the other hand, if the wage-workers cannot afford to buy the commodities produced by capital, the profit is not realised.

The contradiction is reflected, also, in the relations between different capitals, for example between banks and industry where the latter tends to be more inclined to protect the use-values of, for example, the machines, premises and labour power while the former looks more to the exchange-values, regardless of from where they are derived. Therefore, capital needs to be regulated due to its inherent contradictions, but also due to its incompleteness (Jessop, 2002: 18; Liedman, 2015: 428). As Gamble (2016: 105) puts it, "capitalism is a dynamic economic system but only because there are institutions outside the capitalist market which perform functions which allow the conditions on which it depends to be reproduced."

The capitalists cannot themselves close the circuit of capital accumulation. It must be closed, however, because otherwise the wheels would stop spinning and capital would no longer be accumulated, and it would then cease to be capital. Capitalists cannot decide what the wage-workers do besides the job. To be sure, wage-workers sell their labour power, but only for a limited time. Without the time limit, they would in practice sell themselves and turn into slaves. Capitalism presupposes formally free people who, when their labour power is not used by capital, can do what they themselves want. It is, however, in the interest of capital that the wage-workers use this time to recover and reproduce their labour power but they cannot make sure that they do so.

Furthermore, it takes people to buy the commodities that capital produces. If people do not want or cannot buy the commodities, commodity capital is not turned into money capital and accumulation stops. For the circuit of capital to be concluded, therefore, it takes people who can and want to buy the commodities. But capital cannot determine this. The individual must always have the last word, at least seemingly, otherwise capital undermines itself. Capitalism presupposes that people own their own labour power but also take their own decisions about what they want to consume. Therefore, there is no guarantee that capital will accumulate; capital accumulation may well fail.

Capitalists can only decide about what has been transformed into commodities. The limit for the commodity world changes constantly. New objects, events and services are commodified, for example in recent years even intimate relations through Facebook (Blackburn, 2011: 34). If commodification goes too far, it can trigger reactions and perhaps even threaten the continued accumulation of capital. There are limits to what can be commodified. Everything cannot be commodified because that would undermine capital itself. Capitalism assumes that not everything is commodified, but at the same time it is precisely capitalists that aim to push the boundaries and draw new use-values into the accumulation of capital. Due to the tendency of the profit rate to fall, that is necessary for capitalists to continue to accumulate and thus to remain capitalists.

The boundaries of commodification may be materialised institutionally. Another thing is the perception of the boundaries. The prevailing discourses may well make it look as if the limits are somewhere else other than where they actually go. That is probably the case with Facebook, which represents a more profound commodification than perceived. It could be to the advantage of capital but also to its disadvantage if any particular event led to the illumination of the differences between real and perceived boundaries. It can get many people to suddenly feel as if they have far fewer rights and freedoms than they previously perceived. This may in turn lead to calls for restrictions on capital. Young people are often the ones who reveal commodification. That criticism is very important.

5.1.3 Fordist economies

Despite all these inherent difficulties, including the conflict-prone and antagonistic character of capitalist social relations, capitalism has continued to exist. It proves the success of bringing about specific forms, called regimes of accumulation (Aglietta, 1987; Jessop & Sum, 2006). That means long-term patterns of relationships between production and consumption (see also Becker et al., 2010: 227). For such long-term relationships to emerge, single forms of regulation are not sufficient. It requires entire modes of regulation, that is, contexts of norms, institutions, organisational forms, social networks and behaviour. As Jessop (2002: 5) states: "seen in integral or inclusive terms, specific forms of capitalism can be interpreted as an 'accumulation regime + mode of regulation'". These forms can be called growth models (Jessop, 2013b).

The concept of Fordism refers to one such growth model. First of all, however, it refers to a type of work process, with mass production based on the assembly line technique performed by semi-skilled labour (Jessop, 2002: 56). As mass production became related to mass consumption during the post-war decades, a particular Fordist regime of capital accumulation emerged. Wage-workers were thereby involved in the capitalist economy even as consumers. It differed sharply from previous periods prior to Fordism, when wage-workers were only involved as producers and consumption needs were provided for by small business or their own housework.

Several of the neighbourhoods in Citispyce were part of the Fordist development and still bear the mark of it. One of them is Marghera in Venice, with its 29,000 inhabitants (Campomori et al., 2014). After being repeatedly bombarded during the Second World War, the area was reconstructed and subsequently became one of the most important industrial districts not only in Italy, but also in the whole of Europe (Campomori et al., 2014). The main industries were petrochemicals and shipbuilding, both so crucial for Fordism. Young people grow up in the legacy of this development, including the consequences of its decline since the 1970s.

This legacy is expressed nowadays as the highest proportion of households dependent on social assistance and in particular of children distanced from their families, compared to the city average. Other similar characteristics are drug dependence among the young and also very young people. Another main feature of Marghera, mentioned by Campomori et al. (2014) is the "strong sense of community and a strong engagement of the citizens towards the common good: there is a lively civil society either in terms of informal committees of citizens or in formal organisations." This has its background in a strong working class, still predominant, according to Campomori et al. (2014).

A strong working class was significant for Fordism to develop into a growth model; it required a certain mode of regulation which included collective agreements. Through the latter, unions were recognised as legitimate representatives of the wage-workers, and as a counterpart in negotiations. In return, the unions gave up their struggle for power over production and wages were linked to productivity. Through collective bargaining, wage increases spread to other parts of the economy, which also led to increases in both demand and the tax base. Of similar importance was the position of industrial capitalists on the other side of the negotiating table. They had the power among capitalist fractions during the Fordist era, not the financial capitalists. This secured the use of the increased profits for investment in large-scale industry and not for speculation.

Regarding the systemic causes of inequality, defined in the previous chapter, the Fordist wage relation regulated the first one, the capitalist relation of exchange, in favour of seeing workers as a source of demand, not primarily as a cost. Wage increases, thus, were in the interests of both capitalists and workers as it increased demand, actualised the profits and kept the wheels spinning. Even if the wage relation tended to cause inequality, the actualisation of it in the Fordist mode of regulation, modified it in favour of an increasing equality.

The Fordist regulation of the second systemic cause of inequality, the capitalist relation of production, meant that workers were more rapidly worn out. An active labour market policy was supposed to compensate for that and also for the effects of the third systemic cause of inequality, the tendency of the organic composition of capital to rise. When workers protested in the 1960s, it was against the effects of these two latter systemic causes of inequality, typical for Fordism. This also made the existence of these causes tangible, although the effects of them were not yet called inequality. Still, the first systemic cause of inequality, the one inherent in the capitalist wage relation, was regulated in favour of an increasing equality.

5.1.4 The Keynesian welfare state

The Keynesian welfare state was crucial in regulating the Fordist growth model, using the increased tax base to expand the public sector as well as infrastructure. That also made people feel safer and contributed to the development of other norms, focused on mass consumption. In addition, it created higher demand and thus stimulated the continued expansion of mass production. It was not obvious that people would become mass consumers, but it required that the traditional ways of life were replaced by norms of mass consumption and the Keynesian welfare state contributed to that. It was also not obvious that the state would use the increased tax base to expand the public sector, but once it was done, it contributed to the regulation of the Fordist growth model. The establishment of all these forms of regulation had historical backgrounds with conflicting wills and failed attempts. It was not clear that they would be established, but once that had happened one could experience it as if they fitted together.

A Fordist growth model existed when this regime of accumulation was coherently combined with its associated mode of regulation. Fordism, however, was developed unevenly across Europe. In Britain, Fordism has been described as flawed, while an export-oriented flexi-Fordism developed in Germany (Jessop and Sum, 2006: 128–133). The countries in southern Europe, except for some parts like Barcelona and Northern Italy, did not develop Fordist growth models due to their large agrarian sectors and late industrial development. Yet, they were affected by the general crisis of the Fordist growth model during the 1970s. When new growth models eventually appeared, it turned out that the differences between the European economies had increased. It also became apparent that the welfare state across Europe differed substantially.

These differences were conceptualised by Gösta Esping-Andersen in his seminal book from 1990 *The Three Worlds of Welfare Capitalism*. There, he introduced a typology of welfare regimes, partly deriving from quantitative criteria concerning the decommodification of labour-power in eighteen OECD countries, which became widespread in the 1990s and 2000s. Inspired by Karl Polanyi (2001), he meant by decommodification (1990: 3) the degree to which social rights "permit people to make their living standards independent of pure market forces". This is how Esping-Andersen formulated (1990: 21) the basic principles that the welfare state is based on:

> The welfare state cannot be understood just in terms of the rights it grants. We must also take into account how state activities are interlocked with the market's and family's role in social provision. These are the three main principles that need to be fleshed out prior to any theoretical specification of the welfare state.

With these three principles as the basis – market, state and family – Esping-Andersen identified three different types of welfare regimes. With the liberal regime, also called Anglo-Saxon, he referred to means-tested social assistance under minimalist standards. Support is based on demonstrable needs and not on status or how much one has previously worked. With the conservative regime, characterising countries particularly in Central Europe, he referred to welfare rights that are set in relation to status and based on social insurance. With the social democratic regime, the one that has dominated Northern Europe, he referred to a welfare state with universal rights attached to citizenship and mainly financed by taxes. The social democratic regime seeks equitable redistribution of society's wealth and includes a contributions system in accordance with maximalist standards.

Jessop (2002: 53) has elaborated the theory by linking the welfare state to capitalism, suggesting a distinction between four dimensions in the analysis of the forms and functions of the state. Firstly, the welfare state should be seen as linked to the reproduction of capital through economic policy. During the first post-war decades, this appeared as support for large-scale industrial production, for example road construction or expansion of electric power. Secondly, the welfare state was linked to the reproduction of labour power through social policy by the support for collective agreements, the generalisation of mass consumption norms and demand management. The welfare state can be classified as Keynesian when its economic policy favours large-scale mass production and its social policy (in the broad sense) favours large-scale mass consumption.

In addition to the above, Jessop maintains a third dimension, which concerns the structured coherence of the various scale levels of the policies, i.e. local, regional, national and international. This structured coherence is accomplished through spatio-temporal fixes. It means the spatially and temporally defined boundaries within which a given social-order is preserved and secured (Sum & Jessop, 2013: 247). The fourth dimension concerns how the different forms of regulation are governed.

It is with respect to these four dimensions (i.e. economic policy, social policy, scale and control) that Jessop can clarify the differences between the various types of the capitalist state. The welfare state has been such a type of capitalist state. With respect to the four dimensions, Jessop calls it "Keynesian Welfare National State" (KWNS) unlike the "Schumpeterian Workfare Post-national Regime" (SWPR), also called the competition state, which has spread in recent decades. A major difference between these two types concerns the relationship between the first and second dimension (Jessop, 2002: 251). In the SWPR, social policy (second dimension) has become subordinated to an expanded notion of economic policy (first dimension).

The first three systemic potential causes of inequality, referred to above, can be seen as included in what Jessop calls the first dimension of the KWNS, dealing with economic policy. They could also be said to concern what Gunnar Olofsson has called the exchange-value side of living conditions, concerning wages, prices, rents, taxes, etc. (1979: 133). Similarly, the second dimension can be associated with what Olofsson has called the use-value side of living conditions, concerning the quality of food and housing, health, working hours, education, holidays, etc.

The fourth and the fifth potential systemic causes of inequality have a bearing on this use-value side.

The fourth potential systemic cause of inequality, defined in the previous chapter as the individualistic outlook on people which is inherent in the state, privileges those with the potential to assert themselves as individuals while tending to violate the human rights of the others. That may happen if the state, at the same time, does not include compensatory policies. The welfare state has, however, included such policies. This becomes clear in the following quote by Andreas Novy where he describes the welfare state as one of the biggest achievements of the 20th century (2011: 249):

> Differences in housing, education and health were seen no longer as private concerns, but as public responsibilities. Diversity in access to health, education and housing was denounced as inequality. The public sphere was widened and the private domain of difference restricted. It was a huge step towards a society that gives the equal right to be different to all its citizens.

The welfare state compensated even for the fifth systemic potential cause of inequality, associated with an intellectualising approach to knowledge. Such a compensatory policy has echoes in, for example, the *Swedish National Curriculum for the Compulsory School, Preschool Class and the Recreation Centre 2011*, referred to in chapter 1.3, presenting knowledge as expressed in four forms (the four fs in Swedish), which presuppose and interact with each other. This division into four forms expresses an approach to knowledge which was developed during the heydays of the welfare state but inserted in the curriculum after austerity already had begun to pounce. The four fs are still there, but many teachers find them hard to comply with due to the pressure on them to control and grade.

5.2 The neoliberal revolution

During the first post-war decades, industrial capital dominated. This changed as a result of the crisis in the 1970s. In recent decades, finance capital has dominated, and with a global coverage, not national (Foster & Magdoff, 2009: 18; Therborn, 2011: 53 and 108). Large corporations have become much more engaged in the financial markets, based on speculation and rents (Arrighi, 2007: 230; Becker et al., 2010: 228). Banks have been transformed. With the proliferation of financial capital institutions, money-capital has become king, as Gowan (2009: 22) describes it:

> It entails the total subordination of the credit system's public functions to the self-expansion of money capital. Indeed, the entire spectrum of capitalist activity is drawn under the sway of money capital, in that the latter absorbs an expanding share of the profits generated across all other sectors.

Finance capital thus liberated itself from its previous close links with industrial capital, and thereby did the overall social relations of capital change. Through this financial capitalist-driven globalisation, capital has in general strengthened its position against both the wage-workers and public authorities (Ryner, 2013), but with finance capital in power (Guttmann, 2008: 10). As Pettifor (2017: 46) highlights:

> It is not just workers who are hurt by finance capital's exploitation of their labour and the extraction of wealth by way of high rates on debt. Firms, entrepreneurs, hospital administrators, university chancellors, inventors and engineers, innovators and artists of all kinds find their efforts thwarted by bankers or 'private equity investors' demanding higher rates of rent, and a larger share of the returns on investment, creativity, skill, hard work and innovation.

Thus, changes have been enforced to favour the increase of profits but this has also aggravated the internal contradictions of capital. The threat of climate change and increasing inequality indicate an erosion of labour power: i.e. our common ability to produce, solve problems, think anew, etc. A major redistribution of wealth has taken place, confirmed by many reports, among them the comprehensive one from the OECD, *Divided we stand – why inequality keeps rising* (OECD, 2011) and, of course, Piketty (2014).

5.2.1 The three principles of neoliberalism

This development has been associated with neoliberalism, but what is that? As a term, it is quite old. In *Encyclopedia of globalization*, Bob Jessop (2012b) traces the term neoliberalism back to the 1930s when it was introduced in Germany as Neoliberalismus. The term signified a revival of classical, laissez-faire liberalism and called, in short, for a free economy and a strong state. That was also how Andrew Gamble (1988) in a book with the same name, *The Free Economy and the Strong State*, summarised the politics that Margaret Thatcher pursued after she had been elected leader of the Conservative party in the UK. Thatcher and Ronald Reagan, after their historic election victories in 1979 and 1980 respectively, were at the forefront of the neoliberal revolution that began around 1980 (see also Callinicos 2010: 54ff), based on a strong support from economics. In the mid-1970s, two of neoliberalism's foremost economists had been awarded the Nobel Prize in economics; first Friedrich Hayek (1974) and then Milton Friedman (1976).

I will use a definition of neoliberalism suggested by Jessop (2012b), seeing it as a "political project that is justified on philosophical grounds and seeks to extend competitive market forces, consolidate a market-friendly constitution, and promote individual freedom." Similar definitions have been suggested by others, for example Harvey (2005: 2). While Harvey calls it "in the first instance a theory of political practices", Sayer (2015: 16ff) distinguishes neoliberalism as an academic theory from the political use of it where ideas from the theory are bent to political ends. Fairclough (2003: 4) describes it as a "political project for facilitating the re-structuring and re-scaling of social relations in accordance with the demands of an unrestrained global capitalism."

Jessop's definition has the advantage that it consists of three clearly identifiable main principles, mentioned in the quote above. Firstly, neoliberalism extends competitive market forces, amongst other things, by deregulations and privatisations. That has been accomplished by combatting organised labour and weakening the labour movement, as Therborn (2013: 128) puts it "an almost universal trend of increasing violations of basic labour rights from the mid-1980s to the early 2000s."

It has also implied an emphasis on exchange-values at the expense of use-values. High unemployment and low growth occur, according to neoliberals, because the market is not free enough, and deregulation has thus been demanded as a remedy. The markets must be made more free and people must be encouraged or forced to apply for a job, regardless of the quality. Activation, it has been called. Safety is less important. The state should focus on supporting the supply side and not on strengthening demand, whereof the latter has been characteristic of the Keynesian policy (Morel et al., 2012).

> According to the New Labour rhetoric, the unemployed needed to be 'helped back to work', but in practice this meant being disciplined – put under surveillance and required to train for non-existent jobs.
>
> *(Sayer, 2015: 165)*

Secondly, neoliberalism consolidates a market-friendly constitution by strengthening the surveillance, controlling and repressive functions of the state. That has been expressed in austerity measures and welfare retrenchments. Austerity has been permanent since the end of the 1970s (Gamble, 2016: 2). From the perspective of neoliberalism, social policy has been seen as a cost and inequality a natural part of a market, even being necessary to motivate the economic actors (Morel et al., 2012: 7). The resulting inequality is shown for example in Rotterdam where the "Buzinezzclub is one of the few remaining provisions in the 'landscape of provisions' of the municipality of Rotterdam that are specially designed to help young unemployed, vulnerable people between 17–27 years of age to find (further) education or a job and receive substantial financial support." (Davelaar et al., 2015a: 13)

This principle of neoliberalism has materialised in the approach to running public service organisations known as New Public Management and its associated quantifications. Our lives are being increasingly measured and quantified (Power, 2004). Grades have become more important as reference objects than the referent objects that they are supposed to represent; i.e. the knowledge of young people. All of this has paved the way for an underlying approach to knowledge which associates knowledge with the quantifiable and therefore tends to give priority to one of the four forms of knowledge, namely factual knowledge. As one of its characteristics, emphasis is put on results at the expense of processes.

This approach to knowledge has favoured the phenomenon called financialisation (see chapter 6.1) and the demand that it should be possible to count everything of value. It has also, I would suggest, reinforced the cultural inequality basically caused by the approach to knowledge inherent in the state: the one which associates knowledge with the mind at the expense of the body. It becomes an inequality as it violates the human rights of those who might be very knowledgeable but whose knowledge sits primarily in the body and cannot easily be quantified. In the light of this context of meaning, the latter category of people appears as less meaningful than the former. That makes it cause a cultural inequality.

Thirdly, neoliberalism promotes individualism. On the basis of many interviews with young people, Gehrke et al. (2014b) in the report on young people in Hamburg draw a conclusion which confirms the success of neoliberalism in this respect:

> Their coping strategies can be summarised as learning and working harder than the rest, and a clear career orientation, modelled on middle-class ideals; these strategies come with a whole array of tactics to circumvent encounters of discrimination by individuals and institutions.

The authors interpret these tactics as "signs of individual resilience, but they do not go beyond this individual level". In addition, I interpret it as a symptom of how the systemic cause of cultural inequality, inherent in the state, has been reinforced. It privileges those with the strength to assert themselves as individuals, while at the same time violating the human rights of those without that strength, due to their position in society. It is a cultural inequality because it makes the former category appear as more meaningful than the latter.

The effect of this cause can also express itself when young people are asked to explain the causes of inequality. As Tan & Spies (2014b: 7) report from the interviews in Rotterdam, "many young people told us about their problems and how inequality affected their daily lives, but only a few of them were able to formulate causes on a more abstract level". When better-educated and/or employed people were asked what were the reasons why so many young people from these neighbourhoods were unemployed, they basically all came up with the same list and nothing really concerns society and how it works:

> lack of education or motivation of the person himself, lack of parental support/not being raised properly, growing up in a disadvantaged neighbourhood with easy access to criminal activities, a culture of wanting expensive (Gucci, Prada) clothes and cars, peer pressure, lack of chances both regarding education and the labour market, no network that gets them inside labour via informal contacts, short term strategies and discrimination on the labour market.

Such a lack of structural causes shows the success of neoliberalism and, thus, inequality has not increased by coincidence. It should not be seen as an unfortunate outcome or a failure. On the contrary, neoliberalism justifies inequality and sees it as necessary (Morel et al., 2012: 7). However, neoliberalism is not the origin of inequality. It does not come with neoliberalism. All three of its principles cause inequality by actualising the potential causes mentioned in chapter 4. In these three respects, neoliberalism pushes for and justifies certain actualisations of the potential causes inherent in the capitalist economy and the capitalist type of state. Neoliberalism has prescribed and justified a development of social forms to actualise these systemic causes. To explain inequality, therefore, it is not enough to understand neoliberalism; it also requires an understanding of the potential systemic causes that it actualises.

Neoliberalism has put its imprint on all the countries included in the Citispyce project, although to different extents. Jessop (2012b) identifies four main types of neoliberal regimes that developed in the 'neoliberal epoch' beginning in the 1970s. All of them emerged in reaction to the crisis of post-war settlements. The most radical was the neoliberal system transformations in the states that emerged from the former Soviet Bloc, among them Poland, the Czech Republic and Bulgaria. Next follows the neoliberal regime shifts of which Thatcherism is the prime expression. The third form comprises restructuring processes that were primarily imposed from the outside (southern Europe), while the more pragmatic neoliberal policy adjustments constitute the fourth type. Germany, The Netherlands and Sweden belong to this last group.

All these institutional changes testify to the success of neoliberalism. Furthermore, as a context of meaning, neoliberalism seems to have become the basic grammar all across Europe (Anderson, 2009), for example indicated by the conduct of austerity policies. Neoliberalism has succeeded with what Stuart Hall once described as the hope of every ideology, namely "to naturalize itself out of History into Nature, and thus to become invisible, to operate unconsciously" (1988: 246–247). Very significant for this success is its basis in neoclassical economics. This foundation and its implications is what I now seek to highlight.

5.2.2 On the basis of neoclassical economics

Neoclassical economics had its break-through in the 1870s. Economists like Jevons, Menger, Marshall and Walras pushed through a shift of focus from production to market. They claimed that the price of a commodity should not be seen as determined by production but by the relationship between supply and demand in the market, in accordance with Say's law (see 5.1.2).

This was based on a liberal outlook, inspired by Jeremy Bentham, seeing people as driven by egoism and the maximising of utility. The neoclassical revolution of the 1870s consolidated the emerging divisions between economics and the other social sciences, as Ben Fine (2007: 48) puts it, "with the former tending to offer an individualistic approach (economic rationality) to market relations, and the latter focusing on holistic approaches to non-market relations (and/or 'irrationality' in individual behaviour)." In this way, the economists made economics their own subject while other sciences were expected to deal with the rest, understood by the economists as the social.

That is the background to the development that began in the 1960s, characterised by Fine as another revolution. Since then, economics has exceeded the old limit and become more focused on the social, but on the basis of its own outlook on people. One of those who took the first step was Gary Becker with the theory of human capital, published as a book in 1964 with the same name. In brief, the theory implies, according to Liedman (2006: 519), "that an individual put so much time and money into his education which she expects to get back in the future in the form of higher standards of living" (my translation). According to the theory, we thus increase our human capital and it is our self-utility that drives us to it. The theory of human capital is, thus, based on the same outlook on people as neoclassical economics. In fact, Becker pushed the economistic outlook to the extreme and made it an explanation of many different phenomena such as discrimination, education, crime, marriage, divorce, suicide and childbirth.

5.2.3 The twisted promise of social capital

Another prominent expression of this outlook is the concept of social capital. The current use of this concept has its origin in the second half of the 1980s. Two researchers have been commonly cited as the originators: Pierre Bourdieu and James Coleman. Indeed, both were sociologists, but, in important respects, they represented different perspectives. Contrary to Bourdieu, Coleman was heavily influenced by neoclassical economics and was one of the instigators of the revolution in economics that began in the sixties with the theory of human capital. Coleman's theory of social capital is a continuation of this development, which Fine (2001: 10) describes as colonisation by economics of the social sciences. Coleman was also one of the initiators of another expression of this neoclassical imperialism, namely, rational choice. Inspiration was very much provided by Gary Becker, and facilitated by both of them being employed at the University of Chicago, the residence also of Milton Friedman and the centre for so much of neoliberal thinking.

In recent decades, the concept of social capital has been associated with Robert Putnam. According to Fine, Putnam has not taken sides regarding the important differences between Bourdieu and Coleman. Therefore, Fine sees him as rather unclear in his basic outlook. Thus, in a time when social capital has become a major concept, it lacks any deeper anchorage in scientific theory. The important differences between the originators have been smoothed over (see for example Field, 2008). How has such a mediocre concept become so popular? David Halpern (2005: 2–3) suggests a plausible explanation, whilst also defending the use of it:

> The term captures the political Zeitgeist of our time: it has a hard-nosed economic feel while restating the importance of the social. It implicitly counters the crude economic political fashion of the 1980s and early 1990s especially

characteristic of the USA, UK and New Zealand, as captured in Margaret Thatcher's famous pronouncement that 'there is no such thing as a society'.

The concept seems to strengthen the social and become part of the critique of neoliberalism; instead it has been the opposite. What the concept does, above all, is to justify the definition of capital as an asset and resource. Such a definition of social capital is also what all its advocates seem to have in common. As John Field writes in his book *Social Capital* (2008: 44): "surely, if the concept does add anything new in analytical terms, it lies in its focus on networks and relationships as a resource".

On the basis of the other definition of capital, the one that I represent in this book (see also chapter 4.1), the concept of social capital is a prime example of an oxymoron (Fine, 2007), according to Britannica "a word or group of words that is self-contradicting, as in bittersweet or plastic glass". Capital is namely social in itself. At its core, capital consists of a special social relation, albeit contradictory and incomplete. It is therefore logical and at the same time revealing that the concept of social capital only refers to social relationships outside capital, as here in the definition suggested by Halpern (2005: 38–39):

> The term refers to the social networks, norms and sanctions that facilitate co-operative action among individuals and communities.

Where do all the other social relations take place, those that have to do with, for example, the workplace, trade unions and the state? The most serious problem with the concept of social capital, in my opinion, is its highly effective concealment of capitalist social relations. It makes it difficult to understand the critique of the other definition, the one of capital as an asset and resource. Instead, it provides the ones critical of neoliberalism with a space of their own, but still within the frames of neoclassical economics. That ensures their continued power.

5.3 But also other ways

Above is not the whole story of the last decades. As I have underlined many times, the social world does not only contain constraints but also opportunities. Actors who see other meanings with their lives than the one prescribed by neoliberalism have used the opportunities to make a difference. Several such long-lasting efforts are described in the reports from Citispyce. One of them is "Casal dels Infants" in Barcelona which has existed since the early 1980s. It is probably the largest organisation in the area and described as a reference point. With the arrival of migration, it has oriented its services to foreign children and youth. A very comprehensive and integral set of programmes is offered.

> According to an interviewee, the most innovative approach of this organisation is training young people to promote the development of abilities and

skills which involve participation in the public space, and the development of identities linked to the territory. A clear example would be an Initial Programme of Professional Qualification (PQPI) on illumination to other activities. Young people learn how to make a creative illumination installation in a public space which has a deficit of illumination, where children can also play. Apart from learning technical issues, they gain an artistic sensitivity and how to work in team. This is also a way to foster community participation as these young people will probably later on engage with other activities happening in the area. This in turn has an impact on their self-esteem and competences to be more autonomous.

(Jubany et al., 2014a: 29)

Another example is Sofielunds Folkets Hus, the centre of civil society in Malmö. It is located in an old building and former school, built in 1902 and owned by the municipality. In the early 1990s, the building was decaying and the municipality had plans to knock it down. At that time, an association had started in the area with the ambition of creating a meeting place, especially for young people. There was very little for young people to do in the area and that caused a lot of problems, both for the young people themselves and for others. In 1995, the association got the opportunity to dispose of the old school and they thereby established Sofielunds Folkets Hus (SFH). Since then it has developed into a multicultural, flourishing and vibrant meeting place, as well as a basis for a wide range of activities.

The main activities in the building are run by another association, called Glokala folkbildningsföreningen (GFF) (trans. Glocal "folkbildning" association), initiated in the late 1980s. The Swedish term "folkbildning" means the enlightenment ("bildning") of people ("folk") and refers to the folk high schools and study associations, i.e. the organisations that constitute the non-formal and voluntary educational system in Sweden. Both folk high schools and study associations receive substantial state grants that make it easier for civil society to take care of needs and initiatives among young people regardless of priorities inside the municipal structure.

SFH and GFF have been closely intertwined over the years. From the early days in the mid 90s, GFF initiatives have supplied the house with a lot of activities, daytime as well as night-time. A major initiative was the establishment in 2005 of a "folkhögskola" (folk high school) in the house, called Glokala Folkhögskolan (GFH) with GFF as responsible. Since then, a wide range of courses have been held in the house, offered, for example, to young people without a completed formal education as well as to immigrants. Furthermore, GFH offers generic folk high school courses but here with a 'glocal' profile, short-term courses for the general public (urban art and hiphop, glocal media, etc.), general lectures, etc.

As part of the Citispyce project, we carried out a lot of interviews with people associated with SFH and GFF. Our interviews focused on the value of the SFH: in the first place its use-value and thereby the type of value which, in contrast to exchange-value, cannot necessarily be measured in money. The management highlights the implications of people in general being made welcome and on the voluntary basis of the activity. In SFH, trust and confidence are created, says one of the members of the board. A board member with an immigrant background relates how much he learns in SFH about Swedish society, due to the fact that he feels welcome. Feeling welcome is something that several of the members of the board highlight. That strengthens your self-confidence. A member says that here *"you get support to get ahead in life in a dignified way"*. He is seconded by another member who finds the statement right on target. *"You grow by the trust you get and subsequently can give."*

SFH has been the basis of many different initiatives over the years, including some larger ones such as the Brewery. In the late 1990s, a group of young skateboarders got the opportunity to take over a large part of the old Brewery. Before that, they had been accommodated at the SFH where the ideas about creating something much greater were generated. The young skateboarders built up a large indoor skateboard park called the Brewery, then and today considered one of the best and largest in northern Europe. The skateboard park attracted not only skaters, but also many young people just hanging out, discussing and listening to hip hop. Thus, since then, the activities in the Brewery have been under a constant remodelling to explore new possibilities, according to the wishes of the young participants.

5.4 Conclusions: Neoliberal constraints but also new opportunities

During the first post-war decades until about 1980, inequality did not increase but on the contrary equality increased. In this chapter, I have explained why and with regard to the five systemic potential causes of inequality. They were actualised in other ways compared to those in later years. Revolving around collective agreements, the so-called Fordist wage relation actualised and regulated the capitalist relation of exchange, relation of production and tendency of the organic composition to rise. These systemic potential causes of inequality were actualised in favour of industrial capital and a function of the wage as a source of demand. That made it profitable for capitalists to increase wages, expand the public sector and thus, in these ways increase demand.

The Keynesian welfare state contributed with an economic policy which included an active labour market policy, but also with a social policy that compensated for both the individualist and the intellectualist causes of inequality inherent in the state. Because of these settlements and power relations, an increasing equality was in the interest of all.

This was no longer the case when neoliberalism came to the fore. Neoliberalism can be defined as a political project, characterised by extending competitive market forces, consolidating a market-friendly constitution, and promoting individual freedom. These three principles have guided institutional changes. The first principle (extending competitive market forces) has led to new forms for actualising the systemic causes of resource, health and structural inequality. These new forms will be identified in chapter 6. The second (consolidating a market-friendly constitution) and third (promoting individual freedom) principles, in their turn, have provided the systemic causes of cultural inequality with new forms for its actualisation. These will be dealt with in chapter 7.

In this chapter, I have also shown how neoliberalism has derived strength from philosophical support in neoclassical economics with its liberal outlook on people. As a context of meaning, neoliberalism has benefited from the development of concepts like social capital which provides the ones critical of neoliberalism with a space of their own, but still within a framework set by neoclassical economics. The concept of social capital can be seen as one of the moments in this context of meaning. Using the concept of social capital tends to reproduce neoliberalism and ensure its continued rule.

However, actors have not been equally constrained by neoliberalism. Actors who see other meanings with their lives than the one prescribed by neoliberalism have used the opportunities to make a difference. Several such long-lasting efforts are described in the reports from Citispyce. One of them is "Casal dels Infants" in Barcelona which has existed since the early 1980s. Another example is "Sofielunds Folkets Hus", the centre of civil society in Sofielund, Malmö. Such organisations have concentrated on creating use-values which, in contrast to exchange-value, cannot necessarily be measured in money; e.g. trust and self-confidence. Thereby, they have resisted the neoliberal revolution and its commodifications, insisting that everything of value cannot be measured and particularly not in money.

6
FINANCIALISED ECONOMIES

This chapter pinpoints and compares the situation of young people in the ten countries with regard to the economy and deals with growth models. As defined in chapter 5.1.3, a growth model comprises a long-term pattern of relatively stable relationships between production and consumption. It also comprises forms of regulation. In this book, I have focused on the forms that regulate the wage relation and the ones that involve parts of the state. The latter consists of institutions and organisations that belong to economic policy: i.e. the first of Jessop's four dimensions (chapter 5.1.4). It is associated with what Olofsson has called the exchange-value side of living conditions (chapter 5.1.4). A further rationale for the chapter is that it traces the effects of the first principle of neoliberalism, as presented and explained in chapter 5.2.

Chapter 5.1 explored the Fordist growth model with its national boundaries. It has been replaced by a variegated capitalism, as Jessop conceptualises it. This means that different variants of capitalism coexist and co-develop in the context of the world market. At the same time, it is this interaction that makes the world market develop, rather than any pre-determined overall logic (see e.g. Jessop, 2012c). This also means that different variants of capitalism cannot obviously be considered national, because they are not necessarily confined within national borders. Yet, large and decisive national differences remain, due to the differences in forms of regulation. That makes a difference concerning the actualisation of the systemic causes of inequality. Even if these latter potential causes are the same ones across Europe, the actual causes that emanate from the context-dependent actualisation of them could be different. The focus of this chapter is, therefore, these actual causes and the differences between them in Europe.

To understand the differences between the European national economies, industrial relations as classified by the European Commission (2008) may serve as an entry point. The European Commission starts by highlighting some commonalities which the western member states of the European Union share and which distinguishes the EU from other regions in the world. In post-war western Europe, the industrial relations arrangements and their achievements in contributing to growth and publicly secured social protection have rested on four institutional pillars (European Commission, 2008: 19); "strong or reasonably established and publicly guaranteed trade unions; a degree of solidarity wage setting based on coordination at the sectoral level or above; a fairly generalized arrangement of information, consultation, and perhaps co-determination at the firm level based on the rights of workers and unions to be involved; and routine participation in tripartite policy arrangements." From the perspective of regulation theory (see chapter 5.1.3), these four pillars are associated with the so-called Fordist mode of regulation.

The European Commission has also tried to classify the differences that have emerged (2008, 2013a). The report identifies five models of industrial relations, associated with different geographical areas. The Nordic model is characterised by being inclusive and coordinated as well as having a high union density and collective bargaining coverage. The Central European model is also coordinated, but dualistic and it has a middle-range union density, although quite a high bargaining coverage. The Western model is uncoordinated and market-oriented as well as characterised by a low union density and also low coverage of collective bargaining. In the Southern model, described as state-centred and dualistic, union density is extremely low but bargaining coverage rather high. The Eastern model has both an extremely low union density and a low bargaining coverage. Citispyce contains representatives for all these five models.

From the perspective of regulation theory, these five models concern the structural form called the wage relation. As such, the categorisation is useful. In order to make the categories even more useful, these five different forms of wage relations will be linked to different regimes of accumulation. As Becker and Jäger (2011: 4) maintain "to understand the crisis of the EU and the Eurozone and the responses to the crisis it is necessary to analyse the content of structural forms, their interaction and territoriality together with the regimes of accumulation." Together these five different forms of wage relations and their structurally coupled regimes of accumulation constitute five models of growth. Each one of them will be dealt with in turn to clarify how they have been actualised. The aim is to highlight the model-specific causes of inequality and more precisely, how the models actualise the systemic potential causes of inequality.

6.1 Dependent financialisation in the south

Countries in the south of Europe have pursued an import oriented regime of capital accumulation, depending on borrowed money and indicated by current account deficits in Spain and Greece from at least the mid-1990s. The increasing indebtedness has been driven by consumption but also by rising prices of real estate (Lapavistas et al., 2012: 19). The main reason for increasing debt has been the loss of competitiveness, which has forced peripheral countries to focus on boosting domestic demand, above all, through investment in real estate and consumption (Lapavistas et al., 2012: 92).

This regime of accumulation has been called dependent financialisation (Becker and Weissenbacher, 2012). With the support of Fine (2011), I may define the concept of financialisation by referring to the phenomenal expansion of financial assets and financial activity relative to the rest of the economy over the last thirty years (see also Callinicos, 2010: 23; Foster and Magdoff, 2009). Financialisation has comprised "the proliferation of different types of assets, not least through the expansion of securitisation, derivatives, exchange rate speculation and corresponding futures markets for currencies as well as for many commodities". Moreover, this proliferation has occurred at the expense of the real economy. Financialisation "has been perceived to be dependent upon consumer-led booms based on credit in which the housing market in particular has been the basis for a central speculative asset". It has also penetrated generally into "ever more areas of economic and social life such as pensions, education, health, and provision of economic and social infrastructure." A similar definition, highlighting eight features, has been suggested by the FESSUD project (see Stenfors et al., 2014: 16).

In addition to the definition suggested by Fine, financialisation has to be treated in conjunction with the finance-dominated regime of accumulation (Guttman, 2008: 2). This differs from the Fordist regime of accumulation, where productive capital dominated and the wage functioned as a source of demand. Therefore, increases in real wages were in the interest of both capital and labour. In the finance-dominated regime of accumulation the wage is regarded as a cost and has to be kept as low as possible. As Boyer (2000: 118) notes, "accumulation has become mainly extensive and based on the differentiation of modes of consumption and increasing inequalities". Hence, the wage share has declined in all OECD countries, according to Stockhammer (2013: 1) on average from 73.4% in 1980 to 64% in 2007, constituting "a major historical change as wage shares had been stable or increasing in the post-war era". The results of Stockhammer's study indicate that financialisation has been the main cause of the decline in the wage share (see also Therborn, 2013: 129; Pratschke & Morlicchio, 2012: 1892).

> Of course, the declining wage share has during the last quarter of century been compensated for by falling personal saving rates and rising levels of consumer debt, another important aspect of the growth dynamic in finance-led capitalism.
> *(Guttmann, 2008: 4)*

In Spain, the continuous economic growth for 14 years, from 1994 to 2008, and the veritable economic boom in the last decade of this period, was built on loans. As Lapavistas et al. (2012: 93) show, "aggregate Spanish debt has risen dramatically as a proportion of GDP since the late 1990s. The bulk of growth has been in private debt, driven mostly by rising debt of the financial sector". In contrast, Spanish public debt has actually declined in relative terms since the late 1990s. Money was mainly invested in construction and its subordinated industrial production, not for example in export oriented production or increased productivity (Lapavistas et al., 2012: 27). This made the growth model vulnerable to changes in borrowing conditions. Accordingly, and as Roiha et al. (2013) highlight, sectors closely related to the previous economic growth were affected more severely by the crisis.

In Greece, the public sector debt has been a far more significant part of aggregate debt than in Spain and Portugal. This has been a feature of the Greek economy since the 1980s with the initial growth of public debt being an outcome of the expansion of public expenses and mismanagement (Lapavistas et al., 2012: 95). For instance, Avatangelou et al. (2013: 11) describe that although the National Health System, founded in 1982, was originally a breakthrough concept at the time, gradually, great administrative loopholes, mismanagement and lack of monitoring resulted in poor public health services, worsening during the time of the crisis. The Greek welfare state in general has for a long time been described as dysfunctional and inefficient. Obviously, despite the great expectations of certain legal provisions, operation mechanisms remained ineffective and the welfare state did not manage to support the development of a competitive economy deserving its place in the international division of labour.

In Italy, the general government gross debt as a percentage of GDP has exceeded 100% every year since at least the mid-1990s. Dependent financialisation has not, however, engendered the same dynamic as in Spain and Greece. Italy has suffered from slow growth since the late 1990s. As Tridico (2013: 18) concludes, "Italy used to be a richer country, with an average GDP above the EU15 (the richest club), and today it is far below this average level". According to the detailed analysis made by Tridico, this depends on the past reforms of the labour market, in particular the labour flexibility introduced in the last 20 years.

The development of the welfare state in Greece can be interpreted as an attempt to catch up with regard to modes of regulation instituted in other countries during the heydays of Fordism. Another such attempt was made to establish the kind of wage relation associated with Fordism when pressures by the Unions led to the establishment of some 'protective' laws restricting the use of fixed-term contracts. Accordingly, in 2007 Greece's rate of fixed-term contracts was below the EU27 average, Avatangelou et al. (2013: 8) report, but "nevertheless, after the eruption of the crisis, temporary employment came dynamically to the forefront and permanent employment declined, within the general measures taken for the enhancement of 'flexible work'."

The restrictions on fixed-term contracts in Greece did perhaps alleviate the effects of the division between insiders and outsiders, characterising the southern form of wage relation. By contrast, in the labour market of Spain a tendency to rely on temporary work contracts, especially for young people, has been the norm. As Roiha et al. (2013: 6) state,

> a key reason why temporary contracts do not lead to permanent employment in the Spanish context is the large difference between dismissal costs for

temporary and permanent contracts, making companies reluctant to convert fixed-term contracts into open-ended ones. ... This means that many young people are trapped in precarious employment or unemployment, with unfavourable effects for their long-term employability and large costs for society as a whole.

The dualistic division and the concomitant existence of a market for low skills seemed to have made it legitimate for a substantial share of young people not to educate themselves. As Roiha et al. (2013: 7) mention, a high percentage of youth (15–24) in Spain have attained at most lower secondary education (see also chapter 2.2), but yet "until 2007, the unemployment rate of low-skilled workers was not much higher than that of skilled workers, indicating a great deal of low-skilled jobs in the construction and hospitality sectors in the past". The first to lose their jobs during the crisis, however, were these low-skilled youths and "they are also likely to be in a disadvantageous position in terms of accessing new jobs when the economy recovers, considering the growing demand of high and intermediate levels of skills".

In general, young people have been particularly vulnerable, due to the southern form of wage relation with its dualistic labour market dividing workers into insiders and outsiders. They do not seem to have had any legitimate representatives in the labour market. Union density is extremely low in the southern form of wage relation. As Avatangelou et al. (2013: 19) maintain, "participation of young people in labour unions is minimum in Greece, mainly due to the neglect and lack of good practices for attracting youth." The Greek trade unions have failed to offer a fresh view to young people and tend to have restricted themselves to safeguarding the insiders.

Accordingly, young people from both the areas studied by Tryfona et al. (2014b: 14) "mentioned that the majority of jobs offered to young people are low status positions in the service sector, such as coffee shops, restaurants, bars, and clubs". As indicated by all the interviewees, the working conditions have deteriorated in recent years. Tryfona et al. (2014b: 15) relate how a new category called "job contractors" has appeared, offering jobs for young people in exchange for money or a percentage of their wage. In addition, employers may take advantage of subsidised employment programmes that exist:

> Overall, these programmes offer only limited professional experience to a small number of young people. Furthermore, many companies take advantage of them in order to employ low-cost workforce, with limited employment rights. Basically, all that is achieved is high unemployed turnover among available job positions aiming at keeping low youth unemployment rates.
>
> *(Tryfona et al., 2014b: 16)*

Yet, in Spain and Greece this growth model seemed to have been successful. In 2003, Greece had the highest growth rate among the countries in the European

Union, 5.9%, compared to −0.4% in Germany. As Avatangelou et al. (2013: 2) state, "an unexpected growth throughout the 1990s, also continued into the new millennium, involving a major improvement in employability, welfare and citizens' living standards and providing immense opportunities to young people at the time." Yet, just a few years later, everything had been turned upside down and the growth model had proved to be unsustainable.

6.2 Superior export-orientation in the centre

The Central European model consists of an export-oriented regime of accumulation, regarding both goods and money capital. In contrast to the countries with dependent financialisation, Germany has had a surplus in its account balance since 2001, rising until 2007. This surplus has not depended on superior productivity growth, which has been weaker than for example in Greece (Lapavistas et al., 2012: 26), but on a favourable situation in the Eurozone as well as an internal pressure on pay and conditions. Growth in Germany has, in fact, been mediocre. In addition, investment has been flat, consumption stagnant, savings rising and household debt falling. The question arises about what has engendered growth. As Lapavistas et al. (2012: 21) underline, "the only source of dynamism has been exports" and two thirds of German trade is with the Eurozone (2012: 30). As the leading country of this growth model, Germany has become very rich.

As mentioned in Chapter 1, the Euro has been crucial in the neoliberal project. It has urged the member states to strengthen competitiveness by increasing flexibility as well as promoting temporary and part-time work. This race to the bottom has been won by Germany. Lapavistas et al. (2012) highlight two main reasons. Firstly, peripheral countries entered the Eurozone at high exchange rates which gave German exporters a competitive advantage. In that way, the competitiveness of peripheral countries was reduced at a stroke when joining the Eurozone.

Secondly, Germany has been much more successful than the peripheral countries in squeezing its own workers and in that way increasing its competitiveness. Lapavistas et al. (2012: 30) describe the Euro as a "'beggar-thy-neighbour' policy for Germany, on condition that it beggars its own workers first". German capital has also, since the early 1990s, taken full advantage of cheaper labour in Eastern Europe. A complex pattern of pathological interdependencies has arisen which causes a lot of inequality.

One of the most important industrial centres in Germany, and indeed of this growth model, is Hamburg. It shows all the benefits of this growth model. As Gehrke et al. (2013: 7) state, "never before has the number of people in employment been as high". In fact, Hamburg is one of the richest cities in Europe, ranking fourth of the 271 NUTS-2 regions with regard to GDP comparison per capita. The Hamburg report gives the impression of a city with a lot of space for the type of work organisation associated with discretionary learning and to which I will return below:

> The City of Hamburg has a prosperous and innovative scene that spans across the arts and creative industries, including services and production related to new technologies and software development, media and journalism, advertising and design. Beside the typical hot spots in which young urban professionals have already established centres for multimedia and all types of creative and independent arts and technology (Schanzenviertel/St. Pauli/Ottensen), many new creative cells are spread all over the city.
>
> *(Gehrke et al., 2013: 4)*

The report also highlights, however, the costs of this model because "at the same time, precarious jobs (short-term or part-time contracts – with less protection than in previous decades when permanent contracts were the norm) are increasingly common, even for middle classes, causing uncertainty and unease" (Gehrke et al., 2013: 8). Gehrke et al. (2013: 9) mention subcontracted temporary employment, "which increased by 95% during 2000–2011 up to 3.4% of all formal employment contracts (the national average is 2.9%). Half of these contracts are for less than three months and typically, the wages are much lower compared to average wages in regular employment contracts". Since 2000, the low wage sector has increased by 38% and in 2010, it comprised 19% of all employees working with an income of less than 1,890 Euro per month. People in general have benefited from the regime of capital accumulation but a substantial proportion of the population has not been favoured by its form of wage relation. As Becker and Jäger (2011: 6) emphasise, the low wage sector is as important in Germany as in the USA. According to Eurostat data for 2014, the proportion of low-wage earners among all employees is among the highest in Europe, 22.5%, slightly higher than in the UK (21.3%).[1]

Rotterdam with its harbour is certainly a very important node in this growth model. As the Rotterdam report (Spies and Tan, 2013: 7) maintains, "from the 19th century onward the harbour and the economic activity that comes with it, has been the most important source of employment in the region". A lot of the low-skilled work, associated with the harbour and traditionally dominating the labour market, has however disappeared. The Rotterdam report tells us how the labour market has changed, also in terms of the wage relation. Flexibility is increasing and fewer people have a permanent job. Nevertheless, the Dutch economy seems to have positioned itself successfully in the international division of labour, indicated for example by a surplus in the current account balance for decades and by low levels of unemployment. The Netherlands has one of the highest percentages of employees working in organisations characterised by discretionary learning, 64% in 2000, although it has decreased since then. Obviously, that makes the Dutch economy competitive and allows it to provide job opportunities for young people.

Yet, the systemic causes of inequality, inherent in the capitalist system, are actualised even in this seemingly successful development. This actual cause of inequality is called accumulation by dispossession, a concept introduced by David Harvey, who has derived it from the concept of primitive accumulation used by

Marx (1996) in his explanation of the rise of capitalism (Arrighi, 2007: 224). In order for the capitalist social relation to arise, it required owners with enough money on the one hand, and on the other, free workers who basically did not own more than their labour power and therefore had to sell it to make a living. With the concept of primitive accumulation, Marx referred to the historical process that deprived the producers of their means of production, that is, opportunities to earn a living. It could be done, for example, by the expropriation of peasant farms or by new laws (see also e.g. Polanyi, 2001). Another method of primitive accumulation was the slave trade which made Liverpool a metropolis (Marx, 1996).

By updating the concept of "primitive accumulation" to "accumulation by dispossession", Harvey (2010: 48) wants to highlight that primitive accumulation does not only belong to the earlier stages of capitalism. It continues to happen and indeed, puts an imprint on contemporary society, by the use of illegal means, "such as violence, criminality, fraud and predatory practices of the sort that have been uncovered in recent times in the subprime mortgage market". But also legal means are deployed, including "privatisation of what were once considered common property resources (like water and education), the use of the power of eminent domains to seize assets, widespread practices of takeovers, mergers and the like that result in 'asset stripping', and reneging on, say, pension and health care obligations through bankruptcy proceedings".

Accumulation by dispossession should be seen as the normal way of accumulating capital in an era when finance capital dominates. As such, it constitutes an actual cause of inequality, actualising the potential cause inherent in the capitalist relation of exchange. Thereby, people's relationship to the accumulation of capital has changed. Earlier, people contributed to the accumulation of capital mainly through the production of values, but now we are contributing increasingly by being dispossessed of values, for example by big differences between lending rates and deposit rates, transaction costs, pensions, insurances and the stock market.

An example of accumulation by dispossession is the largely privatised sector of labour re-integration in the Netherlands, which the report on the case study called "Rotterdam-Buzinezzclub" tells us about:

> The reputation of Dutch commercial enterprises active in the field of job-re-integration and activation is – to put it mildly – not very good. Re-integration businesses are often described as 'cowboys', mainly active in the field to 'make easy money', albeit under conditions (contracts) set by the public authorities.
> *(Davelaar et al., 2015a: 26)*

The "Rotterdam-Buzinezzclub" claims to be "the opposite of the acclaimed 'hit and run' mentality of many re-integration firms", as the report puts it, "there is ample evidence that this is true, in theory and practice". The authors may be right, but when many companies turn into an accumulation of capital by dispossession, it seems important to scrutinise the selectivity of these social structures.

As the authors of the report write, the "Rotterdam-Buzinezzclub" in Rotterdam "addresses the unemployment of young people with few chances in the labour market. It is a private, for profit, initiative aimed at developing entrepreneurship among young people on social assistance by broadening their network and their skills." The young participants receive support in "developing their ideas into realistic business plan, or towards new plans for picking up education again or for more successful ways of trying to enter the labour market." A partnership has been formalised by the use of a Social Impact Bond (SIB). This is a financial construction in which private parties invest in solving a social problem that costs the local government a lot of money. The local government pays back with the money it is saving, including possible interest. The faster young people move out of the allowance system, the higher the interest. On the other hand, the "Rotterdam-Buzinezzclub" and investors run the financial risk; the municipality does not. To the extent that the re-integration of young people fails and they do not move out of the allowance system, the "Rotterdam-Buzinezzclub" and its investors have to pay the cost.

This construction puts a pressure on the "Rotterdam-Buzinezzclub" to succeed in accordance with the predetermined goals and also to do it as fast as possible. That raises several urgent questions. What space does this enable for the young people to be critical? How can they be fostered to become critical citizens? Will such a fostering not contradict the demands for a profit as it takes too much time? Obviously, the "Rotterdam-Buzinezzclub" does not address the causes of inequality, but does it not actually entail an interest in preserving the causes? The whole business idea relies on the existence of causes that generate a constant flow of affected young people. All these participants are unemployed and without basic qualifications. They are all selected by the municipal Youth Coaches. That makes the "Rotterdam-Buzinezzclub" dependent on the municipality and its employees at the Youth Counter. According to the Director of the Buzinezzclub, this is a key problem and he describes the municipality as monopolist. "At the same time", the authors of the report remind us, "the fact that the Buzinezzclub is one of the few organisations allowed to deal with the 'monopolist' gives it a clear advantage."

But what happens if the "Rotterdam-Buzinezzclub" loses its own monopoly and the municipality opens up for competition? That would probably increase the pressure on the companies to succeed with the predetermined goals even faster, probably then also to the detriment of fostering young people to become critical citizens. There may then also arise a competition for investors. Investors want to invest in the business which can give the highest profit and that does not necessarily have to be in favour of young people with often complex problems and in need of long-term solutions. That is how the structure works.

Another form of accumulation by dispossession is the normalisation of debt (Sayer, 2015: 62). It is a social relation, allowing the creditor to dispossess the debtor (Sayer, 2015: 66), which certainly makes it more difficult to become and remain included. It puts an effective barrier between the ones that can borrow money and the others who cannot, either because they are not entitled to it or they cannot pay it back. Furthermore, indebtedness includes its own mechanisms which may tend to exclude.

One of the case studies, called "Rotterdam-Challenge Sports", highlights this problem and indicates how extensive it has become. The aim with "Rotterdam-Challenge Sports", according to the report (Davelaar et al., 2015b: 2), is to train and coach "young people on benefits in the hope that this can direct them towards school or work within a short period of time (3–6 months)." One of the challenges is the financial problems of the young people. The manager states that "almost all our participants have debts, ranging from €1,000 up to €30,000". According to the report (2015b: 12), "Rotterdam-Challenge Sports" has the contractual obligation to work on financial problems, "but in many cases, according to public officials, they do not manage to do so." The report describes the financial problems as standing in the way of a sustainable positive societal integration of young persons.

6.3 Dependent export-orientation and financialisation in the east

The Czech Republic, Poland and Bulgaria have in common the legacies of the severe recessions and de-industrialisation that occurred in the early 1990s as a result of the transformation to capitalism. It took until the late 1990s until the growth models became more neatly defined. Becker and Weissenbacher (2012: 5) characterise the accumulation regime of the Czech Republic and Poland as a combination of dependent export-oriented industrialisation and financialisation. "These growth models corresponded to the accumulation strategies of West European companies – the outsourcing of production by German manufacturing companies and the export of money capital."

The key sectors, export industry and banking, became dominated by Western European companies. In that way, the Czech Republic and Poland were closely linked to the German export industry and productive system. As Sirovatka and Valkova (2013) reaffirm: "the economy of the country is very much tied to the performance of manufacturing industries, the exporters in particular, strongly influenced by the development of the economy in Germany". Due to this dependence, the growth model has proved to be highly vulnerable, Becker and Weissenbacher (2012: 9) conclude, "but it has at least a productive base – though usually a very narrow and extraverted one". The expansion of domestic demand has relied significantly on increasing household debt.

Regarding industrial relations, union density is below 20% in both the Czech Republic and Poland, while bargaining coverage is higher in both countries, around 40%, but yet much lower than the average of the EU 27 (European Commission, 2013a: 23). Active labour market policies have been rather underdeveloped. As Sirovatka and Valkova (2013: 7) put it: "the Czech Republic prefers rather to have an increasingly flexible labour market and force the unemployed to take any job available than to invest into job creation and employability".

In contrast, financialisation was the main motor of the growth regime in Bulgaria, Becker and Weissenbacher (2012) maintain, relying on huge capital inflows.

During 2001–2007, Bulgaria attracted considerable amounts of Foreign Direct Investment. This led to the emergence of an unsustainable current account deficit. The pre-crisis growth model proved compatible with increased labour force participation, a significant jump in employment levels and much lower unemployment. Hajdinjak and Kosseva (2013: 17) explain what happened:

> The limited construction of new housing in combination with the increased demand pushed the housing prices progressively upwards. With the stabilisation of the economic situation in Bulgaria and a clear course towards EU membership, the Bulgarian property market became interesting for foreigners. In addition, numerous Bulgarians who emigrated during the 1990s started investing in property in the country, giving a push to a construction boom from 2000 to 2008, during which property prices increased dramatically.

That made the Bulgarian economy vulnerable in a way similar to the countries with dependent financialisation. Hence, the global financial crisis led to a considerable decline in the economy. Both private consumption and foreign investment declined rapidly in 2009 and 2010. Although a very modest growth resumed in 2010, both private consumption and investment remained quite low even by 2012, when they began to recover in most EU countries. Today, the most important obstacles for foreign investment and economic growth remain low productivity and competitiveness in the European and global markets, which are a consequence of inadequate R&D funding and a lack of a clearly defined development policy.

Bulgarian households are under a heavy burden of low incomes, high unemployment, declining property prices and the fear that the jobs market will deteriorate further. Severe constraints on access to credit, concerns about liquidity in banks with strong linkages to EU15 countries and very high real interest rates are also major factors inhibiting investment. Wage levels remain the lowest in the EU and the low-wage sector comprises 18.2% of all employees (2014).[2] As a result of low average wages, Bulgaria enjoys substantially lower unit labour costs, which means that Bulgaria has to rely on industries with low added value – a factor preventing a catch-up with the more advanced countries of the EU. For example, the majority of Bulgarian exports are products with very low skill content (clothing, footwear, iron and steel, machinery and equipment).[3]

6.4 Superior financialisation in the west

After the election victory in 1979 for the Conservative (Tory) party and its leader Margaret Thatcher, Britain came to spearhead a neoliberal societal transformation. It turned out to promote the emergence of a new model of growth: the finance-driven. Increased debt came to be a measure of that and it did not decrease after the Tory government's electoral defeat in 1997. During the Labour government's 10 years in power after 1997, the private sector's total debt increased from 133% of

GDP to 227% (Turner, 2008: 26). British society made itself debt-dependent. At the same time, more and more of the industrial sector disappeared. When the Labour Government took office in 1997, still about 4.2 million worked in the industrial sector (manufacturing). Ten years later, the figure had dropped to below 3 million (Turner, 2008: 68).

The UK has gone through the neoliberal societal transformation called by Jessop the neo-liberal regime change. This means that neoliberalism has led to a more profound change than in countries such as Germany and Sweden (Jessop, 2012b: 6). It has made the British economy particularly vulnerable, which showed itself during the 2008–2009 crisis when Britain experienced its first run on the banks (i.e. where an unusually high number of savers quickly take out, or try to take out their money from a bank) since 1878 (Turner, 2008). Some banks went bust and had to be rescued by large government initiatives and bail-outs, "socialism for the rich", as Sayer calls it (2015: 227). Real estate bubbles, an extensive banking sector and high household debt are the symptoms of an extreme financialisation with a background in the Thatcherism of the 1980s, especially in its second half, making the UK and particularly London an international centre of finance capital.

Doreen Massey (2007) has written a book about this change in London. The book is called *World City*, and that is what London has become. It has its roots in the mid-1960s, when London could establish itself as a market for the growing supply of dollars that were owned by people other than Americans, so-called euro dollars (2007: 45). Thanks to favourable tax rules, London could become an offshore to New York (Gowan, 2009). Thatcherism built on these new conditions, particularly through the change called the "Big Bang" in October 1986 when market forces were let loose on the London Stock Exchange (Callinicos, 2010). This opened the doors for an emerging new elite. At the same time, the old imperial symbols were retained, which made it particularly attractive for foreign companies to establish themselves in London.

In London, there was previously a large manufacturing base, but it disappeared, mainly in the 1980s and 1990s. Instead, London has become "the world's leading international financial centre" as The City of London describes itself on its website. There are 251 foreign banks in London and 588 foreign companies listed on the London Stock Exchange. London is by far the dominant centre for hedge funds in Europe, managing around 85% of European hedge funds' total assets. Britain also has the largest insurance sector in Europe and the third largest in the world. As Massey describes it, London reinvented itself based on what happened during the mid-1980s. Since then, Britain has had a deficit in its annual current account balance (Turner, 2008: 64). The Thatcherism of the 1980s got Britain to embark on a course that also included a weakening of the unions and led to high unemployment.

> Many of those out of work were low-skilled manual workers with minimal or no qualifications and had no tradition of self-employment. They were ill-equipped to access new opportunities which required higher levels of literacy

and numeracy. They were in no small part victims of the structural shift in economic policy espoused by the Thatcher government in the 1980's. This was the case across the country, where the emergent neoliberal economic settlement significantly altered the cultural as well as economic bedrock of Britain.

(Robinson et al., 2013: 4)

Currently, Britain has a low union density and one of the lowest bargaining coverage rates in Europe (European Commission, 2013a: 22). Another legacy of the Thatcher governments in the 1980s is the emphasis on flexibilising wages, hours and working conditions, instead of reskilling workers (Jessop, 2006: 135). The UK displays the lowest level of spending on active labour market policies in the whole of the EU (European Commission, 2012b: 96). Thus, the victims of the structural shift, mentioned in the quote above, have not got much support to cope with the new flexible conditions and instead become permanently socially excluded, sometimes for generations.

Youth unemployment in the UK was quite low before the crisis and lower than the average of the EU27. It has been argued that the deregulated labour market makes it easier for young people to get a job. It certainly makes it easier to lose jobs as well. Besides an excessive resource inequality, a structural inequality exists in the labour market with many young people working on precarious conditions. An example mentioned by Robinson et al. (2013: 7) is the so-called zero hours contract, "whereby people agree to be available for work as and when required but they have no guaranteed hours or time of work".

This gives expression to another actual cause of inequality; one which actualises the systemic cause inherent in the capitalist relation of production. To identify it, we may use a distinction made by Lundvall and Lorenz (2012: 237) between four different forms of work organisation; discretionary learning (DL), lean production, taylorist organisation and traditional organisation. These forms differ with regard to problem solving and learning on the job as well as the degree of freedom that the worker has to organise his or her work. Discretionary learning is the form where employees are engaged in work activities involving problem solving and learning. That matters, Lundvall and Lorenz claim (2012: 237), because "… the key to economic success for a national or regional economy is its capacity to renew competencies in order to be able to move into activities that are less exposed to global competition." It is simply less efficient to operate in a hierarchical organisation when the environment changes rapidly. The patterns vary considerably across Europe but the share of work organisation characterised by discretionary learning has in general decreased. This affects young people in particular (Eurofound, 2012).

According to Lundvall and Lorenz (2012: 250), the UK belongs to the countries with the lowest frequencies of discretionary learning. They relate that to income inequality and claim that "the countries with the highest degree of income inequality (the UK and Portugal) are amongst those that are most unequal in terms of access to discretionary learning and that those countries (Denmark and the

Netherlands) that have the most equal income distribution also offer the most egalitarian access to jobs with discretionary learning." This means that young people who get a job in the UK are more likely than in other countries to also get a low income and are less likely to learn something useful for a future career.

The growth models in the south consists in turn to a high degree of hierarchical organisations. In 2000, only around 20% of the employees in Spain and Greece worked in organisations characterised by discretionary learning and since then it has further decreased.[4] In Italy, the corresponding figures have been higher (30% in the year 2000), but yet far below the shares in the Netherlands (64%), Sweden (53%) and Germany (44%) (Lundvall and Lorenz, 2012: 249).

The idea that our work makes us who we are is actually quite old. It was fundamental for Hegel and also for Marx (see for example Karlsson, 2013). Again, Marx may provide us with an illuminating explanation of what this means (Marx, 1986: 29):

> Hunger is hunger, but the hunger satisfied by cooked meat eaten with knife and fork differs from hunger that devours raw meat with the help of hands, nails and teeth. Production thus produces not only the object of consumption but also the mode of consumption, not only objectively but also subjectively. Production therefore creates the consumer.

For this reason, we should ask what it means that young people are helped to survive in the labour market, as some of the case study reports from Citispyce put it. What will happen to young people who do not get the opportunity to develop on the job? What kind of people will they become? We cannot expect them to be able to create many new ideas. Furthermore, we cannot expect them to become more ecologically minded consumers, contributing to the demand so well needed to make society more sustainable. Can we expect them to open their hearts to the refugees and retain a belief in democracy?

6.5 Export-orientation and financialisation in the north

The growth model in Sweden is characterised by export-orientation, just like the German one, and Sweden has had a surplus in its current account balance every year since 1994. In contrast to the German growth model, however, households in Sweden have become heavily involved in financialisation through both assets (pensions and insurance) and liabilities (mortgage and unsecured debt). Financialisation in Sweden is, what Becker and Jäger (2011) call, mass-based. A part of the pension system has been privatised via the implantation of capital based schemes. Housing prices have increased almost constantly since the late 1990s and households are heavily indebted, among the most in Europe. In fact, the Swedish financial system has since the early 1980s been transformed from one of the most to one of the least state regulated in the world (Stenfors et al., 2014).

Financialisation in Sweden has its roots in the deregulations that were implemented in the 1980s. In addition, changes to the tax system, increasing profits, the new pension system, tax cuts, cuts in the public sector and privatisations have made an increasing amount of assets available for speculation. For a long time, large financial assets have been moved from production and the public sector to financial and speculative investments, (largely as a result of political decisions), in line with the first principle of neoliberalism, which calls for the enlargement of market forces. Those who speculate are the rich and they do it because they have too much money. Even those who do not like it are caught up because they have to protect their capital by investing part of it in speculation. Otherwise, you risk being ousted.

The unions are, however, still quite strong and the collective agreements do still cover a considerable part of the labour market. This has contributed to strengthening competitiveness, but not, as in the German case, through reduced wages and the preservation of a low-wage sector. According to Eurostat data for 2014, Sweden has the smallest low-wage sector in Europe.[5] The proportion of low-wage earners is only 2.6% of all employees, compared to 17.1% in the EU28. Instead, work has been made more efficient. This has been the old-fashioned principle in operation since before the Second World War and defended by the parties in the labour market.

In recent decades, however, competitiveness has also been increased by the reduction in the relative labour costs. Compared with the average for the OECD countries, labour costs have dropped by as much as 39% during the period 1981–2010. In Germany, during the same period, they increased by 16% and in Greece by 20% (Ehrenberg & Ljunggren, 2011: 260). Part of this can be explained by the sharp decline in the value of the Swedish krona. In comparison with the euro and the previous ECU, the krona has almost halved in value since 1970 (Ehrenberg & Ljunggren, 2011: 318). This decrease in the value of the krona has also helped to increase competitiveness.

Yet and regardless of this, Sweden has a rationalised economy, reflected in a high share of jobs which Lundvall & Lorenz (2012) characterise as discretionary learning. At the same time, this has heightened the barriers around the labour market and made it more difficult for young people to get a job. The demands for a formal education have been sharpened. Among the young people interviewed in Sofielund, the few who have a job are employed in the low-skilled service sector (e.g. cleaner, receptionist, etc.). Many of the unemployed are pessimistic about getting *any* job, Grander and Alwall (2014) report, and some "never apply for a job since they have a low self-esteem. Many believe that they can't handle a job, because their friend – who may have been better in school – hasn't got one. At the same time, they can be confident in what they do for a living – crime".

Due to this growth model, not many low qualified jobs remain in the labour market. This increases the risks of unemployment for those who do not fulfil the requirements. To avoid this, well developed labour market measures have been a part of the growth model since its early days. In 2014, Sweden spent 1.33% of its

GDP on active labour market measures, which is among the highest in Europe.[6] These measures have, however, not been fully sufficient to meet the increasing unemployment. This was a major reason why the Social Democrats lost in the general election of 2006.

The response of the succeeding right-wing coalition between 2006 and 2014 was to dismantle labour market measures even further and in general increase the divisions, in particular between those with and without a job, in the hope of thereby strengthening the motivation of the unemployed to seek work. This was achieved by major tax reductions. In the absence of a low-wage sector, this has led to higher barriers around the labour market than in the other countries. The barriers were there even before this, however, and should basically be seen as an actualisation of the potential cause of inequality inherent in the tendency of the organic composition of capital to rise. This causes structural inequality as it enables jobs for fewer and fewer people. The previously more active labour market policy counteracted the actualisation of these barriers and thus kept them much lower. The heightening of the barriers and indeed also extensive financialisation indicate an abandonment of the previous growth model and a transformation to something else (see chapter 8).

6.6 Conclusions: Diverging economic contexts

In this chapter, I have highlighted how the economic realities look like in the ten cities across Europe and the differences between them. I have used the concept of growth model to capture the different combinations of forms of regulations and regimes of accumulation. At least five such growth models have been identified, although not contained within national boundaries, yet creating different conditions in the cities. My main concern, however, has been to find out how the systemic potential causes of inequality get actualised and in what forms. I have also paid a special attention to how the appearance of these forms differs between the countries.

To reconnect to chapter 4, the first systemic cause of inequality is inherent in the capitalist relation of exchange. Capitalists need to make a profit from their exchanges and continue accumulating their capital. If that accumulation stops, they run the risk of not remaining capitalists. This chapter has shown how this potential cause becomes actualised in forms called accumulation by dispossession. One such form is the dependent financialisation that characterises whole countries in the south of Europe. Other forms of accumulation by dispossession highlighted in this chapter are the use of Social Impact Bonds (SIB), normalisation of debt, ballooning of housing prices and privatised pension systems. The examples also show clearly the dependence of this capital accumulation on power, in particular of those who control the allocation of credit (Sayer, 2015: 82). Accumulation by dispossession both presupposes and causes inequality.

These forms should be seen as actual causes of inequality but if it was not for the potential cause inherent in the capitalist system, they would be quite hard to explain. Why would so many actors accumulate by dispossession? If we do not believe that such a behaviour belongs to the human characteristic, which I do not, it must inhere in the system and I have identified the particular capitalist relation of exchange as this mechanism.

The second systemic cause of inequality, explained in chapter 4, is inherent in the capitalist relation of production, tending to cause health inequality. This chapter has shown how this potential cause gets actualised in labour markets with precarious working conditions and low incidences of discretionary learning. Thus, the precariat is not only a category of people; the concept also refers to certain working conditions where the actual cause and effect coincide. As young people work under these conditions, it does something with them.

The actualisation of the third systemic cause of inequality, inherent in the tendency of the organic composition of capital to rise and tending to cause structural inequality, has a particular prevalence in an economy like the Swedish one with strong trade unions and a high coverage of collective agreements. This has erected barriers around the whole of the labour market, though previously it was much better compensated for by labour market policies.

Due to the variety of growth models and how they differ in the actualisations of the systemic causes, inequality affects young people differently. The kind of barriers in Sweden around almost the whole of the labour market, affecting young people in particular without a formal education, do not exist anywhere else. The vulnerability of young people due to employment in sectors most dependent on financialisation is concentrated in the south of Europe. Other forms of accumulation by dispossession, however, seem to exist across Europe. The actual cause of health inequality associated with precarious working conditions and a lack of discretionary learning is particularly prevalent in the UK. Everywhere, young people are subjected to the strong powers of employers and their associates in politics, administration and the media. Without the backing of power, quite a lot of the current inequality would probably not exist.

Notes

1 Available at: http://ec.europa.eu/eurostat/statistics-explained/index.php/Main_Page (accessed 6 July 2017)
2 Available at: http://ec.europa.eu/eurostat/statistics-explained/index.php/Main_Page (accessed 6 July 2017)
3 Important additional information has been provided by one of the authors of the Sofia report, Marko Hajdinjak.
4 According to a lecture given by Bengt-Åke Lundvall at the international Helix conference in Linköping, 12 June 2013.
5 Available at: http://ec.europa.eu/eurostat/statistics-explained/index.php/Main_Page (accessed 6 July 2017)
6 Available at: http://stats.oecd.org/Index.aspx?DatasetCode=LMPEXP# (accessed 6 July 2017)

7

AUSTERITY AND INDIVIDUALISATION

The focus in this chapter will be on the actualisations of the fourth and the fifth systemic potential causes of inequality, the ones that are inherent in the state (see chapter 4.2). The chapter positions young people across Europe with regard to welfare provision and it deals with welfare regimes. This is another main context in which young people live and which has a fundamental impact on their lives. As defined in chapter 5.1.4, a welfare regime is a constellation of state, market and family institutions and organisations in the management of social risks.

The theory has been elaborated and restated by many social scientists after the introduction by Esping-Andersen in 1990. It has also been criticised, for example by Jessop (2002: 68), who highlights the restriction of Esping-Anderson's original typology to only the decommodification of men's waged labour. The equally important relation of the state to women's waged and unwaged labour was not considered. Nor were other dimensions of the state's involvement in social reproduction examined, such as housing, health or education, although Esping-Anderson has extended into these areas in later work. Jessop wants to retain the concept of welfare regime but broaden its definition, emphasising "how welfare regimes are structurally coupled with modes of economic growth (including their insertion into the international division of labour) and more encompassing modes of regulation".

In my attempt to put a welfare regime in place, I will relate it to the second of Jessop's four dimensions, the one dealing with social policy (see chapter 5.1.4). A welfare regime is about what Olofsson (1979) has called the use-value side of living conditions. Besides using the tools of this quite well-known theory to understand the differences for young people across Europe regarding social provision, I will supplement the theory itself by incorporating approaches to social exclusion. Such approaches express outlooks on people and that becomes especially important in social practices that deal with the management of risks.

7.1 The conservatives and their "misérables" in the centre

The term social exclusion stems from France in the mid-1970s (Amin et al., 2002: 17). At that time it referred to the growing number of people who, for various reasons, were not covered by the social insurances of the welfare system. The title of Victor Hugo's classic from 1862, *Les Misérables*, accords well with those designated in the original definition of the concept of social exclusion. This definition was broad, but it did not include the unemployed, which Amin et al. (2002: 17) highlight:

> Interestingly, given the subsequent history of the term, this list encompasses a wide range of individual conditions and problems and social ills and pathologies but does not explicitly refer to the unemployed or any other group whose exclusion might be attributed primarily to *economic* deprivation.

Amin et al. (2002) explain the omission of the unemployed in the definition as time-bound. The concept emerged at the end of the long period in Europe characterised by full employment. Mass unemployment did not yet exist, nor deregulated labour markets nor low-wage sectors.

An additional explanation has been put forward by Atkinson and Davoudi (2000: 429). The fact that the original definition did not include the unemployed depends on the welfare model developed in France (see also Levitas, 2005: 21). This welfare model has been tailored for well-paid industrial workers with lifetime employment capable of paying into the social security funds and thereby safeguarding both their own and their entire family's situation. The model also includes a concern for solidarity with the disadvantaged in society; however, from a conservative basis. Not only working men constitute the pillars of the model, but also their home-working wives. Although in the formal sense unemployed, the home-working wives are not counted as excluded.

This model has been called a conservative or Central European welfare regime. In this regime, economic security is built on a mix of insurance and family. It relies primarily on the breadwinner, usually male. Welfare rights are attached to status, based on social insurances rather than taxes and directed at the family. The principle is that unemployment compensation has to be earned, either through insurance payments or housework. Compensation levels can, therefore, vary widely. The regime also rewards long-term employees and well-paid men with home-working wives. Single people, especially women and young people, have it much more difficult. Germany is usually described as the prototype of the conservative, "Bismarckian" regime and the Hamburg report from Citispyce highlights its principle of subsidiarity:

> An important principle that stems from the Christian background of the German welfare model is subsidiarity: the state should only come in as a last resort, family and civil society should be the first to turn to in times of need.

This principle is reflected in the governance and provision of social services and in the power of the big non-governmental welfare associations.

(Gehrke et al., 2013: 11)

In a conservative regime, the housing systems usually have a unitary character. This means that public and private sectors are treated in a co-ordinated way to encourage affordable housing provision across tenures. In Germany, and thus, Hamburg, various policy instruments exist to provide affordable housing, including housing benefits to low income and unemployed households, and subsidies to housing providers who offer apartments at a low price (Gehrke et al., 2013: 16). Social housing constitutes an important part of the system, with access determined by income ceilings and priority criteria. According to Gehrke et al. (2013: 18), "nearly half of the households in Hamburg (46%) would be eligible for social housing due to their low income".

The Dutch welfare regime has been classified as conservative. As Spies and Tan (2013: 5) explain, "over the last 20 years the Dutch welfare state, however, has been in transition, partly guided by elements from Anglo-Saxon welfare state models, partly guided by populist sentiments, and partly through windows of opportunity arising from among others changing political constellations". As part of this transition, the obligation to work has been increased, and "almost all municipalities in The Netherlands have adopted a form of 'work first' policy, partly substituting the right to a benefit with the right to a (subsidised or created) job. This is especially true for young people." Furthermore, benefits and access to social support have been limited; more pressure has been put on people to become self-reliant; services have been privatised; and rights and responsibilities have been individualised, instead of being attached to the household. This causes inequality as it privileges those with the potential to assert themselves as individuals and makes the others look useless:

> Many social and cultural services were closed in recent times, due to austerity measures following the economic crisis. Respondents mention a community centre or library where young people used to get together for a chat or get rid of some energy by playing sports. Now, people gather in the streets. Some facilities that are still open attract another type of people now, which makes our respondents feel less at home. Many young people complain that there is nothing to do anymore.
>
> *(Tan & Spies, 2014b: 16)*

This is one of the two systemic causes of cultural inequality, which I identified in chapter 4.2. The other one causes cultural inequality by violating the human rights of those whose knowledge cannot be quantified and expressed properly in writing. It is a context of meaning which makes the one appear as meaningful and the other as meaningless. A typical example of how this approach to knowledge operates is provided by Tan and Spies (2014b: 12):

Another respondent finally knew what he wanted, namely to become a train machinist, and passed all sorts of test (physical, psychological, responsiveness, intelligence) except for the one with the Dutch synonyms. He speaks Dutch fluently and made a verbally and communicatively strong impression in the interview. However, not passing the test simply meant no access without a possibility to improve his knowledge of Dutch synonyms and retrying.

In Germany, similar changes have been carried out, starting in the early 2000s when "the German Government, then led by Social-Democrat chancellor Gerhard Schröder, introduced far-reaching labour market reforms, driven by the principles of activation and workfare. These reforms also set a new focus for the field of youth work. Institutions for child and youth work are now asked to build coalitions with the jobcentres for an integrated support of young people on their way to the labour market" (Gehrke et al., 2013: 6).

7.2 The liberals and their obstacles to economic growth in the west

In Britain, another welfare regime came to dominate, called liberal or Anglo-Saxon, characterised by a low level of decommodification (see chapter 5.1.4). This regime implies a reliance on market solutions (Esping-Andersen, 1999). The state provides a minimal level of support, usually means-tested and therefore also predominantly selective, as opposed to general. The same compensation is paid to all, regardless of previous income. Risks are considered social only in a narrow sense and preferably individualised. The family does not play any substantial part in the management of risks.

The UK is usually regarded as the most clear-cut representative of a liberal welfare regime in Europe. It also exemplifies the significance of the social economy in a liberal welfare regime. Amin et al. (2002) define social economy as "non-profit activities designed to combat social exclusion". Indeed, that is a very British definition, which Amin et al. (2002) admit, at least implicitly, by presenting a typology of four models. They make distinctions between the Rhineland, the Nordic, the Mediterranean and the Anglo-Saxon models. A particular emphasis upon tackling social exclusion is a typical feature of the Anglo-Saxon model.

The orientation of the state in a liberal welfare regime is residual which means that it limits its involvements in social reproduction to the most urgent needs. Such a residualisation of housing started with the Thatcher government and Robinson et al. (2013: 16) tell the story.

> The lack of affordable social housing in Birmingham – as in other cities in the UK – can be traced back to the 'right to buy' policy of the 1980s which encouraged tenants to purchase their Council homes. This depleted the stock of social housing and neither local authorities nor government have been able to replenish the supply. Local authorities have also found it hard to fund repairs to much of the remaining stock.

This was the largest privatisation in Britain, according to Sayer (2015: 99), as it allowed the tenants to buy their homes at massively discounted prices. The notion of social housing has its origin in this 'right to buy' policy. It "helped the growth of a new stigma attached to council housing and its tenants" (Sayer, 2015: 100). That reinforced the systemic cause of cultural inequality inherent in the state, characterised by an individualistic outlook, as it made the remaining ones in council housing appear as meaningless in contrast to the meaningful ones who had bought their homes or lived somewhere else.

In 1997, Labour won the election but that did not lead to any fundamental changes (Wood, 2010). The Labour government carried on the policies of deregulation and reduced state intervention. The British attitude to the concept of social exclusion was however modified. As Jessop (2003) highlights, the attitude of the previous Conservative governments had been marked by indifference and denial. Unemployment and social exclusion were considered the price that had to be paid in order to control inflation.

Immediately after its accession to power, the Labour government set up a special unit dealing with issues of social exclusion, called the Social Exclusion Unit. Thereby, the problem was put on the agenda, but, according to Jessop (2003: 16), on the basis of an essentially neoliberal ideology. Social exclusion was seen as an obstacle to growth and appeared on that ground as a problem.

> Thus, in contrast to the Thatcherite view that economic growth would solve any residual problems of social exclusion, New Labour sees social exclusion and the existence of an underclass as obstacles to economic growth.

Central to this approach was the introduction of the Index of Multiple Deprivation (IMD). As the Birmingham report from Citispyce (Robinson et al., 2013: 13) presents it, "the IMD provides a single overview indicator of how all English areas compare on levels of deprivation measured by a broad concept of 'multiple deprivation', made up of several distinct dimensions, or domains, of deprivation". It is utilised in policymaking to compare areas and also trends over time. As the Birmingham report puts it, "with the introduction of multiple indices of deprivation, income redistribution (through welfare benefits) was given a back seat in the government's welfare agenda …"

The British sociologist Ruth Levitas makes a distinction between three different definitions of social exclusion (Levitas, 2005). The definition that emerged in France in the 1970s, which she calls MUD (moral underclass discourse), associates social exclusion with deviant behaviour and lower morale. The definition pursued by the Labour government since its election victory in 1997 focused on unemployment and Levitas calls it SID. She means by that a 'social integrationist discourse'. Here it will be called a 'system integrationist discourse', drawing on the important distinction between social and system integration, represented by David Lockwood (1992: 400). So SID – yes – but as an abbreviation for a system integrationist discourse. Furthermore, Levitas identifies a third definition, called RED (redistributionist discourse), which associates social exclusion primarily with poverty, and as Levitas (2005: 27) summarises it "to oversimplify, in RED they have no money, in SID they have no work, in MUD they have no morals".

The British Labour Party used to be a representative of the definition which Levitas calls RED, but in the 1980s and 1990s, the Labour agenda was gradually remoulded. In the liberal welfare regime problems tend to be individualised. "Risk and responsibility are transferred to the individual" (Sayer, 2015: 17). Young people are encouraged to see themselves as marketable commodities, and to work on their CVs. Those that cannot assert themselves as individuals in these forms appear as meaningless in the light of this context of meaning. This is how neoliberalism reinforces the systemic cause of cultural inequality, inherent in the state.

Society is not seen as a problem. The problem is those who find themselves in a condition of social exclusion and are too weak to assert themselves individually. They have to get included, if not otherwise so, then by the use of coercion (Levitas, 2005: 141). The rich have not been exposed to the same pressure and intrusive scrutiny:

> There is no discussion of how to persuade them to pay existing or higher taxes, how to dissuade them from buying their way out of common institutions, or how to induce them to reduce car and air travel and thus contribution to global warming.
>
> *(Levitas, 2005: 228)*

No matter what kind of work, it simply has to be paid. Although paid work in different ways may impede inclusion, for example for people working long hours, little attention is paid to that (Levitas, 2005: 169).

7.3 The constant transitions in the east

Hajdinjak & Kosseva (2013: 12) paint in their Citispyce report on Bulgaria a background which also applies to the other new member states:

> Under the communist regime, medical and social care were 'owned' and controlled by the state. As such, they were provided to all citizens at no cost, since they were fully covered by the state budget. In general, the communist-era social and health care is still considered as very good, mostly on account of its universal accessibility and highly educated medical personnel.

The political changes in 1989, however, led to a profound transformation. In a study of Eastern European countries, Zsuzsa Ferge (2001: 131) concluded that "most of them seem to share just one feature: the absence of a project for a welfare system …". During the 1990s, the Eastern European countries were pushed by international organisations like the IMF and the World Bank to pursue neoliberal policies, including the withdrawal of the state, deregulation and privatisation.

Existing universal benefits "including price subsidies, the health service, and family benefits were curtailed across the region. They were either simply withdrawn or transformed into public or private insurance, or into means-tested benefits" (Ferge, 2001: 140).

In Bulgaria, the current welfare systems are managed by the state at the national level and financed mainly by compulsory contributions by the employers, the employees and the self-employed. The contributions, however, are insufficient due to the exceptionally low level of incomes in Bulgaria, and accordingly the systems suffer from a chronic underfunding. This has worsened the quality of the service. Instead, "private medical practice has boomed in the past decade and high quality health care is easily available to those who can afford it" (Hajdinjak & Kosseva, 2013: 12). Moreover, an increasing number of people are not entitled to welfare benefits and services. Because of unemployment, they cannot afford to pay the compulsory contributions due to the poverty in which many of them live or they do not qualify to receive benefits. That shows clearly how the welfare state, in the words of Esping-Andersen (1990: 165), is "an active force in the ordering of social relations", contributing to causing the problems it is supposed to solve.

This is probably part of the explanation to why Bulgaria "has the second highest levels (after Romania) of poverty and social exclusion for children and young people (but also for the total population) – between 40 and 45%" (Hajdinjak and Kosseva, 2013: 15). Furthermore, Bulgaria has the highest severe material deprivation rate in the EU. The Bulgarian report refers to the formation of an extensive youth underclass, in which unemployment is not an exception but a norm. "A logical presumption is that if abandoned by institutions and the society, such young and jobless underclass represents a social time bomb, which might explode in a very near future" (2013: 15).

Due to their transitional character, the new member states have been difficult to classify, as reaffirmed by Chrabąszcz et al. (2013) in the report on Krakow. In the report on Brno, Sirovatka & Valkova (2013: 10) describe the transitional character of the Czech welfare state:

> It started as a conservative Bismarckian model inherited from the pre-war period. Later it was modified by the communists who implemented more uniform elements as well as workplace-related measures. After 1989, the post-communist governments again modified it by imposing rather modest standards in social insurance, in combination with selective and targeted measures in the final result generous enough to effectively alleviate poverty. Since 1990s the Czech welfare state has gradually moved in a more liberal, residual direction through the decaying of benefit levels and by a series of partial reforms, labelled as a trajectory towards a 'low social expenditure' welfare state.

As Sirovatka and Valkova (2013: 15) state, "access to housing is one of the key preconditions for the effective inclusion into society". Housing in the Czech Republic, Poland and Bulgaria, however, does not seem to offer such an effective inclusion for young people. In the Czech Republic, a large proportion of the population owns a dwelling. The share of tenants has fallen and a higher proportion of them rent at market prices which reflects the process of rent deregulation. Social housing exists but it "comprises an integral part of the transition model of housing. It is intended among others for young people who cannot afford to pay for standard municipal housing or rent on the open housing market", according to Sirovatka & Valkova (2013: 18) (see also Housing Europe, 2015: 42).

Also in Poland and Bulgaria, social housing hardly exists. Hence, in all three countries, housing can be described as residual and dualist, making it hard for young people to leave the parental home. Consequently, the average age of leaving home is high, around 30 years. In the Czech Republic, 53% of young adults aged 18–34 live with their parents (Housing Europe, 2015: 19). In Poland and Bulgaria, it is even higher, 60% and 62% respectively. That can be compared with, for example, 23% in Sweden and 48% in EU-28.

7.4 The reliance on the family in the south

A fourth type of welfare regime prevails in southern Europe. As it relies primarily on the family, it could be called the familial welfare regime. Welfare is provided by inter-generational care within the family, supported by a low retirement age. Concomitantly, the familial welfare state is less generous than the conservative one with regard to unemployment benefits. As Roiha et al. (2013: 9) explain regarding the characteristics that states in southern Europe share: "they have smaller and less developed welfare programmes; a segmented social insurance model, building on the concept of an insider/outsider labour market; weak safety nets and a strong reliance on families for care and support".

Familism is explained by Campomori et al. (2013: 18) as "based on the idea that family can and has to work as social security cushion for its members and, therefore, that it can carry out a number of functions like child, elderly and disabled people care, guarantee an income in case of unemployment or other events that produce an absence of income. The state gives very few services and some money transfer in order that families can eventually find caregivers on the market". In their report on Venice, Campomori et al. (2013) highlight the inequalities this causes among immigrants, who often do not have wide family support.

The familial welfare state has directed a considerable amount of its resources to generous pension schemes, also in terms of early retirement, favouring a passive approach to employment management, just like the liberal and conservative states. As Mary Daly (2001: 91) has stated, "government and social partners have preferred passive transfer payments over active labour market policies, have maintained high wage rates, and reduced labour supply by relying on early retirement." Old age risks have been favoured at the expense of other risks, particularly in Italy where more than 60% of social benefits have been spent on old age and survivors every year for decades, compared to the average of around 46% in the EU25 (European Commission, 2010c: 280).

The Greek welfare state may have been a dream for those who worked there, but not in terms of the services it has provided. Avatangelou et al. (2013) describe it as an imbalance and inequality in terms of the provision of social services, benefits, pensions and healthcare related to the different number of insurance funds that existed until recently, involving different rules, conditions and criteria. This has been aggravated by the economic crisis. "The main deficiencies young people mentioned during the interviews and the focus group in Piraeus", reported by Tryfona et al. (2014b: 12), "relate to the lack of proactive services and programmes that could inhibit young people's criminal or reckless behaviour".

Just like other welfare states across Europe, the Greek one has been exposed to changes guided by neoliberal principles. In the interviews with young people, this becomes obvious in their descriptions of the educational system. It seems to be oriented towards exams, grading and thus employability, in line with the approach which associates knowledge with the quantifiable and therefore tends to give priority to one form of knowledge, namely factual knowledge.

> "... The Greek educational system is very much disorganized and exam oriented ... They do not target at promoting knowledge ... I can tell from myself ... I cannot remember many of the things I learned, let's say, in the 2nd or 3rd grade of Lyceum, because I did it with the sole purpose of taking the exams. It's not just me; there are many children who learn by heart just to pass the exams ... there is no critical thinking. When they teach you something they do not ask for your opinion, there is no discussion, they do not teach you to think ... therefore, many children who are very smart do not progress at school"
>
> *(Tryfona et al., 2014b: 17)*

According to the authors of the report, most of the interviewees support the view that the existing educational system does not promote critical thinking. As the authors (2014b: 18) see it, "this, gradually but steadily, leads them to adopt the role of a 'follower' by depending on others to decide on various local and national issues that are affecting not only everyday affairs but also their life perspectives. Unfortunately, this is an inhibitory factor for reinforcing young people's engagement with civil society and supporting them to be active citizens." The direction of this development is wisely summarised by one of the young interviewees: "I believe that I am not in position to tell a politician what he/she should do ...". It indicates the very effective operation of an approach to knowledge, which causes a cultural inequality between those who run society and the others who have been diverted from learning the knowledge needed on how to assert their human rights.

A striking figure for Greece is the decrease in the proportion of young people (Avatangelou et al., 2013). That started already during the period when the growth model flourished, before the crisis. From 2001 to 2012, the population aged 15–24 years decreased its share of the total population from 14.3% to 10.2%. Avatangelou et al. (2013) mention low fertility rates as one of the causes, but behind the low fertility rates probably lie the problems of the familial welfare regime. The welfare states of the familial regime have not been designed to support female employment. The family is still expected to care for welfare, and as the labour market protects the privileges of males, women find it hard to combine employment and parenthood. Thus, young people have perhaps not dared to have children, because the familial welfare regime has not been replaced by a regime with a welfare state that provides the support and security needed to develop a competitive economy, for example decent unemployment benefits and child care.

> Despite the fact that the 'Greek Family' is considered as an over-protective structure that in many cases can be held responsible for the 'castration' of young people, it is also the primary supportive network during the times of the crisis.
>
> *(Tryfona et al., 2014b: 21)*

In Italy, devolution has further weakened the welfare state and instead exacerbated the already existing differences among the regions. In this way, Italy has spearheaded the emergence of what Andreotti et al. (2012: 1926) propose to conceptualise as Local Welfare Systems (LWS). By that they do not refer to any fixed and stable structures, but to "dynamic processes in which the specific local socio-economic and cultural conditions give rise to: different arrangements of formal and informal actors, public or not, involved in designing and implementing welfare policies; and different profiles of people in need". Such Local Welfare Systems have emerged in the absence of a framework of rules to guarantee homogeneous access to services across the country. According to Campomori et al. (2013: 9) in the report on Venice, the welfare system in the Veneto region is centred on cash transfers to families while the systems in, for example, Piedmont or Tuscany are more oriented towards the provision of services.

In the familial welfare regime, young people's housing is the responsibility of the family. Accordingly, in Greece, Spain and Italy, but also in Bulgaria, the Czech Republic and Poland, young people do not leave the parental household until they are on average around 30 years of age. This is probably also a reason why young people are considered young up to such a high age, 35 in Greece as well as in Spain. As Avatangelou et al. (2013: 14) maintain, it depends on traditional cultural patterns, "placing family bonds at the high scale of life principles".

The important role of families, as highlighted by Roiha et al. (2013: 13), is "somewhat shaped by religious habits, and the perception of co-residence of parents and youth during the latter's transition into adulthood as part of family life in the Spanish context". Therefore, housing in Spain has been treated as an economic rather than a social policy because it is perceived as part of family wealth. According to Housing Europe (2015), social housing is very tiny, as in Spain, or non-existent, as currently in Greece.

Most of the young people interviewed in the neighbourhoods of Piraeus and Elefsina still live with their parents, although not by choice, and are financially dependent on them. This has been aggravated by the lack of employment opportunities, Tryfona et al. (2014: 11) underline. At the same time, the study identified many cases of young people "who have taken over the responsibility of contributing financially to the parental household undertaking low paid and/or part time jobs in order to support their families and to alleviate them from the financial burden".

The small rental sector, lack of social housing and scarce opportunities for affordable housing also make it difficult for young people to leave the parental household. In addition, as emphasised by Campomori et al. (2013) in their report on Venice, young people find it difficult to obtain credit and loans to purchase a house. As touched upon in chapter 1, this has forced young people in Venice to move from the Old Town to the Mainland, creating what Campomori et al. (2013: 20) refer to as an "exodus".

In the south of Europe, the combination of the familial welfare regime and the growth model of dependent financialisation has left space for quite a comprehensive informal sector. Avatangelou et al. (2013: 9) regard as a characteristic feature; "the extensive informal work flourishing within the context of the 'grey economy', which was especially intensified since the 1990s with the mass flow of undocumented immigration. The informal labour regime that tends to be widespread in Greece, is flourishing in Athens particularly, in all types of work, especially in blue-collar work." Avatangelou et al. (2013: 9) refer to the establishment of 'grey economy networks', "creating especially precarious working conditions for a significant number of young people". Also Campomori et al. (2013: 18) underline the significance of the informal economy, "which Italian governments have tacitly accepted for many years, despite workers in marginal and black economy not benefiting from the social insurances and their job is extremely precarious".

The crisis has exposed all the weaknesses of the familial welfare regime and its backbone, the family itself, as "more young persons (15–24) nowadays are seeking employment in order to help their families to cope with everyday difficulties; a practice that tended to operate in the opposite way in Greece before the crisis, when most youngsters were financially supported by their parents until the end of their studies" (Avatangelou et al., 2013: 8). The already weak structures and operations of the welfare state have deteriorated further through austerity measures carried out because of the crisis. The Athens report gives the impression of a welfare state about to vanish.

> Unable to find a job for long periods, in combination with the almost unbearable taxation and increased prices in products and goods, those youngsters de facto cannot sustain a private household. Thus, more of them are delaying their transition from family home to independent living, which in turn creates further feelings of inability and depression for many of them. On top of that, the apparently weakened and dysfunctional national welfare system, not only fails to support young adults' independent living, but also fails to protect them against the risk of poverty or exclusion in cases of very low or

no income. A large number of young people are constantly complaining about the social welfare state in Greece, which intensifies their insecurity.

(Avatangelou et al., 2013: 20)

In Barcelona, the crisis has resulted in many evictions. "One of the neighbourhoods in the district of Nou Barris – Ciutat Meridiana – has earned the popular name of 'evictions city', as it gathers the highest rate of evictions per neighbourhood in Spain" (Jubany et al., 2014b: 9). The housing market in Spain is based to a great extent on ownership, and due to easy access to loans, many families bought property before the crisis, but "now, a great number have lost their jobs, making it difficult or impossible to keep up with mortgage payments; hence, many families have become homeless" (Roiha et al., 2013: 12). The Spanish government has reacted by changing legislation towards easing the pressure for those in debt; "however, these measures are likely to be 'too little too late' for too many families, focusing only on the debt issue and not on housing as a basic human right".

7.5 The social democratic hesitancy in the north

In countries like France and Britain, the concept of social exclusion has for quite a long time played an important role in both policy and research. In Sweden, the concept has led a more obscure life. This is related to the welfare regime characterising Swedish society. It is neither conservative nor liberal. It is, therefore, not easy to adopt either the French or the English meaning of the term.

In Sweden, the welfare regime called social democratic or Nordic has been predominant. In this regime, the state is primarily responsible for providing economic security and welfare. Unemployment benefits are linked to previous income and are not means-tested. Thus, welfare provision could be characterised as general; financing is secured by taxes, not insurance. The Nordic regime can, therefore, be said to be based on the citizen, not the family, as in the conservative regime or the individual, as in the liberal one. Every citizen receives the same assistance in relative terms, regardless of class, status or earlier achievements. Risks are socialised in a comprehensive sense. Vicente Navarro (2016) highlights the significance of the distinction between the social democratic and conservative welfare states:

> It was the latter (established by Bismarck) that based the funding of the welfare state on labor market contributions. That welfare state, rooted in the insurance system, was more a characteristic of the conservative road, rather than the social democratic one. Based on that tradition, benefits were not universal and funding was not according to the ability of each, but rather to the type of work that each does. The contribution was not from each one's ability and capacity, but rather according to each one's job. This distinction is important.

Despite the significance of the state, the social economy is a deep-seated part of the social democratic welfare regime. Although the term social economy (reference object) has not been used for very long, the phenomenon (referent object) has a background in the popular movements. Basically, the social democratic model of social economy has not been designed to combat social exclusion, although the significance of it in tackling social exclusion has grown in recent years. Instead, it rests on the idea of organised self-help. As such, the social economy in various areas shares the responsibility for welfare provisions and delivery with the welfare state. For example, in Sweden unemployment funds run by the trade unions provide unemployment benefit, not the state.

Public housing constitutes an important part of the Swedish welfare state. In Malmö, public housing accounts for 15% of all dwellings; these are owned by the public housing company MKB, which in turn is owned by the city of Malmö. Sweden has, however, by definition no social housing, since the apartments in the public housing are available for everyone; not only for people with low income or other special needs. Furthermore, rents have been regulated by norms set by these public housing companies for the rent in general, with which private housing companies have had to comply. The public housing companies have been a significant part of the welfare regime with their apartments available for the general public. Due to its availability to the entire population, public housing in Sweden has also been characterised as universalist. It should be seen as a potential that tends to counteract the individualising cause of cultural inequality, inherent in the state. It modifies this systemic cause to the advantage of the ones with a lack of resources to assert themselves as individuals and prevents an appearance of them as less meaningful.

The proportion of public housing in the South Sofielund neighbourhood (further described in chapter 8.3.1) is rather high (Grander & Stigendal, 2014). Yet, the fragmentation of the property ownership structure in South Sofielund is a major challenge in developing a safe and attractive living environment. Some of the property owners have a history of not taking care of their houses and apartments. In the debate, they are referred to as 'slumlords', i.e. landlords who accumulate their capital by dispossession, through buying apartment blocks, mismanaging them and then selling them on at a profit. Since Malmö, much like other major cities in Sweden, has a shortage of housing, young people feel obliged to take whatever is offered. Thus, many young people have become tenants among the 'slumlords', living in poor conditions and not being able to influence their housing. In many cases, they are illegally sub-letting at very steep rents, as the slumlords do not regulate the sub-letting. Many of the inhabitants living in sub-let apartments in these areas were paying a rent higher than that for a newly built apartment in Malmö's high-end areas.

The shortage of rental housing, in particular small apartments suitable for young people, has weakened the potential to counteract the individualising cause of inequality, referred to above. The financialisation of the sector has made it even harder for young people without any income to buy a cooperative housing apartment and thus assert themselves individually. As a result, many of the young people are involuntarily living with their parents or with friends. As individuals, and in relation to the existing possibilities to exercise their human rights, they have become weakened and thus affected by the increasing inequality. It is a resource inequality in the sense that they lack a home of their own. In addition, it is a cultural inequality as living with their parents or in houses owned by the 'slumlords' make them appear as meaningless, particularly in the light of the neoliberal reinforcements of an individualistic context of meaning.

Public cultural institutions like libraries and the local cultural schools, run by municipalities, have traditionally been an important part of the social democratic welfare regime. As such, they have counteracted the other potential cause of cultural inequality, inherent in the state: i.e. the approach that intellectualises knowledge. On the border between North and South Sofielund, two public institutions of this kind are situated: Arena 305 and The Garage.

Arena 305 is a municipal leisure time youth club attracting young people from the whole city. In this sense, Arena 305 is different from ordinary municipal youth clubs. The regular youth clubs are open for young people (up to the age of 16), living in the proximity of the club and offer a wide range of activities after school hours. They are funded by the city district's budget. Arena 305 is different; it could be seen as an after school centre directed to the creation of all kinds of music, aimed at all young people in Malmö between the ages of 16 and 25 and is financed by central funding from the municipality. Arena 305 is incorporated into an old renovated factory which now includes rehearsal rooms equipped with instruments, amplifiers and a sound reinforcement system: there are two recording studios, a dance studio, a DJ room, a café, and three different stages; the largest stage has space for an audience of 350.

When walking around the spaces of Arena 305, it is easy to become impressed with the attractive rooms, the cosy café and the high standard of the equipment. But why is the city of Malmö putting a lot of money and effort into this kind of place? And why is it placed in Sofielund? What problems does it solve? The aims of Arena 305 are rather vague, the manager tells us in an interview. However, the basis for the activities of Arena 305 could be said to be empowerment. According to the manager, young people in Malmö do not lack meeting places, but are in need of meeting spaces which "lift them". Thus, the management has tried to develop Arena 305 into "*a place where young people should feel that they are able to do whatever they dream of, but with support from the staff*" and where they "*can build on their own potentials*".

Located in the same building as Arena 305, The Garage is a meeting place and a city district library, also run by the municipality. Here, visitors of all ages can read and borrow books and magazines in different languages; borrow laptops; exchange and mend clothes; do craftwork; or just meet others over a cup of coffee or tea. The Garage has a language cafe for those who want to practise their Swedish in an informal setting. The manager of The Garage tells us in our interview that she likes to address The Garage as a "creative living room" for all citizens not only from the area but from the whole city. The aims are to be a local meeting-place, to provide a variety of cultural events and to encourage the visitors participate. Using the same bottom-up approach as Arena 305, The Garage's various activities have taken shape based on an on-going dialogue and participatory process with the visitors. The personnel act as counsellors more than librarians. *"The visitors can get help with virtually everything, as long it is in our competence. And if it is not, we can arrange something. For example, free juridical counselling or mother tongue education"*, the manager says.

The supply of books and other resources available for loan is based on the wishes of the participants. Another key element in the participatory approach of The Garage is the availability of the spaces in the evenings and at weekends. Everyone can arrange activities and events at The Garage after regular opening hours. The events are always free and open to the public. The personnel at The Garage provide the spaces, advice and help with marketing. During 2012, over 300 events were arranged in the evenings and at weekends.

The social democratic welfare regime with universalist institutions like public housing has made it difficult for the concept of social exclusion to take hold. The existence of social exclusion is contrary to its fundamental principles. A general welfare based on citizenship makes it quite unthinkable. Any 'miserables', as in the conservative sense, are not supposed to exist. And those who get into trouble should not have to be treated as obstacles to growth. Therefore, there was a lack of a typical Swedish breeding ground for the concept when the right-wing alliance launched it in the election campaign of 2006. To be sure, the alliance put into words a reality that was too little talked about, to some extent unimaginable, given the principles of a social democratic regime. Yet, the breeding ground for it has emerged steadily since the early 1980s due to how profoundly neoliberalism has penetrated Swedish society (Stenfors et al., 2014). Accordingly, the concept used by the alliance parties has rather to be seen as an Anglo-Saxon import; it is the liberal meaning of the term that has been used, i.e. what Levitas (2005) calls SID (see chapter 7.2).

After the change of regime in 2006, the new right-wing alliance government highlighted "a reduction of social exclusion" as its main task. The concept has, however, not been properly defined but used in different ways. This prompted criticism from the National Audit Office which, on examining the concept, focused on the lack of a clear definition. Yet the concept has continued to play a key role. Its importance stems from its seeming flexibility and that is precisely why it is such a powerful concept, as Levitas (2005: 178) claims. It draws the attention away from the injustices and disparities among the included, while "… the poverty and disadvantage of the so-called excluded are discursively placed outside society" (Levitas, 2005: 7).

7.6 Conclusions: Converging welfare provisions

In this chapter, I have highlighted how welfare is provided for in the ten cities across Europe and the differences between these provisions. I have used the concept of welfare regime to capture the different combinations of market, state, family and social economy. At least four such welfare regimes have been identified, creating different conditions in the cities. My main concern, however, has been to find out how the two systemic causes of cultural inequality inherent in the state are actualised and in what forms. I have also paid special attention to how the presence of these forms differs between the countries.

I have claimed that the forms of the state materialise an outlook on people, which tends to cause a cultural inequality in so far as it makes the ones with the potential to assert themselves individually appear as meaning more and the others as meaning less. That is the one systemic as well as potential cause of cultural inequality inherent in the state. In this chapter, we have seen how austerity measures have dismantled the compensating potentials and thus weakened many young people in the sense of their potential to assert themselves individually. Instead, they gather in the streets and perhaps assert themselves collectively. This does not, however, make them recognised as subjects. On the contrary, they tend to be subjected to increasing discipline and surveillance.

Not only have the compensatory potentials been dismantled, but the individualising cultural inequality inherent in the state has also been reinforced by the approach to social exclusion, called SID (the system integrationist discourse). This context of meaning considers risks as social only in the narrow sense and instead transfers the responsibility for managing them to the individual. It encourages young people to see themselves as marketable commodities, and to work on their CVs. Those that cannot assert themselves as individuals in these forms appear as meaningless in the light of this context of meaning. The context of meaning expresses an outlook on people which can be summarised as 'blaming the victim'. Included in this context of meaning is also the 'work first' policy, which substitutes the right to a benefit with the obligation to accept the first available job, regardless of its quality.

Another form for the actualisation of this cause consists of social housing, particularly prevalent in the UK. It reproduces a context of meaning which makes the ones in social housing appear as meaningless in contrast to the meaningful ones who had bought their homes or live somewhere else.

As examples from Malmö have shown, however, this individualising cause of cultural inequality can be counteracted by universalist public housing. It prevents an appearance of the weaker individuals as less meaningful. Developments in Malmö, however, also show how this counterforce can be weakened by a shortage of rental housing and financialisation. Thus, a resource inequality has emerged due to the difficulties for young people of getting a home. It becomes also a cultural inequality, as living with their parents or in houses owned by the 'slumlords' makes them appear as meaning less, particularly in the light of the neoliberal reinforcements of an individualistic context of meaning.

The other systemic as well as potential cause of cultural inequality inherent in the state is the approach to knowledge which violates the human rights of those whose knowledge cannot be expressed properly in writing, according to the standards set by the state. This systemic cause of cultural inequality is actualised and reinforced by educational systems oriented towards exams, grading and thus employability, in line with the approach which associates knowledge with the quantifiable; therefore tending to give priority to one form of knowledge, namely factual knowledge. Such an educational system does not empower young people to tell a politician what he/she should do, as a young person in Athens wisely puts it. Instead, it tends to cause a cultural inequality between those who run society and the others who have been diverted from learning the knowledge they need on how to assert their human rights.

This potential cause of inequality is actualised also by the so-called Index of Multiple Deprivation (IMD) in the UK. It should be seen as linked to the individualising cultural inequality caused by SID as it focuses on the losing side of inequality only. The winning side is not exposed to the same intrusive scrutiny, regarding, for example, tax avoidance, exploitation of labour, use of power, contributions to global warming, etc. The focus on the losing side makes the symptoms appear as the causes. Furthermore, this excessive use of an index signals that everything worth paying attention to in these neighbourhood can be quantified. It is a very effective way of disguising all the positive potentials and, thus, an illuminating example of selectivity (see chapter 3.3).

8
INEQUALITIES IN THE CITIES

As part of the global economic order emerging since the 1980s (Therborn, 2011), the responsibilities of cities have been much enhanced. On the one hand, globalisation has put cities at the forefront, strengthening them with regard to their regional and national territories and, generating new prospects. Every employment hub, city or region, has to compete with the others to attract and keep investments in its area. As Doreen Massey (2007: 12) describes it, neoliberalism is made in the city. This has not just happened by coincidence, but "the organisation of consumption through urbanisation has become absolutely central to capitalist dynamics" (Harvey, 2010: 175).

On the other hand, "cities have become concentrations of inequality" (Therborn, 2013: 24), where different forms coincide, often also with segregation. This development laid the foundation for a fear which, as highlighted by Novy et al. (2012: 1876), "became explicit when causes and symptoms of 'new poverty' – partly due to the transition to the post-Fordist economy – were conceptualised and discussed at policy level under the label of social exclusion". But what is social exclusion? What should be meant by it? Can a use of it be justified? Yes, I believe it can. I will explain why and how in this chapter. Defining social exclusion as both a process and a condition puts us on track towards an understanding of how new societal borders have arisen and how that has happened in cities. It justifies a reformulation of the problem of inequality into a problem of societal causes of social exclusion.

8.1 The polarisation between exclusion and inclusion

As clarified in Collins English Dictionary, the term social exclusion has two different meanings: the one referring to a process and the other to a condition. While in English, one and the same term (signifier) carries both meanings (signified), different terms are used in Swedish, for example. The previous right-wing Swedish government, 2006–14, often used the term 'utanförskap' (being excluded). That corresponds to the use of the English term social exclusion as a noun, referring to a condition that some people are in.

8.1.1 Processes of exclusion

This is not how many scientists define it (for example Byrne, 2005; Madanipour et al., 2003: 22). It is usually seen as an on-going process and Byrne (2005: 2) stresses the benefits of such a definition: "When we talk and write about 'social exclusion' we are talking about changes in the whole of society that have consequences for some of the people in that society." Byrne asks us to pay attention to the inherent dynamics of the term because it points out something that happens in time. The term is also clearly systemic, Byrne claims, as it is about the nature of social systems and also has an implication for agency. "'Exclusion' is something that is done by some people to other people". In this sense, the term social exclusion refers to a process and that can be called a process definition of social exclusion.

This is similar to how one of the projects studied in Citispyce, "Barcelona-Forn Teatre Pa'Totohom", defines exclusion, namely as "the consequences suffered by some people because of society's economically oriented philosophy, thus defining 'vulnerable' as whoever doesn't have the possibility to defend herself or himself against social exclusion" (Jubany et al., 2015b: 8).

This sense is lost in translations of the English word 'social exclusion' into 'utanförskap' in Swedish. Then the term is used precisely in the sense of a condition which Byrne (2005: 2) opposes and which can be associated with the term underclass, "that miserable conditions are self-induced – the poor do it themselves". Byrne is not alone in defining social exclusion as a process. It is probably a fairly common definition among international researchers: for example Ali Madanipour, Göran Cars and Judith Allen in *Social Exclusion in European Cities*:

> Social exclusion is defined as a multi-dimensional process, in which various forms of exclusion are combined: participation in decisionmaking and political processes, access to employment and material resources, and integration into common cultural processes. When combined, they create acute forms of exclusion that find a spatial manifestation in particular neighborhoods.
> *(Madanipour et al., 2003: 22)*

The EU used a similar definition as part of the original Lisbon process in the early 2000s. The EU definition of social exclusion at that time was described by Atkinson and Davoudi as a peculiar combination of a liberal, Anglo-Saxon concern with poverty (SID) and a more conservative, continental interest in the moral and social order (MUD). This meant that the European definition of social exclusion was quite broad and hence vague. Atkinson and Davoudi (2000: 437) saw it as a prerequisite for being able to agree.

In this sense the very vagueness of the term social exclusion may actually be an advantage, as it allows the Commission to bring together Member States with different welfare regimes and a range of potentially conflicting interests to construct a 'coalition against exclusion'.

The fight against exclusion was made a key part of the Lisbon Strategy. At its meeting in December 2000, the European Council decided on common objectives. In order to meet the objectives, each country elaborated in 2001 NAPs (National Action Plans), which then formed the basis of a joint report adopted by the European Council in December 2002, called the Joint Report on Social Inclusion. The report begins with a grand statement: "It is the first time that the European Union endorses a policy document on poverty and social exclusion" (European Commission, 2002: 9). The report had also agreed on a definition of social exclusion, as clarified in the next version of the Joint Report on Social Inclusion from 2004:

> Social exclusion is a process whereby certain individuals are pushed to the edge of society and prevented from participating fully by virtue of their poverty, or lack of basic competencies and lifelong learning opportunities, or as a result of discrimination. This distances them from job, income and education opportunities as well as social and community networks and activities. They have little access to power and decision-making bodies and thus often feeling powerless and unable to take control over the decisions that affect their day to day lives.
> *(European Commission, 2005: 10)*

This definition differs in important respects from the liberal SID. Based on SID, social exclusion appears as a condition, but in the above EU definition it is described as a process. It is something which affects individuals, "pushed to the edge", and apparently is nothing for which they should have to bear the blame themselves. They are prevented from participating and it is said to be due to poverty, which is reminiscent of RED and it is also said to be due to discrimination. Society is obviously not faultless, which by contrast mainly SID appears to contend.

Furthermore, participation is not just about paid work, but also about "social and community networks and activities". Here are traces of a conservative solidarity thinking, which is what MUD is based on. It is, in any case, a different approach from the restriction SID places on paid work, thereby it also, as Levitas (2005: 26) says: "tends to reduce the social to the economic, and simultaneously limits understanding of economic activity to market activity." Particularly noteworthy in the quote above is the EU definition's emphasis on power.

8.1.2 The condition of being excluded

In British politics a definition of social exclusion as a condition came to prevail, according to Fairclough (2000: 54), as "in the language of New Labour social exclusion is an outcome rather than a process – it is a condition people are in rather than something that is done to them." It is used to present people and places as excluded but without the slightest trace of someone causing it, other than themselves. Fairclough (2000: 65) concludes that New Labour replaced the quest for equality with the desire for more inclusion.

> The objective of equality in left politics has been based on the claim that capitalist societies by their nature create inequalities and conflicting interests. The objective of social inclusion by contrast makes no such claim – by focusing on those who are excluded from society and ways of including them, it shifts away from inequalities and conflicts of interest among those who are included and presupposes that there is nothing inherently wrong with contemporary society as long as it is made more inclusive through government policies.
>
> *(Fairclough, 2000: 54)*

This is the definition that the previous Swedish right-wing government imported before the election in 2006 by translating social exclusion as 'utanförskap'. It is also the definition used in the EU's social inclusion agenda and I will return to that in chapter 9.1. Levitas traces the roots of this view in the sociology of Emile Durkheim. Characteristic of this "neo-Durkheimian hegemony", as Levitas (2005: 188) calls it, is that the existing social order is taken for granted. This is exactly one of the main approaches that C. Wright Mills criticised in his book from 1959, *The Sociological Imagination*, and which the neo-classically inspired economists represent. The societal order is seen as obvious and natural, and the individual must adapt to it. Disorder depends on individuals who have not adapted and, therefore, should be blamed. Thereby, the critique of capitalism is removed from the political agenda (Levitas, 2005: 188).

Will a process-definition of social exclusion be sufficient to bring the full potential of that critique back in? I do not think so, because the process-definition also tends to take society for granted, although not necessarily the contemporary one. It conjures up the vision of a society that does not exclude and where social exclusion becomes the exception. It makes us believe that we are all basically included, but we are not. Being included is never unconditional. As I explained in chapter 3.2, society and the social world does not consist of isolated individuals but of social relations. Being social means to take part in social relations, which may then also enable us to develop as individuals. Just being a human being does not necessarily make us included in society, which Marx emphasised in the Grundrisse (Marx, 1986: 195):

> Society does not consist of individuals, but expresses the sum of interrelations, the relations within which these individuals stand. As if someone were to say: Seen from the perspective of society, there are no slaves and no citizens: both are human beings. Rather, they are that outside society. To be a slave, to be a

citizen, are social characteristics, relations between human beings A and B. Human being A, as such, is not a slave. He is a slave in and through society.

This is a conception of individuality, which goes further than that of Durkheim, as Robotham highlights. While "Durkheim still retains notions of self-subsistent individuals brought into inter-dependence by the social division of labour", for Marx "sociality enters into the very constitution of the individual" (Robotham, 2005: 17). To be included in society, thus, you need to participate in the relations and processes that society consists of. According to the indicator called NEET, included in the dashboard of EU Youth indicators, quite a lot of young people do not do that in crucial senses.

As Figure 8.1 shows, the NEETs were fairly numerous even before the financial crisis that started in 2008. In 2005, the average for the 28 EU member states was 12.7%. Since then, the average has not changed a lot. It peaked in 2012 with 13.2% and has thereafter decreased gradually to 12.0% in 2015. Among the ten countries which Citispyce has focused on, however, the patterns differ substantially. In five of them, the proportion of NEETs has gone down between 2005 and 2015. The NEET percentage has remained particularly low in the Netherlands and has decreased to low levels also in Germany and the Czech Republic. In contrast, Italy is the only country where it has increased, from 17.1% in 2005 to 21.4% in 2015. Italy has now the highest share of NEETs among the ten countries. This means that in Italy, more than 1 in 5 young people neither have a job nor do they participate in education or training. In the EU28 as a whole, the percentage of

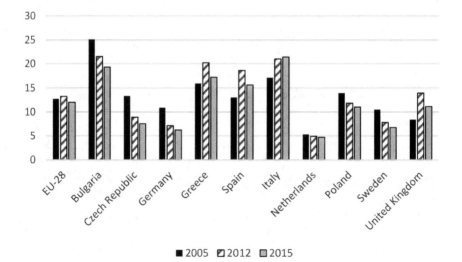

FIGURE 8.1 Young people (15–24 years) not in employment, education or training (NEET)
Available at: http://ec.europa.eu/eurostat/web/youth/data/eu-dashboard (accessed 6 July 2017)

NEETs corresponds to 6.6 million young people, thus more than the population of a country like Denmark, for example.

These worrying figures prove the need for recognising the existence of being excluded, at least from crucial societal systems, which then obviously means the violation of human rights. This should not, however, let us limit our focus to those socially excluded young people. More important is to find out how society has become such a condition of social inclusion that makes it difficult for many young people to become and remain included. Just as social exclusion, the term social inclusion may have two different meanings, the one referring to a process and the other referring to a condition. It is because society has developed into a new condition of social inclusion that people may become excluded from it. Characteristic of the 'neo-Durkheimian hegemony', mentioned above, is the use of social exclusion as a noun and social inclusion as a verb. That conceals, effectively, both why people have become excluded and how society has become a condition of social inclusion, with barriers and conditions that make it difficult to become included. Therefore, both these two concepts, social exclusion and social inclusion, should be defined as both processes and conditions.

8.1.3 Causes of social exclusion

The two definitions of social exclusion and social inclusion, respectively, seeing both as a process and a condition, can be associated with two types of causes, firstly the processes that exclude and secondly the conditions that make it difficult to become included. People could, thus, live in a condition of social exclusion both because they have been excluded and because they do not fulfil the conditions for being included. Accumulation by dispossession is an example of the first type of causes of inequality. Let us call them process-causes of social exclusion. All the systemic causes of inequality, presented in chapter 4, belong to this category.

Correspondingly, I propose the second type be called condition-causes of social exclusion. They can be clarified by using Levitas' distinction between the three definitions of social exclusion, but seen as three different forms of such conditions for getting included. If you cannot get included, it may depend on that you do not have, do and/or mean what is required. This distinction has also the advantage of being compatible with the forms of inequality, presented in chapter 2. The ones on the disadvantaged side of resource inequality, those who do not have what is required to be included, belong to the have-nots; i.e. the aspect emphasised by RED. Similarly, SID is concerned with the disadvantaged side of structural inequality and thus the ones who could be called the do-nots. MUD, in its turn, deals with the disadvantaged side of cultural inequality and thus the mean-nots; i.e. those who do not express the "right" morals. At least one more aspect needs to be added, however, concerning those who do not want to be included and who can, therefore, be called the want-nots.

As I see it, making this distinction between process- and condition-causes of social exclusion paves the way for that fundamental critique of capitalism and contemporary society that Levitas (2005: 6, 187) regards as implicit in a broader idea of inclusion, because "beyond the question of who is included and on what terms, lies the question of what they are included in". This is the question, or rather what they are not included in, to which I will now turn.

8.2 Societal causes of social exclusion

As we have seen in previous chapters, neoliberalism has put its imprint on all the countries and cities, although to different extents because of differences in histories, institutions, relations of strength between social forces, etc. As I will claim, neoliberalism has led to the rise of a particular societal model, which can be called the neoliberal one. Inequality is, thus, not accidental. It is not a deviation or a failure. Instead, I will claim that it is inscribed in this model as one of its moments (i.e. constituent parts). Without inequality, it would not work. This model has to a great extent been actualised in the UK.

In the definition pursued here, the concept of societal model refers to the potential for relatively coherent, orderly and stable societal development. Such a model may contain a complexity of various moments but here I will restrict myself to what I have written about in the previous chapters. Hence, a societal model, as I will treat it here, contains a combination of a growth model and a welfare regime. Given the findings in the previous chapters, at least three such societal models can be defined. In line with the three main ideologies, I will call them the neoliberal, the conservative and the social democratic societal models. None of them goes beyond capitalism.

Each one of the societal models actualises the systemic causes of inequality, but in different ways. With regard to the losing side of inequality, they may also tend to exclude differently. These are the first type of causes, mentioned above. They can be called systemic process-causes of social exclusion. The second type of causes, referred to above, emerge from the specific combinations of growth models and welfare regimes. They are the ones associated with certain conditions for what you need to have, do and mean in order to become and remain included. They will be called model-specific condition-causes of social exclusion. None of these societal models are actualised in full anywhere. Actors may, however, strive towards one of them precisely because they enable relatively coherent, orderly and stable societal development. Concrete societies may, thus, be more or less characterised by a particular model.

8.2.1 The neoliberal model

This societal model includes a growth model where causes of inequality in the forms of accumulation by dispossession operate in a quite unrestricted way due to extensive deregulation. Basically, this has unleashed the growth imperative of capital and the systemic cause of resource inequality inherent in the capital exchange relation. It has acquired more forms through which to operate. A relatively large part of the economy has also arisen to make this kind of profits, the ones acquired through accumulation by dispossession. Similar to the growth model called dependent financialisation, the economy is not very competitive, indicated by a long-term deficit in the annual current account balance, but in contrast to dependent financialisation, this is not a big problem. The model does not earn its supremacy by being competitive, in contrast to the export-oriented model, but by hosting a centre of finance capital. The supremacy of such a centre has to be maintained.

The neoliberal societal model consists to a large extent of precarious and low-paid jobs, which tend to cause health and resource inequality. This low-wage sector can be said to be a counterpart to the much more developed labour market policy in the social democratic model. The jobs in the low-wage sector do not usually imply any discretionary learning. It is, therefore, easy to get stuck there, maybe also because of the need to take several jobs in order to get by. The low benefit levels offered by the welfare state reinforces this. They could hardly be higher, because then people would try to get benefits instead of a job. There is a logic behind the link between the low-wage sector of the growth model and the benefit levels of the welfare regime.

The neoliberal societal model differs from the other models as its growth model does not consist of barriers, neither in the labour market between inside and outside, as in the conservative model, nor around the labour market as a whole, as in the social democratic model. Instead, its labour market could be described more as a continuous deterioration of working conditions. This reinforces structural inequality between the ones with good and bad jobs respectively. Due to the modest increase in productivity, the rising organic composition of capital does not tend to cause unemployment to the same extent as in the social democratic societal model.

The model allows for both extreme wealth and extreme poverty. This is not due to an inherent selfishness of people, but basically it is about the unleashing of the systemic cause of resource inequality. Capitalism has become increasingly influential for societal life and to secure a position in society, you have to hang on and perhaps even make yourself part of the capitalist class. The fate of the losing side deters people from opting out. It encourages actors to seek wealth individually and therefore also contributes to reproducing the societal model.

The main type of inequality in this society, I would say, is resource inequality (see also Therborn, 2013: 43). The societal model in itself causes a lot of it. It is inscribed in how the model operates, indicated by, for example, a low coverage rate of collective agreements. The trade unions must be kept weak because otherwise the societal model would not function. The lack of regulations means that some people can become extremely wealthy; this has strengthened the rich as a class. Pettifor (2017: 58) explains one of the processes through which resource inequality increases:

Pensioners dependent on their savings for income similarly go in search of assets that will generate sufficient income to keep pace with inflation. As a result, savings and surpluses are poured into a small group of assets regarded as safe by investors, including, gold, jewels, stocks and shares, and government bonds. This has led, predictably, to the inflation of these assets as well. As it is the rich who on the whole own assets (i.e. stocks and shares, but also football clubs, public hospital car parks, land, brands, race-horses, works of art, yachts, etc), the rich have grown richer. And as the value of their assets has risen, so have the rents they charge on those assets.

The welfare state is not particularly decommodifying and thus fails to contribute to making people less dependent on selling their labour power. It does not compensate for the low wages but on the contrary, reaffirms them. Therefore, the welfare state can be said to contribute to resource inequality. It does not contain any significant investments in labour market policy and thus does not compensate for the lack of discretionary learning in the workplace. The combined effect of a low percentage of jobs with discretionary learning and inadequate labour market policies constitutes sustained low skills, but also a weak potential to act collectively. Instead of educating people further, they are referred to jobs in the low-wage sector, which means that they remain low-skilled.

The housing situation is significant in this societal model because housing has become part of financialisation and, thus, the actualisation of the first systemic potential cause of inequality; i.e. the one inherent in the capitalist relation of exchange. A favourable condition for this is a high proportion of owner-occupiers. Have-nots can thus only afford to live in a few places. This cause of inequality is not counteracted by the welfare state but instead aggravated, as it refers people to social housing where only have-nots are allowed to live. In order to end up in these areas, you need to be a have-not in the sense of lacking money, labour power and training/education. In addition, the ones who live there do not usually do what it takes, i.e. have a paid job, to support themselves. A different mentality and culture probably then develops in these areas; Owen Jones has written about this in his book *Chavs* (2012) and it is also what *Benefit Street*, the TV series based in Birmingham is about.

Thus, in this way the welfare regime of this societal model contributes to stigmatisation. If not previously, then it is by living in such places that people become part of the mean-nots. In other words, housing in these areas means stigmatisation (Sayer, 2015: 100). It also certainly implies that many despair and do not care about their behaviour. There is no favourable context for a culture of respectability but on the contrary. In the liberal model, the welfare state consolidates the societal borders.

This makes the societal borders very clear and it makes social mobility even more difficult. The combination of the growth model and welfare regime tend to make the low-wage sector and poverty permanent, i.e. the have-nots in the sense of money but also labour power. A reserve army of low-wage workers is reproduced. The model can also be seen as very effective individualisation in accordance with the liberal outlook on people presented in chapter 4.2. It allows individuals to become very rich without being questioned or their wealth redistributed. The poor are questioned, however, and the blame is put on them individually for their situation.

This societal model is essentially based on inequality. On the one hand, it has been necessary to allow some to become very rich. When market forces were released and finance capital took advantage of it, golden opportunities were created for some. The country and the city that aspires to be the centre of this power and provide residency for such people must allow them to get rich. Otherwise, they might move somewhere else; and it would not be very difficult for them due to the volatility of their capital. On the other hand, it has been necessary to make others very poor because otherwise it would not enable the creation of a reserve army of workers for all the poor jobs in the service sector which has arisen as a result of the new rich.

In this model, it does not really matter how you earn your money, only that you earn it. It need not be through paid work. Even the housewife of a rich man is included, not because she works at home, but because the husband is rich. Regardless of whether she works at home or not, this has no bearing on her position. The family, thus, has no relevance in this model. It is only through your activity in the market you societalise yourself. It is not, however, sufficient for you to earn your living through gainful work/employment. You are also supposed to manage your own risks by paying for insurances in the market.

To facilitate this societalisation, the barriers around the labour market are much lower than in the social democratic model and it does not comprise an internal division as in the conservative model. People are supposed to compete in the market and if they do not succeed, there is little support and this is limited by being needs-based and individualised. Instead, the pressure is put on the individual, who is held accountable for her/his own situation. The inadequate welfare state has created a need for civil society initiatives but they are rooted in precisely this need and therefore tend to be compensatory. It is to compensate for the shortcomings of the welfare state that they arise, not to complete it.

8.2.2 The conservative model

In this societal model, the dualistic division between insiders and outsiders is used to strengthen competitiveness by making the conditions for the losing side worse; thereby increasing structural inequality between the ones with good and bad jobs. This has favoured the expansion of a low wage sector, affecting young people in particular, not indirectly as in dependent financialisation but directly due to political decisions. These decisions have been taken in a deliberate attempt to strengthen competitiveness, whereas in dependent financialisation, the struggle for competiveness has been lost and the expansion of the low wage sector depends on the capitalist dynamics. In the conservative model, it is important to preserve structural inequality as it sustains competitiveness.

The logic is that people should, in the first place earn their living by gainful work/employment. Those who do that are rewarded with stronger safety nets and a strengthened position in the family (if they have one). Those who do not earn their living by gainful work/employment become dependent on the family, and not in any form but in a patriarchal one, where the husband's supremacy is reproduced by him earning his living through gainful work/employment. This dependence also concerns the housewife who, by being a housewife and accepting her husband's supremacy also has a position in society.

The logic makes it difficult for singles, especially women and young people. They have not qualified for any of the predetermined roles, because they do not get recognition in any capacity, either as individuals or citizens. Those who either cannot, or do not want to fulfil these requirements should be pitied and supported, but not unconditionally. The ones supported should recognise their subordination according to the Catholic concept of solidarity, also called normative solidarity (Liedman, 1999: 86). For them there is support to apply for, such as access to decent social housing, so that they can become included.

There are barriers that are equivalent to those in the social democratic model, but in the conservative model these barriers exist within the labour market, not around it. Perhaps one can say that the societal borders that arise originate in a combination of do-not- and have-not-causes. The societal model causes have-nots, because only part of the labour market is regulated and the other part consists of a low-wage sector. The welfare regime confirms this division by safeguarding the good life for those who are inside the barriers and confirming a worse life for those who are on the outside.

In the conservative model, the division within the labour market is decisive due to the dependence of the growth model on competitive exports, not on superior financialisation. Competitive exports are not only achieved, however, through rationalisation but also through a downward pressure on wages; the existence of the low wage sector contributes to this.

The conservative model, thus, includes inequality. It can be said to be a necessary component of the model, i.e. one of its moments. But so it is with the neoliberal model. In both of these societal models, there is a model-created inequality. Is this also the case with the social democratic model of society? No, I do not really think so. Inequality is not necessary for it to function. It does not require, as in the conservative model, a low-wage sector that can help to keep wages down in order for the economy as a whole to become competitive. It also does not require, as in the neoliberal model, a low-wage sector where people cannot do much else than serve the rich and do not learn anything else either.

The low-wage sector, therefore, has different functions in these two societal models. In the neoliberal model, it allows a fairly high employment rate due to service demand from the rich. If the low-wage sector also contributes to keeping down wages generally, this has no great significance as competition with foreign countries does not have such importance for this growth model. It is instead fed by being the centre of finance capital supremacy, exploiting all possible transactions and speculations. In the conservative model, however, the low-wage sector has the prime importance of keeping wages down in general but also in dividing the working class. The latter function is filled by the low-wage sector even in the neoliberal model.

8.2.3 The social democratic model

This societal model is perhaps the one that differs the most from the others. A major difference is that it does not have a large low-wage sector. Other differences are the relatively high density of trade unions and the wide coverage of collective agreements. Because of all this, the model includes barriers, not within the labour market, similar to the conservative model, but more around it, in contrast to the liberal model. They are barriers to entry. To keep this model afloat, labour market measures are necessary. They correspond to the low wage sectors in other growth models, but in contrast to these, they are supposed to equip the individual to take part in an export-oriented economy of high added value.

Resource inequality is not particularly prevalent in this model, in contrast to the other two. The welfare state does not contribute in the same way as in the other models to a resource inequality, but maintains people at decent levels. The relatively high proportion of discretionary learning on the job also means a lower resource inequality, in terms of labour power. The welfare state contributes to this by well developed labour market policies. Instead, this model has probably the strongest potential causes of structural inequality between those with and without paid work, depending on a well regulated labour market and competitive capital. As an emergent effect, societal borders can arise if the actualisation of these causes is not counteracted by a highly developed labour market policy.

Such emergent societal borders fill no function in the social democratic model, I would say, as opposed to the situation in the UK. When low incomes (wages and/ or compensation) are maintained in the UK, as well as individualisation and poor working conditions, people find it hard to do something else and that is exactly what the neoliberal model requires. If people were better off and had the time to start thinking, learning something at work and joining together, then the neoliberal model would break down. This is not the case with the social democratic societal model, because for this model, marginalisation and social exclusion are mostly damaging, and create fertile ground for social forces that could threaten the model. This will ultimately also make it more difficult to include these people in the highly skilled and competitive economy.

This model has higher expectations of the individual to earn her/his living through gainful employment than the other two models. Those who fail should not be blamed for their own situation and receive support under selective conditions, as in the neoliberal regime, nor get support in line with a conservative concept of solidarity, but because they are citizens. It is supposed to be equal for all, according to universal principles. This also manifests itself in the absence of social housing, and the existence instead of public housing that caters for everyone.

The family has no particular function in this model and is not expected to take any significant responsibility. On the contrary, the model tends to undermine the family, as there is pressure on both fathers and mothers to work or at least prepare for it through training. The social economy fulfils its own function as a complement to the welfare state and does not act in a compensatory way as long as the welfare state manages its maximalist commitments. Civil society can instead focus on strengthening the citizen, which is thus the basis of this model. It requires, again, that the welfare state maintains an active labour market policy and thus compensates for the barriers around the labour market. If it does not and instead these barriers are lowered, the individual country where this happens will transform itself into another societal model. The maintenance of these barriers and countering them through active labour market policies are included in the model as moments.

8.3 New societal borders

Different forms of inequality have come to coincide in the cities, often coinciding also with segregation. That makes it important to reformulate the problem of inequality; it should rather be described as a problem which concerns the polarisation between social inclusion and social exclusion. On the one hand, society has turned into a condition of social inclusion with surrounding borders consisting of demands on what to have, to do and to mean in order to be included. On the other hand, spatial concentrations have emerged of people who do not have, do or mean what is demanded to participate in society. They most certainly have, do and/or mean something else, but not that which allows them to participate in society. The socially included and the socially excluded thus tend to live in different parts of cities.

In between, borders have arisen, which I prefer to see as societal. By this, I do not mean to locate people in these socially excluded neighbourhoods outside society in every respect. There is no doubt, however, that a kind of border exists. That is also how many young people in the Citispyce interviews describe it. Referring to the borders as societal should be seen as symbolising the depth of inequality. Many young people across Europe are affected not only by one form of inequality, but by multiple forms. Moreover, the affected ones are often concentrated in certain neighbourhoods. The question of dealing with inequality becomes, thus, a question of dealing with these societal borders and the causes of them.

8.3.1 Segregated neighbourhoods

In previous chapters, I have referred to Fakulteta neighbourhood in Sofia as a pole of both resource, structural and cultural inequality. In Fakulteta, these three forms of inequality coincide. It is not 'only' about poverty, not 'only' about unemployment and not 'only' about discrimination, but about it all. Furthermore, it is about space, which the concept of segregation may help us to understand. A neighbourhood like Fakulteta is certainly segregated, but then in relation to other neighbourhoods.

Segregation should be defined as relational. It arises when different social groups are separated spatially and thus, social difference coincides with spatial separation. This means that segregation always consists of at least two different social groups, which are living, working, and/or going to school in separated spatial areas. These spatially separated different social groups constitute the poles of segregation and the concept of segregation comprises them both. Therefore, segregation is not only about a neighbourhood like Fakulteta, but such neighbourhoods in their relation to neighbourhoods where other social groups live, work and/or go to school. Studies on segregation cannot focus on only one of these poles, but should incorporate both and in their relation to each other.

Young people tend to know this very well, for example some of the interviewees in Birmingham who "pointed to high levels of income and wealth in the city centre as symbolising inequality. When meeting with us in the city centre, young people pointed toward development as symbolising where wealth and opportunity were concentrated, in contrast to their neighbourhoods." (Hussain et al., 2014b: 9).

Many researchers nowadays would also agree that segregation must be defined relationally. Politicians, however, often focus on only one side, the "losing side", as the researchers Andersson et al., (2007) call it. They are harsh in their criticism and believe that focusing on the losing side exacerbates the problems:

> That segregation is relational tends to be hidden. In fact and as mentioned, the self-segregation of the rich is significantly stronger than the poor's – for them less possible to influence – segregation. By proclaiming neighbourhoods and residential areas as vulnerable, one proclaims them also as different and contributes to stigmatisation. The image of 'blame the victim' is likely to be strengthened.
>
> *(Andersson et al., 2007: 67 – my translation)*

The neighbourhood Lozells & East Handsworth in Birmingham may help us to understand what a relational definition of segregation means. It is located in the north-western part of the city, not so far from the city centre. A huge majority, as many as 90%, belongs to an ethnic minority, in particular Pakistani which makes up 25% of the population. In total, 60% belongs to an Asian minority. Besides that, there is also a sizeable Black community, constituting around 20% of the ward's population. The neighbourhood is one of the most deprived in the country. For example, 43% of children in the ward are at risk of poverty.

Given all these indicators, the neighbourhood could be described as segregated but then in relation to other more affluent parts of the city with a less diverse population. In fact, this segregation is reinforced spatially by "the Six Ways roundabout that forms an interchange with neighbouring Aston and Newtown also acts as a 'concrete collar' that disconnects the areas and people living within them" (Hussain et al., 2014a: 11) Interestingly, the authors also mention another divide:

> Community cohesion is also affected within Lozells & East Handsworth by a divide that exists between significant portions of the South Asian and African Caribbean Communities. Some interviewees pointed to this being the result of housing settlement patterns that meant both communities being concentrated across from each other (a road dividing areas of predominant Black or South Asian settlement was often invoked to symbolise the divide).

This is also an example of segregation, although not between rich and poor or good and bad. It is a division between two different groups, quite homogenous due to their respective ethnic identity, but which coincides with housing settlement patterns and the road.

Another example, although between winners and losers, in contrast to the one above, is the pattern of segregation in Malmö between the Sofielund area, in particular the neighbourhood called Seved, and other parts of Malmö (Grander & Stigendal, 2014). The Seved neighbourhood is located in South Sofielund ("Södra Sofielund"). South Sofielund is characterised by mixed settlements, in terms of scale, function and age. Low townhouses and former industrial buildings from late 19th century are mixed with apartment blocks and detached houses from the 1920s and 1930s. There are also three to four storey buildings, apartment blocks built in the functionalist 1950s. The most common form (68%) of tenure in South Sofielund is rental units. 25% of the dwellings are shares in a housing cooperative ("bostadsrätter"), where you buy the right to live in your apartment, owned by a cooperative, where you become a member. The detached houses are condominiums, amounting to 6% of the total housing stock. The single largest property owner is the public housing company MKB, which owns 26% of the total housing in South Sofielund, or a third of the rental apartments. The other rental apartments are owned by a large number of small private landlords.

The population is 4,600 in South Sofielund and 3,700 in North Sofielund (2012). 47% of the population in South Sofielund have been born abroad. The largest immigrant groups come from Iraq, Bosnia-Herzegovina, former Yugoslavia, Poland and Denmark. These countries, however, only add up to around half the population born abroad. Hence, the population is to a great extent multicultural. The local school has a significantly lower percentage of pupils graduating with the grades necessary in order to be accepted at upper secondary school. 52% of the residents (20–64) of South Sofielund were gainfully employed (2015), compared to 70% in Malmö as a whole (including the ones working in Denmark). The results of the City of Malmö's annual safety surveys show that the inhabitants in general perceive a high degree of insecurity, especially in the Seved area. It is primarily disturbances, vandalism/littering and drug problems that seem to be greater in Seved compared to the city district in general.

As a whole, the Sofielund area could be seen as a pole of segregation in Malmö. The situation is particularly precarious in the Seved neighbourhood. It has been the centre of attention for actions in Sofielund during the last decades, as much criminality and social turmoil has manifested itself here. According to a recent report from the national police authority, it is one of the most vulnerable neighbourhoods in Sweden, characterised by serious crime. Yet, Sofielund is quite close to the city centre.

Segregation can be even more divisive when disadvantaged people have been located at a greater distance from the rest. An example of that is the neighbourhood Trinitat Nova in the outskirts of Barcelona. It is a rather small neighbourhood with almost 8,000 inhabitants, built in the 1950s to house migrants from other parts of Spain. Jubany et al. (2014a) describe the houses as badly built and equipped. Most seriously, the use of asbestos led to problems with aluminosis in the 1990s. Because of that, the inhabitants started to protest and organised themselves in a neighbourhood movement. The administration responded by launching a Community Plan, first designed in 1996. Improvements in communications have also been made by the new metro stop "Trinitat Nova", inaugurated in 2000. In recent years, further renewal initiatives have been carried out, co-funded by the European Regional Development Fund (ERDF).

Yet, the previously successful collective organisation has been deactivated and demoralised. Jubany et al. (2014a) attribute this primarily to the permanent bureaucratic problems with the administration. As one of the interviewees describes it:

> "Trinitat Nova is a neighbourhood which has broken down. It was a neighbourhood of housings built by the Obra Sindical del Hogar, social housing with a big problem of aluminosis. The people who lived in there were much organised, but due to this [reform], which was quite demanded by the people, the neighbourhood has broken down. [...] This has happened in a neighbourhood where the population is very old and the young people have left due to the bad housing conditions. This reform, which was demanded by the neighbourhood, has not been well managed. The physical issue of housing has been very negative to bring the neighbourhood together".
>
> (Jubany et al., 2014a: 8)

Among the neighbourhoods in Citispyce, there are also examples of ones where very wealthy and very poor live almost side by side and thus, where no clear patterns of segregation exist. This is the case with Middelland in Rotterdam. The neighbourhood has almost 12,000 inhabitants and is located close to the city centre. It is an old neighbourhood with 73% of the houses built before 1906. As Tan and Spies (2014a) report, it has beautiful grand avenues where double income families live in well-kept ancient houses. "Between those avenues smaller streets were built to house the working- and middle-class. The Dutch working class moved out to the suburbs though and immigrants took their place. Houses are rather small but most of these streets look fine; it does not have a deprived appearance."

> In many respects Middelland is a neighbourhood of extremities. Due to its proximity to the city centre it has a metropolitan feel with lots of shops, coffee shops and restaurants, but also sex clubs, drug-related crime and prostitution. It attracts the creative class, students and criminals alike. Middelland is considered a transit area as couples that want to start a family move out, but also because youth that wants to party in the city centre first stops in Middelland for a drink.
>
> *(Tan et al., 2014a: 28)*

This is a super diverse mixture of not only people with different ethnic backgrounds, but also of rich and poor, where prices of houses have remained affordable and many young people establish themselves there. Middelland shows the importance of analysing inequality from many different angles and not take for granted that it means the same everywhere. Segregation can certainly aggravate existing forms of inequality but not necessarily so.

8.3.2 Spatial causes of inequality

Distancing the winning and losing social categories from each other in terms of segregation should be seen as a spatial cause of inequality. It tends to be aggravated by a large distance. The neighbourhood of Elefsina in Athens constitutes such a pole of segregation, geographically remote and also poorly connected by the transport network to the wider city. If the high cost of transportation is also taken into consideration, Elefsina is seen by Tryfona et al. (2014a) as disconnected to a great extent from whatever happens in the city centre. As the authors (2014a: 8) conclude, "the physical distance, 'isolating' Elefsina from Athens city centre has created a closed community which works as a supportive network enhancing collectivity and mutual support, especially in the difficult times of the crisis". Here, space in terms of territory contains a strong selectivity. It divides different categories of people from each other more than in Piraeus or in Sofielund.

> During the field study we met young people in the area of Elefsina who lived in conditions of extreme poverty. This may relate to the fact that Elefsina is a rather remote community, affected by the industrial decline of the area and restricted by 'physical barriers' that do not allow young people to seize the economic and employment opportunities given in the Metropolis.

However, that does not deplete the opportunities. Even spatial causes operate as selectivities and every selectivity is strategic in the sense that it matters how you deal with it (see chapter 3.2). It is a selectivity for someone, individuals as well as collectives. There is always discretion. And in Birmingham some young people do deal with a selectivity which seems similar to the one in Elefsina (Hussain et al., 2014b: 18):

> Many young creatives or social entrepreneurs who happened to live in the case study areas (or ones similar in terms of deprivation), chose to base themselves or operate from the city centre. The new Birmingham library had become a place young people gravitated to for utilising free internet and spaces to hold meetings. An independent coffee shop on the edge of the city centre some distance from the busy consumer outlets and near the offices of various professional firms was the preferred working space for a surprising number of young people we interviewed.

Besides distance, segregated neighbourhoods can contain other forms of selectivity too. Neighbourhoods should not be seen as empty forms for a structural, cultural and/or actorial content but possess their own content. As geographers have argued including Doreen Massey in her influential book *Spatial Divisions of Labour* (1984: 52), "geography matters. The fact that processes take place over space, the facts of distance or closeness, of geographical variation between areas, of the individual character and meaning of specific places and regions – all these are essential to the operation of social processes themselves".

Critical social theory began to reassert space through this focus on place as relationally constituted processes. The last decades have seen at least four such spatial turns, privileging place, territory, scale and network respectively. Jessop et al. (2008) question any such privileging of a single dimension of sociospatial relations. Instead, they suggest a framework which includes all the four above mentioned spatial turns, called TPSN (Territory, Place, Scale and Network). More such spatial dimensions of social relations may exist, but these four "are arguably the most salient in work on contemporary political-economic restructuring" (Jessop et al., 2008: 392).

Territory is about bordering, bounding and enclosure, for example the construction of divisions between insiders and outsiders. The concept of place deals with how the design and maintenance of houses, streets, parks and spatial forms enable and/or constrain social relations. While place deals with horizontal relations, scale conceptualises the significance of vertical relations, for example the division of political power between municipal, regional, national and EU levels. The fourth dimension in the TPSN framework is network and that refers to, for example, the relationships between different cities. These four concepts make us attentive to the different dimensions in which space both constrains and enables social relations (see also Moulaert et al., 2016: 171). Aspects of these four dimensions were highlighted by young people themselves in Birmingham, as seems clear in this summary from Hussain et al. (2014b: 7):

> The interviews revealed a number of important points about the way young people imagined and lived in their neighbourhoods; how their

neighbourhoods and the ethnic diversity and resultant infrastructures could be both enabling and limiting at the same time; how the city was appropriated as a cosmopolitan place offering unfettered movement in and around the city for some, while for others inhibited by negative effects of deprived neighbourhoods.

As territory, space may reinforce the polarisation between the socially included and the socially excluded by keeping them distant from each other. That may enable social relations to flourish within each one of the categories while it constrains social relations between them. As place, space may enable and constrain due to its individual character. Neglect and decay tend to cause hierarchies between places. As scale, space may eclipse the relation between symptoms and causes, expressing the former at the local scale level and making them look like causes, justifying the blaming on the victims (see next section). In these three modes – distanciation, hierarchisation and scaling – space contains the potential to aggravate the relation between the socially included and the socially excluded (see also Therborn, 2013). They can be very differently combined and actualised in an individual neighbourhood.

In Malmö, walking through the Sofielund area, Grander and Alwall (2014: 18), paid attention to the place which they find attractive due to variations and mixes. "It appears as part of a small town, while at the same time in different ways signalling the presence of the centre of a bigger city in its close proximity." This is also mentioned by the young people and as one of the interviewed says, "[it's] so nice because you can just go to the Seved square and you know that your buddies will hang out there, I mean you don't have to call them or make an appointment, but they are all there".

In the minds of many interviewees, the area's location, physical characteristics and multicultural atmosphere seem to surpass the fact that the standard of housing and the general appearance of the area is poor. "I feel at home here", as one of the interviewees says. At the same time, Grander and Alwall (2014: 18) report, some of the interviewees describe the area as "framed":

> "I feel that the whole of Sofielund is very clearly enclosed by major roads. / ... / If you are experiencing social barriers against society in terms of getting jobs or an education, I believe that physical barriers can reinforce that feeling"

This touches upon what I will refer to as the new societal borders. The street of Lönngatan, dividing South and North Sofielund, appears to be a mental and physical barrier for some of the young people interviewed. North Sofielund is in general regarded as "nicer" and "more clean" by the young people. Yet, Lönngatan seems to be frequently used as a passage way to and from Sofielund. It leads to the bordering area of Möllevången, a highly popular (and still not too gentrified) city district, which is perceived by many as the centre of multiculturalism in Malmö. In general, the young people interviewed appreciate the proximity to this area and – beyond it – the inner city centre. This explains the territorial selectivity of the neighbourhood.

Territorial selectivity, however, does not have the same content everywhere, as neighbourhoods associated with social exclusion are not always distant. Another example of that is Piraeus in Athens. As one of the interviewees says (Tryfona et al., 2014b: 6), "to tell you the truth in every road there is a bus, a railway or a trolley bus stop. The area is not remote …". As Tryfona et al. (2014b: 6) explain, "the proximity to the wider city area and the existence of the commercial port, which implies population movement to and from Piraeus, give young people the opportunity to get in touch with different stimuli, opportunities and mindsets".

8.3.3 Understanding the borders

During the heyday of Fordist economies and Keynesian welfare states, the reach of different societal systems usually coincided with the territorial borders of the nation state. As Novy (2011: 249) puts it, "the unique achievement of universal social rights was linked to a specific form of territory, the nation, and a specific public institution, the state, which was the nodal point of regulation." Therefore, what existed can be called nation-societies.

Those societal borders have been partly dismantled in line with globalisation. Instead, new societal borders have emerged, and I claim that they exist in cities. Although they may not be determined accurately to the millimetre, like the borders of the nation state, yet they fulfil a similar function by constituting the spatio-temporal fixes of contemporary societies (see also Jessop, 2006). It is by establishing these borders that current societies make themselves coherent. By setting these borders, society moves the societal problems outside itself: the very problems that it itself creates. The new societal border in cities thus become a prerequisite for society to hang together.

The existence of such borders is highlighted also by Stephen Graham (2011) in his book *Cities Under Siege: The New Military Urbanism*. Graham characterises those outside, the "outcast proletariat", as "neither consumers nor producers, unintegrated into the dominant corporate system of globalisation, they instead try to benefit indirectly, through 'black economies' and informal labour, from the urban cores they literally surround." Graham's book is about how these urban borders between "inside" and "outside" are being militarised by what he calls the new military urbanism. This development has been part of the neoliberalism of the last decades, Graham contends.

To understand this existence of societal borders in the cities, we need to incorporate the third spatial dimension into the analysis, the one of scale. The significance of scale and the interlinks between different scales in multiscalarities is explained by Miciukiewicz et al. (2012: 1857):

> Urban labour markets may show their local character but are intrinsically spatially articulated through the strategies of corporations, through regional and

national policymaking, through migration, etc. Collective agencies for social change may be locally rooted but regionally and internationally co-ordinated. Local ethics borrow a significant part of their values and principles from national, European and 'global' grand discourses – for example, about the partaking of all citizens in the 'knowledge society', participation in a local solidarity action to eradicate hunger at the world level as the Millennium Agenda proclaims or adopting values learned from international migrants.

If collective action is coordinated regionally, the region is then the scalar level that should be focused upon to analyse the coordination. This does not make it less relevant to analyse the collective action at the local scalar level. The coordination at the regional level designs potentials, which then have to be actualised at the local level. If local ethics borrow a significant part of their values and principles from national, European and 'global' grand discourses, a significant part of the analysis should be devoted to analysing these discourses at a global level. At the local level, however, they exist first of all as potentials which are actualised by actors with their own interpretations of them and for specific purposes. Such recontextualisations need to be analysed in their own right, then at the local scalar level.

It is perhaps easiest to understand these societal borders spatially. In this sense, Fakulteta in Sofia is perhaps the most obvious example among the twenty neighbourhoods in the ten cities of a life excluded from society. However, the border is societal as well. It appears when the inhabitants of Faculteta are told by representatives of society that they do not have, do and/or mean what it takes to be included. Furthermore, it appeared, as Hajdinjak (2014) reports, when "young Roma spoke about Fakulteta as a ghetto, which has been forgotten by every single institution, and said that they felt as if they lived in an autonomous region, where laws did not apply". What these young people are talking about, in my interpretation, is the composite effects of different forms of inequality. An important concept for that is social exclusion. The use of it, however, often contributes to stigmatisation. Therefore, it needs to be carefully defined, which I hope to have done.

Again, the actual is always different from the potential and the former cannot be reduced to the latter. To the extent that societal borders exist, it is because somebody makes them, not just as they please. They are not made under circumstances chosen by themselves, but, to quote Marx & Engels (1979/11: 103) once again, "under circumstances directly encountered, given and transmitted from the past". The agents of the societal borders actualise structures, which have been developed gradually and so they follow in the path-dependent footsteps of others. This does not make their actions fully predetermined; there is always a discretion, as I have underlined several times, and it is this discretion that I will address in chapter 9.

8.3.4 The existence of the borders

It is an empirical fact that disadvantaged people tend to become concentrated in certain neighbourhoods. More interesting is to explain what makes them end up in these neighbourhoods. What causes these spatial concentrations of have-nots, do-nots and mean-nots? What makes these neighbourhoods become poles of social exclusion? An obvious reason is that other people do not move there. The distance and decay of these neighbourhoods, as well as their reputation, influence those that have a choice against selecting them. That does not explain, however, why those who do not have, do and mean have moved in and even stay there. What is needed, thus, are analyses, which do not limit themselves to describing excluded neighbourhoods, and thereby run the risk of further stigmatising them. There is a need of analyses, which highlight how the causes of inequality are actualised.

To give an example of this and show how complex interactions of different tendencies cause the spatial concentration of people, I have drawn on the Citispyce case study of the neighbourhood called Cejl in Brno (Sirovátka et al., 2014). Cejl is a medium-sized area with about 8,000 inhabitants, of whom about 50% are Roma. More than half the population is under 25 years. The area is located near the centre. There are many pubs, clubs, gambling halls and pawnbrokers. Previously there were a lot of bigger factories but most of these have now been closed and abandoned or used for other things. Instead, many small businesses have been set up.

The area consists mainly of older houses, built in the early 1900s and not maintained since the 1950s. Much is thus worn down and in poor condition. At the same time, many improvements have also been made in the last ten years. It is classified as a development area and big investments have been made there. In general, however, the area is characterised by its low quality of housing, overcrowding and debt. The renovations often mean that Roma have to move to even worse houses, because only those without debts are allowed to move back into the renovated dwellings. That shows how the systemic cause of inequality, inherent in the capital relation of exchange is actualised, causing resource inequality.

The formal level of unemployment is very high, which equates to a high structural inequality. There are temporary jobs, however, but especially in the grey economy: paid in cash and without any payments made to taxes. Therefore, many end up outside the social security and health systems, affected thus by a combination of structural and health inequalities. Furthermore, the jobs are usually low-skilled and low-paid. Many who live in the area have debts, for example, to meet housing costs or for consumption. Concentrations of poor people live here. It therefore constitutes, a pole of resource inequality.

Roma in general, and especially when they are concentrated in Cejl, are exposed to much discrimination. They belong, therefore, to the losing side of cultural inequality, by being portrayed as meaning less. That is a reason why they often do not go on to further study at higher levels. Their level of education is generally quite low. Of the two high schools in the area, around 90% of students are Roma. People from other parts of the city regard the area as risky. Segregation is increasing as well as the negative attitudes toward Roma. Although the area is centrally located, its inhabitants are almost completely isolated from life outside the area.

That is what I mean by a societal border. It exists due to both process- and condition-causes of social exclusion as the example makes clear. The Roma people are both excluded and find it hard to get included. Among the twenty neighbourhoods studied in Citispyce, Cejl in Brno and Fakulteta in Sofia are perhaps the most excluded ones. That does not make it irrelevant, however, to talk about societal borders in the other cities. Polarisation processes in line with the division between social inclusion and social exclusion take place everywhere (Pratschke & Morlicchio, 2012).

At one pole, the included people live. By this, I mean those that actually participate in society; a society which has evolved into a condition of social inclusion. They are also often actually participating in forms which favour a sense of participation: it feels meaningful to take part. At the other pole, concentrations of people live whose lives are characterised by social exclusion, precisely because of the condition of social inclusion into which that society has developed. As a result of stricter requirements and higher barriers, these people are not actually involved in important societal structures and contexts of meaning. And to the extent that they are, it is often not in forms that make them feel involved. They might have, for example, low-wage jobs and be employed in precarious conditions.

Tryfona et al. (2014b: 19) conclude in their report on young people in Athens that "there is a strong relationship between the barriers young people face in the employment and educational sector, and the increased level of disappointment and hopelessness including a range of negative feelings, such as lack of interest and self-motivation, frustration, and passiveness".

> "It is not a good feeling. I don't think we deserve at this age to be in this 'roller coaster' ... I don't think there is an appropriate age for that but I don't think it's good at this age to be talking to psychologists, to be thinking if the electricity will come, that we have nothing to eat, things that are not compatible to our age ...."

According to the study made by Tryfona et al. (2014b), young people in the neighbourhoods of Athens have lost their trust in the state and in public authorities. Many even consider the state as the source of the problems and what the interviewee refers to below is exactly the systemic cause of inequality which is inherent in the state (see chapter 4.2), turning to individuals and favouring those who can assert themselves individually, causing a cultural inequality:

> "The laws are (in favour of) for those who write them and not for the rest of the people, the laws help someone who has money to protect better his money and for those who don't have money to never obtain any money"
>
> *(Tryfona et al., 2014b: 20)*

In my understanding, these dividing lines should be regarded as societal borders. They come to fruition, not only spatially, but also socially in the encounters between, for example, on the one side teachers, social workers or even firemen and, on the other side, the young people in these neighbourhoods. The former represents, structurally as well as culturally, a society, which has developed into a condition of social inclusion, while the young people represent a life situation which means that you do not have, do and mean what is required to be included. Furthermore, the location of them in these neighbourhoods contributes to their condition of social exclusion. This seems confirmed by a young person in Sofielund, Malmö:

> "Sofielund is an area that has a lot of social problems. I absolutely think being raised here differs from other areas in Malmö. How your school environment is, what friends you meet when you grow up, how your family situation is, etc. It's really important – it's not as easy to get out into the society. And if you also speak another language at home it may be difficult with the language as well. There may also be obstacles created within the family. Perhaps no one in your family has a university education, which could make it difficult to get the motivation to educate yourself. It's always difficult to break norms. If the norm in your area is crime, unemployment and so on, it's probably easy to end up there"
>
> (Grander & Alwall, 2014: 12).

Crime puts its imprint on many excluded neighbourhoods across Europe and contributes to an image of the residents as being outside. As one of the young interviewees in Birmingham puts it, according to Hussain et al. (2014b: 6):

> "you're asking me if I can't work, how am I gonna make money? I ain't gonna lie to you I would go out there and sell drugs to people… and I will give fake £50 notes to people, sometimes you have to do certain things to live enit. I see it as if I can't get no money from nowhere and the only way I can get money is to sell drugs to people then that's what I'm gonna do to eat, no one else is gonna put food on my table"

Tan & Spies (2014b: 15–16) found from their studies in Rotterdam that young people enrol in crime because "there is a culture of wanting very expensive brand clothes, shoes and cars. The interviewee shows his 200 euro Prada cap and claims everybody in Delfshaven has clothes like that, and if you don't have them you're nobody". As one of the young interviewees says:

> "This is the age of thingies: people look up at people with a very nice car and not at someone who graduates cum laude. The imaging is on the streets and on TV, in video clips and so on. It starts with the clothing: young people rather work for branded clothing than be in school."

8.3.5 Meanings of being outside the borders

The spatial causes contained in territorial distanciation and hierachisation of places are often combined with cultural causes. Grander and Alwall (2014: 15) refer to how several of the young people discuss the role of the media in establishing the image of Sofielund, making it more difficult for young inhabitants to enter the labour market.

> "The media has a strong impact on how we perceive things. They haven't depicted Seved as a good neighbourhood. It is a huge obstacle. The news agencies these days don't base their actions on what is true. They create the headlines that people want to buy. We are suffering from bad publicity at Seved, the effect of which may well be that you are not called to an interview and because of that you can't even enter the labour market".

Although reinforced by the media, there are of course reasons for the bad reputation. The area of South Sofielund is known for having problems with crime and drug traffic. A number of the interviewees have been trapped in drug abuse. They tell stories of being afraid of society, hiding in the area and getting stuck there. Others are telling stories about how the drug dealers are influencing the everyday life of the inhabitants.

At the same time, a sense of belonging is apparent among the young people interviewed, especially regarding the Seved area in South Sofielund. As one of the girls says: "We know most of the people who live here. We never want to move from here. We like our place, yes we like it here" (Grander & Alwall, 2014: 8). Similarly, young people from the Mestre and Marghera neighbourhoods in Venice express strong feelings for their neighbourhoods despite their criticism of the cuts and withdrawal of societal institutions. As Della Puppa & Campomori (2014: 11) relate, "all young people converge in saying that, at last, 'it's not so bad to live here!', 'I like to live in Mestre'".

In Rotterdam, Tan & Spies (2014b: 6) interviewed a young person who discussed the pros and cons of leaving the neighbourhood when he has a family. "On the one hand his future children will have better chances growing up in a white neighbourhood, on the other hand he will have a harder time raising his children in line with his culture. Also he would miss the support system in Bloemhof."

> "In a white neighbourhood one has less problems, but on the other hand, if you have a problem you're all by yourself, while in this neighbourhood 50 people are ready to help you".

Similar strong bonds are reported from Piraeus. It seems to be even stronger in the neighbourhood of Agia Sophia (Tryfona et al., 2014b: 6), "where the majority of the population originates from Mani (south part of Peloponnese) and therefore, tight social and family bonds have been developed among the residents creating a strong local identity". As the authors go on, "these solid social bonds are beneficial to the individuals within this social group, as they have managed to act collectively and to claim things from local authorities." On the other hand, however, these strong bonds and the associated identity have alienated another part of the population:

> "… I will talk to you about Piraeus, because I refrain from going to my neighbourhood, Agia Sophia. I do not like the area, where I live, I never did. There is a certain perception that does not match mine. It is a ghettoised area, there are cliques in which I do not participate for several reasons and therefore, I prefer the centre of Piraeus …"
>
> *(Tryfona et al., 2014b: 7)*

Young people from a certain neighbourhood may also represent a certain meaning in the perceptions of inhabitants from other parts of a city, which makes these young people excluded from going there. This is the case reported from Birmingham (Hussain et al., 2014b: 5) with "the cosmopolitan feel of the city centre, which worked to exclude some of them". As one of the young interviewees said, "basically if you're from Handsworth you can't go to Aston, Newtown, Nechells or other places". This shows clearly how causes of inequality can be inherent in cultures, operating then as selectivities. The existence of a particular neighbourhood with its location, design, individual character, tenures and concentrations of people: all of this materialises a certain meaning – it speaks a language – which favours some and not others. Della Puppa & Campomori (2014: 11) mediate a similar story in their report on Venice and the Marghera neighbourhood:

> "A person that was born in Marghera, since the early age, he or she used to hear: 'Do you live in Marghera!? What a nerve! How do you feel there? – and faces as if to say – How can you feel fine in Marghera guys!?' […] Being from Marghera means being alternative, being 'other', being something else […] People used to say: 'Ah, Marghera!? There is only the lane with the whores'. That is, you know? They think like that about us. Or 'Marghera? Full of immigrants, full of Bangladeshi'. Or once again: 'When I take the bus number six or number three to go to Marghera always feel stinks!' Got it? If you are from Marghera you should be ashamed of that, [instead] in Marghera there's the pride of being from Marghera. We, as people from Marghera, have the pride that makes you say: 'I'm not like everyone, I'm not like all the rest, I am the rebel of society'."

In line with my rephrasing of the problem, the aim to explain the causes of inequality means that we have to explain the causes inherent in society: those that cause social exclusion. I set out to do this in chapter 8.1 by making a distinction between process- and condition-causes. That enabled me to define three societal models and to highlight model-specific causes. The spatially demarcated poles of social exclusion are particularly pronounced in the neoliberal societal model, where the have-nots are referred to specific neighbourhoods with social housing estates where others are not allowed to live. Furthermore, the deregulated market in the liberal model means that it is only affordable for have-nots to live in certain neighbourhoods which are characterised by low standards due to low rents. It is too dear to live somewhere else.

Due to the differences between the three societal models, the existence of such borders in British cities should not be a surprise. They belong to the normal also in countries imprinted with the conservative societal model. It is perhaps more surprising that they exist in a city like Malmö, but, according to the experience of many young people, they do. Due to the legacy and reputation of the social democratic societal model, their experience makes it particularly important to explore and explain. It shows the existence of discretion, but, in this case, to transform the Swedish society from a social democratic to a neoliberal societal model, because such a transformation process has been in operation since the 1980s. This transformation partly explains the existence of societal borders in Malmö as well. In the next three sections, I will show how the creation of these new societal borders takes place in everyday life at the local level.

8.4 The making of the new societal borders

Discretion exists because actions are not fully predetermined by either the social structures or the contexts of meaning (cultures). The constraints and opportunities of structures as well as cultures – together constituting their selectivities – should be seen as potentials and explored as such. As potentials, however, they have to be actualised by individual and/or collective actors. When they do this, it matters how these actors deal with their tasks. That is the implication of seeing their actions as strategic. It also reaffirms the existence of discretion. What causes an effect is thus not the potential causes inherent in the structures and cultures, but the emergent actual causes, operating as strategic selectivities.

Individual actors can certainly use their discretion to consolidate the existing order. Their discretion can also be used, however, to change it, perhaps in different directions. In this chapter, I will show how actors in three different contexts at the very local level use their discretions in ways which contribute to a societal transformation towards a neoliberal societal model. They might not be aware of it and, as the first case shows, the intentions could perhaps even be the opposite. The second case shows how such a transformation has been set in motion by gradually changing the welfare regime. The third case shows how the order of the current growth model can be extended, even without anyone accepting responsibility for it.

8.4.1 Reproducing the old in a new context

Arena 305 and The Garage, presented in chapter 7.5, are important and well-known cultural institutions run by the Malmö city council. Both places are easily accessible. This means that a lot of young people from all over the city can access them without reflecting that they are in Sofielund. Therefore, it is quite remarkable that very few of the young people interviewed from Sofielund talked about, or actually visited these places. Statistics from the two institutions show that most visitors come from other parts of the city. The institutions are placed on the north side of the street of Lönngatan; young people in South Sofielund might simply cross the street, but most of them frown when asked if they attend The Garage or Arena 305.

> "I believe that those who are into various problems see Arena 305 as the state and thus an enemy. They believe going in there means being met by the social authorities who wants to take care of them, in which they have no interest."
>
> *(Grander & Alwall, 2014: 25)*

The young person quoted refers to a perception of Arena 305 as the state and thus an enemy. That indicates the existence of what I mean by a societal border. And this border consists not only of culture, but also of how the welfare state works, as also mentioned in the above quote. The main cause of why it exists here is, as I see it, that the actors of the cultural institutions do not fully know how to reproduce the old institutional logic inherent in these institutions in the new context. The cultural institutions are deeply imprinted by the social democratic societal model. They have the potential to reduce inequalities by their broad, universal approach. In Sofielund, however, they have to operate in another environment from the one which prevailed when the social democratic model was actualised to a greater extent. This requires more knowledge in order to fulfil the universalist aspirations.

Based on the opinions of the young people, it is obvious that they do not manage to do that. It might depend not only on a lack of relevant knowledge among the actors that work in these institutions but also on a lack of discretion. Perhaps they have not got the power in their roles to develop the institutions in order to attract the young people in Seved whilst, at the same time, keeping its universalist aspirations and not becoming selective. As a consequence, the cultural institutions contribute to the reproduction of new societal borders.

8.4.2 Selective measures, compensating for austerity

The borders are also caused by the replacement of universal welfare services, due to austerity measures, by selective and temporary projects. Sofielund has a long history of EU, state or municipally funded area-based projects or measures, associated with social policy, run by the municipality or the city district and often in cooperation with civil society. The URBAN programme from 1997 to 1999 funded the first generation of such projects. Malmö hosted the only URBAN programme in Sweden during the first programming period. "I think it introduced a new mindset", the official who wrote most of the programme, Britta Ström, said in an interview that I conducted with her. By that she referred to, firstly, the link between physical and social changes; secondly, the emphasis on entrepreneurship; and thirdly, the formation of partnerships.

In my interpretation, this new mindset included neoliberal principles, as evidenced by the emphases in the quote on entrepreneurship and partnership. Furthermore, the programme did not cover the entire city but was selectively targeted on specific areas, thus in line with a neoliberal model. The selection was not based on merit but on the problems. It was in these areas that the problems appeared to be expressed, and thus it was also here that they were supposed to be solved. Accordingly, it did not change the structures of the welfare state institutions in response to the new context, while keeping its universal character. Yet, they did change, but in the first place because of austerity measures, and then gradually towards becoming part of a neoliberal societal model. The introduction of entrepreneurship, partnership and selective measures did not accord well with the logic of the social democratic welfare regime, but obviously, the discretion allowed it to be done.

And so it has continued over the years, in Sofielund and in some other areas across Malmö. After the URBAN programme, the 'Seved initiative' was launched, funded by the Metropolitan policy (1999–2004). That led amongst other things to the employment activity 'Youth in Seved', which involved young people living in Seved aged between 15 and 19 years, who maintained and tidied up their local area during the summer. The 'Young in Seved' initiative later became part of the Area programme in Seved, run by the City of Malmö during 2010–2015, with the stated aim of tackling the lack of social sustainability in Malmö. A lot of focus has been on employment and employability, the programme manager said when he was interviewed within the Citispyce project. In a parallel action, the municipality has been coordinating various efforts in Seved where the aim has been to increase citizen participation in society and reduce exclusion. The work has been called 'Turning Seved' and has involved a network of about 40 local actors.

Thus, many new initiatives have been launched: a lot of funding has been spent. And yet, Seved is still one of the neighbourhoods characterised by social exclusion and it seems to have got even worse in recent years, according to police statistics. Why? A major cause, as I see it, is the gradual transformation of Swedish society from a social democratic to a neoliberal societal model, informed by neoliberal prescriptions, and in such social exclusion is not a failure but a constituent part (moment). The austerity of welfare services replaced by selective and temporary measures is part of that. The emphasis has been on getting jobs, but without paying attention to the quality of these jobs. This has contributed to the emergence of the precariat, also a characteristic feature of the neoliberal societal model.

Another important cause of inequality is the approach to knowledge (see chapter 4.2.2). Increasingly, knowledge has become associated with the measurable. Such an approach to knowledge makes it hard to recognise many of the successes that actually have been achieved in all these projects, such as, for example, joy, meaning in life, self-confidence, community, trust, and a sense of belonging: that is, such qualities that are highly regarded as having to do with quality of life. The experience of urban initiatives can in fact be regarded as a particularly rich source of inspiration. Many of the efforts have allowed a fairly wide discretion to develop new forms of work, knowledge, democracy and participation. The big problem is that, instead, this has not been taken advantage of; the reigning approach to knowledge has made the policymakers blind to them.

8.4.3 Extending competitive market forces

Above, I claimed that the cultural institutions, Arena 305 and The Garage, are good at reproducing universal welfare, the characteristic of the social democratic societal model, but they have not managed to adapt the institutions sufficiently to the new context of inequalities and the emergence of social exclusion. Civil society in the Sofielunds Folkets Hus (SFH) has had more success with that (see chapter 5.3). This can be demonstrated, for example, by the fact that use-values are considered at least as important as exchange values and by the long-term as well as the potential-oriented approach. For several decades now, civil society in the SFH has based its efforts on the local context, having faith in people's own ability to create change and develop methods to gather a broad range of actors together. Civil society has also clearly proved to be the best at creating opportunities for those socially excluded who do not have what society requires but certainly have something else; those who do not do what society requires but certainly do something else; and those who do not mean what society requires but certainly mean something else. Civil society in the SFH has also been good at creating opportunities for those who do not want to be involved in society.

The transformation from a social democratic to a neoliberal societal model, however, does not only require an adaption to the new context of inequalities and the emergence of social exclusion. In addition, neoliberal policies have brought about an extension of the capitalist logic, in line with its first principle (see chapter 5.2) which civil society is forced to confront. This is what has happened to SFH. A certain principle has been introduced with huge implications, expressing a change of mindset.

The problem began to affect Sofielunds Folkets Hus in the aftermath of an extensive renovation carried out in 2012–2013 with the support of *Boverket*, the Swedish National Board of Housing, Building and Planning. The remaining cost was covered by the property owner, the municipally-owned company *Stadsfastigheter*, but it was to be paid for via a rent increase. Crucial to the rent increase was the depreciation period. According to the management in a group interview made as part of Citispyce, SFH was first told that the period for depreciation would be 25 years. Prior to the completion of the renovation, the period was changed to 17 years. This meant a much higher rent, which the SFH claimed that it could not cope with.

The management has since devoted much time and energy trying to get the depreciation period increased to 25 years in order to be able to pay the rent. However, neither senior managers nor politicians seem able to change this. No one has been able to provide SFH with a convincing explanation of why it cannot be changed. Thus, SFH has run the risk of going bankrupt for several years now. Such a persistent adherence to economic principles, without any regard for the use-values created in SFH which were at risk of being destroyed in a bankruptcy, should be seen as an expression of a neoliberal strategy. It forces SFH to comply with the logic of a capitalist market economy. But who drives this strategy, how intentional it is and what support it has, is not easy to find out.

For this and a number of other reasons, the management of SFH developed a great distrust of the politicians. "*Some politicians and officials do not seem to want to have a civil society*," said one of our group interviewees. We interviewed the social democratic councillor for labour market and adult education. He said he is very much in favour of how civil society provides spaces for young people's own initiatives. Such a drive will disappear, however, the moment the municipality formalises the initiative and fits it into a decision hierarchy. The enthusiasts may suddenly have no place when the initiative is formalised in the municipality. The councillor described the great benefits of civil society, but believed that there is a lack of a sustainable structure for cooperation between municipalities and associations. "*In the more general discussion of collaboration I do think that we are pretty consistent*," the councillor said.

In our local Citispyce research team, we undertook several interviews about this in order to find out who or what drives this neoliberal strategy and what support it has. We came to the conclusion that it resides in the ensemble of different measures, activities and thinking, such as: the persistent insistence on a shorter depreciation period; a problem-oriented approach; a selective focus; priorities of exchange values at the expense of use-values; unproblematised growth initiatives; unilateral measurements of success based solely on economic indicators; unilateral measurements of results at the expense of processes, etc. Related to each other as moments in a context of meaning, all these together make sense and constitute a convincing potential cause of transforming society to the neoliberal model. Policymakers have not been trained to identify the profound transformation that is going on. This requires a new mindset.

8.5 Conclusions: The new societal borders belong to the neoliberal societal model

This chapter has departed from the concept of social exclusion, defining it in two ways; both as a process in the sense of excluding someone and as a condition in which the excluded find themselves. I have claimed that both these definitions are needed. They lead to a clarification of two types of causes: the ones that exclude and the ones that set the conditions for getting included. I will return to each one in turn below, the first one which I have called the process-causes and the second one the condition-causes. Both raise a question of what people are excluded from and/or not getting included in. My answer is that societies have turned into conditions of social inclusion whose borders coincide with segregation and appear in cities. This relationship between social inclusion and social exclusion, coinciding with segregation, should be seen as the most serious form of inequality.

What are the process-causes; i.e. the causes that exclude the included? Here I want to recall the distinction from a previous chapter between potential and actual causes. The latter are the ones which emerge when the potential causes are actualised. This always happens in a specific context. The actual causes can, therefore, be described as context-dependent and also emergent, which means that they cannot be explained simply by a reduction to potential causes. The actualisation of a potential cause in a specific context means that something new emerges, and that is the actual cause. An explanation of an actual cause, thus, requires knowledge on both the actualised potential causes and the specific context where that actualisation occurs.

Drawing on previous chapters, we can understand that potential causes can be inherent in actors, institutions, contexts of meaning and space. They can also be inherent in systems and in chapter 4, I have identified five systemic potential causes of inequality. In more complex terms and still at a high level of abstraction, I have shown how these potential systemic causes are actualised in growth models and welfare regimes. To the extent that the growth models and welfare regimes can be identified as abstractions, the actualised systemic causes of inequality can also be treated as new and emergent potentials of inequality. As such, they are inherent in the growth models and welfare regimes, belonging to how they work. Similarly, emergent potential causes of inequality can also be inherent in combinations of growth models and welfare regimes. Such combinations have here been called societal models and, on the basis of the previous chapter, I have found it possible to define three: namely, the neoliberal, the conservative and the social democratic societal models. These three concepts refer to potentials for relatively coherent, orderly and stable societal development.

None of these three are fully actualised in any of the cities studied in the Citispyce project. All the cities, however, develop towards actualising the moments of the neoliberal societal model, although from different points of departure and at different speeds. A city like Malmö can, therefore, be understood as a kind of hybrid. Also in Malmö, new borders have emerged, which I have treated as societal. Malmö, the city which I know the best, has been used here as a case study, to show how these borders are made, by what actors and in what situations. The society in which actors in Malmö participate, is gradually being transformed towards actualising a neoliberal societal model. Inherent in this societal model are the main process-causes of social exclusion: i.e. the causes that exclude many young people.

What are the condition-causes: i.e. the causes of this inequality that make it difficult for the excluded to get included? I have concretised three such types of conditions, related to the general types of inequality (see chapter 2). If you cannot get included, it may depend on that you do not have, do and/or mean what is required. The three correspond to the losing sides of resource, structural and cultural inequality, respectively. As the chapter has shown, in societies with an increasing predominance of the neoliberal societal model, you are required to have resources like money, own your house and have power to assert yourself individually. Furthermore, it is required of you to participate in the structures of economy by gainful employment and by being a beneficiary of financialisation. Finally, you need to be associated with the 'right' kind of meaning by not belonging to the 'wrong' ethnicity, by not having the 'wrong' grades and not living in stigmatised housing areas. All of these are conditions set by the structures and cultures of contemporary societies, not of course as prescriptions in some kind of manual but depending on how they work.

The division between the included and excluded tends to be reinforced by potential causes of inequality inherent in socio-spatial relations. That is the case when segregation, i.e. a social difference coinciding with spatial separation, concerns the difference between the winning and losing sides of inequality. Firstly, space may reinforce the polarisation between the socially included and the socially excluded by keeping them distant from each other. Secondly, a spatial neglect and decay tends to cause hierarchies between places. As scale, thirdly, space may eclipse the relation between symptoms and causes, expressing the former at the local scale level and making them look like causes, justifying the blaming on the victims. These three spatial potential causes of inequality can be further reinforced when it coincides with a cultural inequality. The losing pole of segregation can be loaded with a certain meaning which causes a cultural inequality by making the neighbourhood and its inhabitants appear as meaning less (stigmatisation).

9
COMBATTING INEQUALITY

In this final chapter, I will present my proposal for how to combat inequality. More specifically, the proposal concerns the causes of inequality and how they can be addressed at the local level. This differs from the mainstream policies, which, I would say, address the symptoms instead of the causes. This is the case with current EU policies, which I will now present. In brief, the mainstream EU policy, called the inclusion agenda, deals with the inclusion of young people in existing society, without addressing the causes excluding them. Much more profound changes are needed, as I see it, and the second part of this chapter deals with such societal transformations and the urgent need for them.

Policies to transform society, however, often focus on the national and/or EU scale levels. This is, of course, important but a core message of this book is that practices at the local level matter too. The systemic causes of inequality have to be actualised and that happens at the local level. To highlight the required changes, the concept of social innovation has been used in research, administrations and public debate during the last 20 or more years. It has, however, often been associated with the same approach as the inclusion agenda. I will instead reconnect to the approach suggested by many scholars which understands and mobilises the concept of social innovation "in the context of a sociological heritage that challenges conventional economic approaches to development, and that has at its heart a desire for emancipatory macro-social change" (Moulaert et al., 2013: 22).

As I will propose: to become transformative, social innovations should comply with five success criteria. Besides being explained in detail and with examples, the five criteria should be seen in contrast to the other policies, proposals and concepts presented in this chapter. For those who may have the impression that I am spending only one chapter on solutions while the previous eight have dealt with the problems, it will turn out that I see the perspective running through the whole book as part of the solution.

9.1 Current EU policies

The main European solution to the problems of inequality affecting young people is called the social inclusion agenda. A report from Eurofound (2015) *The social inclusion of young people* makes clear how this agenda puts the whole emphasis on getting young people included in existing society without combatting the causes that have excluded them (see for example 2015: 11). This accords with the "neo-Durkheimian hegemony" (Levitas, 2005: 188). Such a focus on those who are excluded from society "presupposes that there is nothing inherently wrong with contemporary society as long as it is made more inclusive through government policies" (Fairclough, 2000: 65).

The inclusion agenda puts its imprint on the *EU Youth Strategy*, and the *EU Youth Report*, mentioned in the introduction. The content of that report may be treated as an expression of current thinking and approaches. I have paid particular attention to what it does not contain. What does the *EU Youth Report* say about the financialisation of societies, often affecting young people who easily get into debt without having had a chance to understand how and why? What does it say about the growing divergences in Europe with increasingly unequal opportunities for young people? Why does it so one-sidedly stress the need to promote the employability of young people and not the need to improve the quality of jobs in the labour market? Why does access to the labour market for young people have to be improved by making changes that weaken the rights of those that work there? How does the *EU Youth Report* want to change the labour market to the extent that it becomes more interesting, stimulating, rewarding and developing to work there?

Unfortunately, the answers cannot be found in the *EU Youth Report*. In Citispyce, we came across many projects, often also called social innovations, which in one way or another were imprinted by the inclusion agenda. A main characteristic of it is the idea of targeting individuals, "motivated to integrate into mainstream society but in need of support" as they were described in a case study report. What about all the other young people, those who are not "motivated to integrate into mainstream society" because they have revealed how being helped to survive in the labour market means that they run the risk of becoming someone else, losing their creativity and critical edge? What about those who understand how society causes inequality and whose criticism it perhaps would be very well worth listening to (see also chapter 5.1.2)?

Furthermore, the inclusion agenda cannot deal with more than just a tiny fraction of all the young people affected by inequality. Does not that imply an inequality in itself? And those that are targeted, how do they succeed? What do the measures lead to for them? The inclusion agenda makes inequality an individual concern. In my view, it should be regarded as a concern for all of us because it is about the future of society. Therefore, the causes of inequality should be tackled and next I will seek some inspiration to what that could mean.

9.2 The urgent need for societal transformations

Capitalism is the given premise. We live in a world characterised by capitalism; i.e. the economic system that is driven by the profit motive. This does not mean that capitalism must exist forever. Yet it exists now, and cannot be ignored and thus a first step of approaching it can be to understand its potential causes of inequality and how these can be actualised differently due to growth models. In recent decades, the finance-driven growth model has been predominant globally. Inequality is an inherent moment in this growth model. Without inequality it would not work. Restricting the operations of finance capital would be an important way to combat the causes of inequality, but still just the actual ones. To combat the potential ones, capitalism needs to be replaced by another economic system and that is of course a very big task.

To combat the actual as well as potential causes of inequality various efforts are needed and at different scale levels. Not only reforms but a transformation of society is required. This should not, however, be seen as a call for revolution. The old dualism of reform versus revolution has to be overcome, in line with the idea of a double transformation, which, according to Andreas Novy (2017), "describes the twofold challenge of civilizing capitalism by overcoming the neoliberal mode of regulation while at the same time taking the first steps towards transcending capitalism and its unsustainable social forms …".

As part of such a strategy, it is important to highlight and reinforce the progressive tendencies that capitalism also contains. Capitalism is both good and bad, as Sayer (2015: 24) says, and we should not deny "that capitalist competition has brought us many of these innovations; it clearly has" (Sayer, 2015: 310). The distinction between the good and the bad sides of capitalism can also be conceptualised in terms of the capitalist form and the social substance, as here by Dan Robotham (2005: 18):

> The enormous possibilities for the development of individual talent and abilities which now exist (at least for some and in the abstract) only exist because of this variegated global specialization in production and global demand in consumption, including productive consumption. One must distinguish this process from the free market process both analytically and in practice. The capitalist form is one thing, the social substance another. Because this enormous extension of sociality is mediated by the market, it presents itself either as consumerist plenitude or, what may well be considered another side of the same phenomenon, as an opportunity for privileged selves to expand their quantity and range of consumption.

Policies are needed that could reinforce the good side of capitalism and restrain its bad. In his book, *Why we can't afford the rich,* Sayer (2015: 121) claims that "the best way to get money to cascade down from the rich to the rest is to tax them – or stop them extracting it in the first place!" For sure, he has a lot of suggestions on how to tax the rich but he also suggests, for example, bringing money supply back under public control to stop them extracting it (see also Pettifor, 2017: 134). Sayer takes it a step further by claiming that "replacing our neoliberal capitalism with a more productive and less unequal capitalism is not the answer" (2015: 337). I certainly agree, but in the shorter-term, the best option, I would say, is exactly to reinforce productive capital at the expense of financial (see also Pettifor, 2017: 159). As Gamble (2016: 81) puts it; "western economies have to move up the value chain which would require increasing investment in education and training."

Anyhow, Sayer's proposals concern a change of politics at the national scale level and this book has not been written to deal with that issue, although it is of course very important. What I have promised to answer is a question on what actors at the local level can do, not only to tackle inequality but to combat the causes of it. Some may believe that combatting the causes is only possible at national and EU scale levels. I disagree. As I have repeatedly stated in the book, the causes first of all exist as potentials and they have to be actualised. That always happens somewhere, in a specific context, at different scalar levels and it is made by actors who always have a discretion to make a difference. This discretion is what I am looking for.

9.3 Transformative social innovations

Inequality has been combatted for decades, but, as Laurent Fraisse (2010) explains, the activity has changed. Previously, stakeholders were mobilised in urban social movements on the basis of a strong collective identity constructed in a relationship of social conflict and aimed at transforming society. Since then, a shift has appeared towards entrepreneurial and managerial concerns in the modes of action, financing and organisation. The mainstream approach, called the inclusion agenda over the last ten years, has tended to reduce local initiatives to the insertion of the disadvantaged without any perspective on reducing inequalities, and particularly not combatting the causes of them. Fraisse (2010: 26) highlights a trend towards the de-politicisation of non-profit and collective action, or even the instrumentalisation of local initiatives by public authorities. This trend expresses itself in individualism, in line with the third principle of neoliberalism (see chapter 5.2.1), which Furlong & Cartmel (2007: 144) criticise:

> Individuals are forced to negotiate a set of risks which impinge on all aspects of their daily lives, yet the intensification of individualism means that crises are perceived as individual shortcomings rather than the outcome of processes which are largely outwith the control of individuals. [...] Blind to the existence of powerful chains of interdependency, young people frequently attempt to resolve collective problems through individual action and hold themselves responsible for their inevitable failure.

The trend also expresses itself in 'localism', which means the limitation of local initiatives to neighbourhoods (see also Robotham, 2005: 17). Solutions are sought in the same neighbourhoods as those in which the problems appear. Because of this localism or 'the localisation of the social', local initiatives have little impact on the causes of inequality. The limitation of local initiatives to certain neighbourhoods may even reinforce inequality as the jobs created contribute to the deterioration of wage conditions. As Cassiers and Kesteloot (2012: 1915) conclude: "policies wanting to combat spatial segregation should target the exclusion mechanisms, not simply assist the poor in targeted areas".

This is the context in which the concept of social innovation has become significant in research, administrations and public debate during the last twenty years. As mentioned above, it often means the inclusion of the excluded in existing society without combatting the causes excluding them. In contrast, I will align myself with the approach which I perceive as running through *The International Handbook on Social Innovation* by Moulaert et al., (2013) where the term social innovation refers "not just to particular actions, but also to the mobilization-participation processes and to the outcome of actions which lead to improvements in social relations, structures of governance, greater collective empowerment, and so on" (2013: 2).

In my view, this means that social innovations have to become transformative, also in line with the idea of a double transformation (chapter 9.2), and thereby combat both the actual and potential causes of inequality. How could local actors contribute to that by using their discretion? After having analysed all the case studies in Citispyce, I have been inspired to propose five success criteria for such an endeavour. Local actors who want to include young people by combatting the causes that exclude them should aspire to change mindsets towards a potential-oriented approach; take advantage of existing experience and knowledge among the young people; give young people opportunities to learn to be critical; make it possible for young people to work in forms of discretionary learning; and empower young people collectively. Such a local mobilisation is absolutely necessary to bring about institutional changes of the state, seen from the viewpoint of Poulantzas (1978) as a "material condensation of the relationship between social forces".

9.3.1 Adopting a potential-oriented approach

This requires, first of all, another approach to young people. They cannot be seen as the problems and blamed for an inequality which they have not caused but of which they are the victims. Instead, young people should be seen and approached as potentials and not only for solving their own problems but for combatting the causes of inequality and developing society.

Several projects show how the potentials of young people could be seen, recognised and taken advantage of. One of them is "Krakow-Free remedial tutoring" where school students provide free tutoring to younger pupils who reside in the district of Mistrzejowice (Chrabaszcz et al., 2015). The practice shows how the informal knowledge of the older youngsters can be taken advantage of. As described in the report, "the tutor is not a teacher or specialist hired on market-based principles, but a person of a similar age and often lives on the same estate". The application of such a peer support mechanism, "contributes to the establishment and development of local social networks, which may pay off in the future in terms of reduced likelihood or intensity of inequality".

In another one, "Barcelona-Educational Demos", previously invisible abilities that the young people have are recognised in the production of hip hop songs. These workshops have led to a professionalisation of the youngsters who have participated for a long time, making them competent to "train the younger ones (as trainers at schools) and awaken their interest for hip hop and for political engagement" (Jubany et al., 2015a: 29).

The main aim of the project "Malmö-Brightful" is "to help and motivate young women and men in believing in themselves and their ability to set (and reach) their own individual goals by providing different activities" (Alwall & Hellberg Lannerheim, 2015: 2). The project directs itself to two groups: lower-secondary school students and young adults, the latter group functioning as mentors. The former group "are helped by connecting with other young people who have already got ahead, inspiring them with their own stories, sharing examples and ideas, helping the school kids grow in self-confidence and an understanding of the importance of setting up and fulfilling their own goals". In this way, "the positive potential of these young people is taken into account and acknowledged".

Recognising the potentials in young people means making a difference between their real qualities and those that appear to be. This concerns the difference between the potential and the actual, which I have pursued throughout the book. Indeed, the book represents a potential-oriented approach and, as I wrote in the introduction to this chapter, the whole book is supposed to be part of a solution. The potential-oriented approach includes not only seeing the positive potential in young people, but also potentials which could be called negative and by which I mean the potential causes of inequality. Furthermore, the potential-oriented approach includes an understanding of how the spatio-social context matters in the actualisation of the potentials. It also recognises that being social means to be related to others and to share a context of meaning. Every such spatio-social context of social relations and meaning is dependent on individuals. Often, contexts have been produced by others and thus precede us. We take part in them by assuming a role, although never fully pre-determined. There is always a discretion, more or less, to make a difference.

I have explained this approach more exhaustively in chapters 1.2 and 3.1. The opposite approach can be called problem-oriented. It is characterised by a limitation to what critical realism calls the empirical and thus associated with empiricism. What appears to be a problem is also seen as the problem that has to be solved. That means that the problem is taken for granted. No particular effort is made to define the problem. Instead, they are perceived as self-defining. If young people appear as excluded, this is seen as the problem, not the societal causes of their exclusion. On the basis of a problem-oriented approach, getting them included in existing society without combatting the causes excluding them appears to be the solution.

The potential-oriented approach combats inequality by providing another context of meaning. It is a context of meaning which, in contrast to the neoliberal outlook, does not take the individual as a point of departure but social relations. It does not take for granted that we as individuals are all equal because we are actually not. This is exactly what the four forms of inequality indicate. We may become equal, however, and that is certainly a very important goal to strive for. It requires an understanding of inequality and in particular explanations of what causes it. This is what the potential-oriented approach represented by this book can provide. Seeing the positive potentials in young people is a first key step. This positive potential was what several of the teams in Citispyce had the pleasure to discover, like here in Athens:

> Despite the low educational status and the difficulty in expression, most participants in this sub-group demonstrated an advanced level of maturity towards several life matters and increased determination and vigour. Furthermore, women participants were more eloquent and demonstrated greater ability of self-expression and critical thinking in comparison to male participants.
>
> *(Tryfona et al., 2014b: 11)*

9.3.2 Building knowledge alliances

To combat inequalities, knowledge on the causes of it has to be produced. The need for such knowledge has been proven to be very urgent. In Citispyce, we experienced difficulties in creating knowledge on the causes. It requires a lot of hard work and thus also human creativity, in the shape of fantasy, engagement, persistence and so on. Many indicators of inequality exist but they concern symptoms and belong to the level of reality called the empirical. We need to go beyond that level and produce knowledge to understand what actually happens and explain why. That requires another approach to knowledge other than the one which restricts itself to the quantifiable. Information, figures, statistics, observations and evidence of various kinds are very important, just as the experiences and stories of young people are, but it all needs to be processed. Otherwise, only the symptoms of inequality will be tackled while the causes continue to generate inequality incessantly.

"Barcelona-Educational Demos" is an example of how the experiences and views of young people can be listened to and taken advantage of; knowledge can be produced in collaboration with the young people and a context favouring creativity can be established by using young people's forms of expression. It is described by Jubany et al. (2015a: 7) in their report as "a wider platform for youngsters to deliver a message to the society through hip hop". On the basis of the analyses, core themes are identified "which relate to the experience of young people in deprived neighbourhoods, how they have been affected by the crisis and display their strength at claiming justice" (2015a: 6). As one of the youth workers puts it:

> "We transmit a message through the lenses of young people because often, these are not taken into account when seeking solutions to social problems. It is a very good tool so that the youngsters say what they think and contribute to society, as they see the world".
>
> *(Jubany et al., 2015a: 15)*

It seems akin to a collaboration which "Malmö-Multisectoral cooperation" formed "aiming to develop knowledge about the causes of social exclusion and testing multi-sectoral cooperation in order to solve problems connected to social exclusion" (Grander, 2015: 2). Such collaborations can be called knowledge alliances. The European Commission uses the same term in its strategy *Europe 2020*. The definition, however, tends to be limited to alliances between "education and business". A broader definition is represented by the influential report *Cities of Tomorrow. Challenges, Visions, Ways Forward* (Hermant-de-Callataÿ and Svanfeldt, 2011). The report builds on a process in which more than fifty experts from various European countries, researchers and experienced practitioners, participated. The report highlights the "neighbourhood-adapted forms of education and knowledge sharing" (2011: 56) as part of a strategy for social cohesion that "requires a revised and more inclusive vision of the knowledge society and the encouragement of knowledge alliances" (2011: 53).

The term was picked up and redefined by the Commission for a socially sustainable Malmö (the *Malmö Commission*) which published its final report in March 2013 (Stigendal & Östergren, 2013). In the first of two overarching recommendations, it proposed that the City of Malmö pursues a social investment policy that can reduce inequities in living conditions and make societal systems more equitable. In the second overarching recommendation, the Commission proposed changes to the processes embedded in these systems through the creation of knowledge alliances. By knowledge alliance, the *Malmö Commission* means collaborations between researchers and many different kinds of stakeholders, e.g. practitioners in general, public sector workers, citizens, policymakers, young people, politicians and volunteers (see also Novy et al., 2013).

"Malmö-Multisectoral cooperation" was a project, funded by ESF, run by the NGO Save the Children and lasting for a year, 2014 (Grander, 2015). It drew on these ideas by setting up a knowledge alliance with representatives from a wide range of organisations and sectors. In a number of workshops, knowledge was created on the structural causes of social exclusion. Young people were also involved in the work to produce the knowledge on the problems of and possible solutions to the causes of social exclusion. This involvement of young people was regarded as particularly innovative as it seldom happens that young people are already involved at the planning stage of projects.

Setting up knowledge alliances with young people and practitioners who work with them deals very much with taking the structural consequences of the potential-oriented approach. As stated in the fourth brief principle of its approach to knowledge (see chapter 1.3), knowledge does not only sit in our minds but also in our bodies. It appears in how we move. We do not just talk about our approach to knowledge. We also practise it, whether we like it or not, think about it or not. A potential-oriented approach enables us to become aware of this and deliberately take advantage of it, for example by setting up knowledge alliances. This also actualises a potential-oriented outlook on people, which makes the young people subjectified, in contrast to the outlook which treats them as objects for pre-designed measures. Thereby, knowledge alliances with young people combat structural inequality, as the young people are invited to assume a role with the purpose of taking advantage of their positive potentials in the development of knowledge on inequality and the causes of it.

9.3.3 Learning to be critical

Education systems across Europe have been badly affected by austerity measures with increasingly unequal chances for young people to educate themselves. The structural causes of inequality inherent in education systems have thus been reinforced. Also contributing to this has been the approach to knowledge, highlighted in chapter 3.3, which privileges the quantifiable, using grading to set the barriers in making society a condition of social inclusion and giving the impression that people with inadequate or low grades lack abilities and use-value. To tackle inequalities, policymakers should learn from education strategies that challenge this approach to knowledge and suggest alternatives.

Such an alternative is "Barcelona-Educational Demos", mentioned above. A major strength of it seems to be that it cross-cuts different types of practices, "offering opportunities, raising awareness of rights and fostering the spirit of community, empowerment through the development of competences and social networks, and bridging social and symbolic distances between the host society and migrant communities (to which most young participants belong) through the work on issues of racism and discrimination" (Jubany et al., 2015a: 1) The educational aspect is, however, essential to the organisation, according to the report, and this is why the project is called 'Educational Demos'. By promoting rap as an educational tool, "the final aim is to educate young people so that they become critical citizens and gain self-confidence" (2015: 14). For that reason, it is an educational project before a musical one. One of the youth workers describes the project as "a resource, a tool to build a critical society, to create critical young people and they make it through music, but they could be doing it through video, theatre, etc." (2015a: 15) According to the youth worker, the project is very successful:

> "These are youngsters who at school have no interest for any subject or for reading and here they are reading the press, documentary … In terms of

literacy skills and expressivity, they make great progress, it is like very evident, and then there is the issue of the initiative of willing to know, of searching for knowledge and information. Their interest is awakened here, but then this must be reflected at school."

(Jubany et al., 2015a: 25)

The authors of the report conclude by proposing it as a "model of education, where the relationship of authority (youth workers versus young people) is based on mutual respect and makes use of referents (the oldest serve as good models for the youngest)" (2015: 31). The success of it is related to the need to approach youngsters at risk of social exclusion. The authors find it difficult to scale it up to the national level as the project "takes place at the local level and is very much connected to the most immediate reality of the neighbourhood". I have another opinion. In my view, "Barcelona-Educational Demos" contains aspects which should serve as a model for education in general, like for example peer-to-peer learning, drawing on the experiences of young people, enabling young people to express experiences of injustices, using the cultures of young people as tools for education, and educating young people to become "critical citizens that want to be politically engaged".

Young people may have a lot of experience and knowledge which can be taken advantage of in knowledge alliances, but they also have a lot to learn. Most important, however, is that the contexts of learning in schools or in associations are characterised by a potential-oriented approach. This means that the preconditions should be created for the young people to make knowledge their own, in line with the third principle in the summary of the approach to knowledge (chapter 1.3). That requires work and a context with favourable social relations. The critical perspective that is so important to learn should be understood in Marx's sense, explained by Sven-Eric Liedman (2015: 267):

> Being critical does not mean to be negative plain and simple. The one who develops critique in Marx's sense analyses an object or phenomenon so that its anatomy and functioning are revealed. The critical analysis opens thereby indirectly a way to a programme of action.
>
> *(my translation)*

9.3.4 Working in forms of discretionary learning

One of the actual causes of inequality, actualising the systemic potential cause inherent in the capitalist relation of production and explained in chapter 6.4, is the poor quality of jobs. As work makes us who we are, what happens to young people when their participation in the labour market becomes a matter of just survival? The quality of jobs should be an urgent concern not only for individual young people but for the future of society. Some of the case studies contain an inspiration for how work organisations in general could be developed in order to enable discretionary learning.

One of them is the project "Sofia-Health and Social Centre" (HSC) which operates in the Sofia neighbourhood of Fakulteta. It is described by Hajdinjak & Kosseva (2015: 2) as "an integrated approach to address numerous interconnected problems of the Roma community (unemployment; low level of education and poor school achievement; poor health; drug use, crime and prostitution; social isolation)". HSC involves young people in its work as health and social community assistants. This is described by the report as one of the most important tools for the empowerment of young people from the neighbourhood. In this way and by being trusted to have an important task, the young people learn and grow. According to the report, a not insignificant number of them have become successful role models. It also "challenges the prevailing views and practices in which Roma are typically perceived as passive recipients of the services, and not as active agents of change" (Hajdinjak & Kosseva, 2015: 21).

Also in "Birmingham-Beatfreeks" young people are involved in work organised and designed in ways which enable them to learn. The stated mission of "Birmingham-Beatfreeks" is to "develop people and spaces through creativity and create a better world through more equipped, engaged, empowered young people able to apply their creativity to affect personal and social change" (Robinson & Commane, 2015: 2). In that endeavour it uses art forms such as dance, poetry, music and media as tools to inspire, engage and empower young people. Funding is attracted from public institutions such as schools, colleges and local authorities to implement projects of various kinds.

> Their 'on the job' training offers a wide range of experiences which can be tailored to individual skills and needs. At the time of interviewing, 150 young people had become paid sessional facilitators for Beatfreeks' projects and programmes as well as undertaking other freelance work.
> *(Robinson & Commane, 2015: 19)*

The actions of "Birmingham-Beatfreeks" connect young people with local policymakers, practitioners and others in positions of authority. It has won the trust of young people through its determination to put young people at the centre and ensuring that these young people are supported in their efforts to connect with others, coaching them to find the right person to contact and then the right questions to ask. "Birmingham-Beatfreeks" seems to be an important role model for others to change their work organisations in order to take better advantage of young people and enable them to develop on the job. As one of the policymakers puts it:

> "We have lots of organisations who do youth engagement but when we ask the question: How are you involving young people in what you do? Or: How

are their leadership skills being developed? Their answers often seem tokenistic – 'we'll consult with young people'. But Beatfreeks is different because young people are actually in there doing it."

(Robinson & Commane, 2015: 22)

Local actors should make sure that the organisation of projects enables discretionary learning for young people. Moreover, they should ask companies to do the same and put pressure on them, to the maximum extent possible. In these ways, they should spread an awareness about this issue: that not only is getting a job important but so is the kind of job you get. Thereby, structural inequality is tackled, as jobs organised to enable discretionary learning empower young people to participate in a more equal way.

9.3.5 Collective empowerment

Empowerment is often seen as an individual concern. However, if causes are to be combatted, not only symptoms, young people should be empowered not only individually but also collectively. An example of such an empowerment, specialised in Augusto Boal's methodology of the *Theatre of the Oppressed*, is "Barcelona-Forn Teatre Pa'Tothom". It is a youth organisation which deals with young people who suffer from inequalities. It is committed to "fighting inequalities in the community and encouraging a critical socio-political vision among its members through social theatre, and through the use of theatre of the oppressed techniques" (Jubany et al., 2015b: 7). "Barcelona_Forn Teatre Pa'Tothom" is grounded in a firm belief that everyone can participate in theatre but "rather than simply teaching youngsters to act, Pa'Tothom seeks to contribute to develop an increased interest on social exclusion issues and to develop sensitisation models for those individuals or collectives labelled as 'oppressed' and which have been marginalised by society, with the intentions of nurturing a critical spirit that facilitates their emancipation and personal growth through values of equality and justice".

> It is through their theatrical plays, that these youngsters explore matters of police abuse and discrimination, social segregation because of ethnicity or place of origin, lack of integration, housing concerns, to vindicate the neighbourhood as a decent one, the problematic of transitioning into adulthood, parting from their own lived experiences.
>
> *(Jubany et al., 2015b: 10)*

"Barcelona-Forn Teatre Pa'Tothom" wants to fight against social structures that cause social exclusion by "nourishing critical thinking, encouraging active political participation and citizenship; they promote the collective reflection of social issues and how to deal with them as a group through theatre" (2015b: 13). For all these reasons, "Barcelona-Forn Teatre Pa'Tothom" should be seen as an important inspiration for others. In contrast, the authors of the report find it difficult to scale it to a national level, "given their closeness to the neighbourhood". In my view, an upscaling should be suggested, yet perhaps not of the practice as a whole, but of different aspects, favouring the empowerment of young people, individually as well as collectively.

The concept of collective empowerment should be related to that of solidarity, but not defined as in European policy. The use of the word solidarity in contemporary European policy has its roots in the decades around the turn of the 20th century (Liedman, 1999). It is a French term, which was written into the Code Civil in 1804 and began to be used a few years later by Charles Fourier, one of the early socialist thinkers. For Fourier, solidarity did not mean an ideal but a real and mutual dependence, based on the division of labour. That approach was later developed by Emile Durkheim, who used it in his understanding of society as a whole. For Marx, solidarity was a concern only for the working class.

Common to Marx and Durkheim, however, is that both mean with solidarity, a reciprocity. That is a different definition than the one that simply relates solidarity to those who suffer, normative solidarity as Liedman (1999: 86) calls it, which means that the fortunate should care about the poor and oppressed, while they in their turn should accept the privileged position of the fortunate. It is a definition of solidarity that has come to dominate, to the extent it is whatsoever spoken about solidarity nowadays. In contrast, I want to reconnect to the reciprocity in the definitions of both Durkheim and Marx but single out the latter's collectivist solidarity as a basis for the understanding of collective empowerment. This would tackle resource inequality and create a transformative agency oriented at combatting the causes of inequality.

9.4 Conclusions: Five success criteria

As I have mentioned above, the design of the book may give the impression that only this chapter deals with the solutions. This is not the case, because the perspective that runs through the book, gradually unfolded, should be seen as part of the solution. This perspective, called potential-oriented in the book, seeks to understand the causes of inequality affecting young people. Causes first of all exist as potentials and to have an effect, they must be actualised. That always happens somewhere, in a specific context, at different scalar levels and it is made by actors who always have discretion to make a difference.

By contrast, the mainstream EU policy, labelled the inclusion agenda, deals with the inclusion of young people in existing society, without addressing the causes excluding them. It presupposes that there is nothing inherently wrong with contemporary society. It simply has to improve its measures to include young people in it. Other characteristics of this perspective, problem-oriented as I have called it in the book, are de-politicisation of collective action, instrumentalisation of local initiatives, localism and individualism. It is limited to what critical realism calls the empirical and thus associated with empiricism. What appears to be a problem is also seen as the problem which has to be solved. That means that the problem is taken for granted. No particular effort is made to define the problem. Instead, such problems are perceived as self-defining. If young people appear as excluded, that is seen as the problem, not the societal causes of their exclusion.

This problem-oriented perspective should not be seen as guidance towards solutions but on the contrary as part of the problem. It is a context of meaning, which actualises the systemic potential causes inherent in the state by reinforcing the individualistic outlook on people and the intellectualised approach to knowledge. It prescribes nothing to prevent financialisation with its accumulation by dispossession or the worsening of job conditions. Instead, it reinforces the systemic causes of inequality inherent in capitalism.

For the potential-oriented perspective, however, capitalism with its contradictions and systemic tendencies to cause inequality is the given premise. The removal of these systemic causes requires a double societal transformation, consisting of efforts which, firstly, civilise capitalism by restricting and counteracting its actual causes of inequality, and at the same time, secondly, gradually transcend capitalism by combatting its potential causes of inequality. In such efforts, I have highlighted the importance of local actors. By analysing the case studies from Citispyce, I have identified five criteria, which should characterise efforts that aspire to be socially innovative in the sense that they combat the causes of inequality and contribute to a transformation of society:

- Adopting a potential-oriented approach: Projects, initiatives, practices and indeed services in general should adopt a potential-oriented approach to young people which means that young people should be seen and approached in the first place as potentials and not only for solving their own problems but for tackling the causes of inequality and developing society. Indeed, this potential-oriented approach is what the book tries to represent and thus, the whole of it is supposed to be part of a solution.
- Building knowledge alliances: On the basis of a potential-oriented perspective, it becomes imperative to produce knowledge on the causes of inequality by taking advantage of the experiences, views and cultural expressions of young people. Producing such knowledge in collaboration with young people and establishing contexts which favour creativity can be called knowledge alliances. In principle, they should include all the ones with an interest in combatting inequality, e.g. practitioners in general, public sector workers, citizens, policy-makers, young people, politicians and volunteers.
- Learning to be critical: This recognition of young people's knowledge does not of course imply that they know enough. Young people have a lot to learn, but education systems should draw much more on their potential and experience of inequalities. The cultures of young people should be used as tools for education. Young people should be encouraged to express injustices in processes that educate them to become critical citizens with a wish to be politically engaged. To be critical means to learn how not to take anything for granted, but instead question the obvious and reveal what lies behind.

- Working in forms of discretionary learning: Wherever young people are involved, attention should be paid to how the work is organised. As work makes us who we are, the expectation of the quality of jobs should be raised. Just to get a job should not be seen as sufficient. The EU should fund projects which show how the potential of young people could be taken advantage of, enabling young people to learn and grow on the job. Such projects should then serve, and be highlighted, as sources of inspiration for the development of work organisations in general.
- Collective empowerment: Practices that aspire to become innovative, should open up opportunities for young people from different parts of a neighbourhood, city and even across Europe to get to know each other and about each other's situations as well as to work together. Young people should be empowered to deal collectively with the problems of inequality, in line with the idea of collective empowerment, based on the notion of collective solidarity. That should be regarded as a concern for all of us and the future of societies.

10

CONCLUDING SUMMARY

The aim of this book is to explain the causes of inequality affecting young people. On the basis of these explanations, it also aims to propose what actors at the local level can do to combat the causes. In this concluding summary, I will wrap it all up. As each chapter ends with a concluding summary, I will keep this final one quite short and instead refer to the different chapters where there is more to read.

I have concluded in chapter 9 by proposing five criteria for transformative social innovations, moreover in line with the idea of a double societal transformation. By the latter, I mean practices of different kind, which contribute to civilise capitalism by restricting and counteracting its actual causes of inequality, and at the same time gradually transcend capitalism by combatting its potential causes of inequality.

Firstly, to become socially innovative in this sense, actors involved in these practices should see and approach young people as potentials. Secondly, the potentials regarding experiences and knowledge should be taken advantage of by involving young people in knowledge alliances to combat the causes of inequality. Many young people knows a lot about how society causes inequality and whose criticism it may be very well worth listening to (see also chapter 5.1.2). Thirdly, young people should learn to be critical, which requires educational initiatives to be designed for that purpose. Fourthly, work opportunities for young people should be organised in line with the principle of discretionary learning, which enables young people to learn on the job. Fifthly, young people should be strengthened collectively to deal with not only the symptoms but also the causes of inequality.

How do these five criteria make sure that causes are combatted? It depends on what we mean by a cause. In chapter 3, I have claimed that causes of inequality are inherent in structures and cultures as well as in society and how it works. Each one of us may cause inequality, but it matters if we do it intentionally or as actors reproducing a role in a social structure. In the latter case, causing inequality has more to do with how the social structures function. Such a cause can, thus, be called structural. That does not mean that our action is fully pre-determined. There is always discretion, by which I mean a scope for variations to deal with the changing 'art of the possible'. If we use that discretion to exacerbate inequality, it has more to do with us as actors. So it is also when collective actors like interest groups push for an inequality which lies in their interest. Such causes can be called actorial/agential, whether pursued by individuals or collectives. We can also cause inequality by reproducing a certain context of meaning. In chapter 3.3, I have shown how such causes, cultural as they can be called, can be inherent in, for example, norms, grading and outlook on people. Again, there is always a discretion to make a difference.

In such structural and cultural roles, we have all, more or less, contributed to a development of society in recent decades, which has turned it into a new condition of social inclusion (chapter 9). This explains why some people have become excluded, many of them being young people. The relationship between social inclusion of and social exclusion from society often coincides with segregation in the cities, which means that the winners and losers of inequality have become separated spatially. Concentrations have arisen in certain neighbourhoods of people who belong to the losing side of not only one but several forms of inequality. Common to these forms of inequality is that they constitute differences between a winning and a losing side, which violates the human rights of the latter. This is how I have defined inequality in chapter 2. On that basis, I have made a distinction between four forms of inequality due to health, resources, structures and cultures respectively.

The development of society into a condition of social inclusion has led to the emergence of new societal borders appearing in the cities. This should be seen as the most serious form of inequality. Most urgent to explain is, therefore, the causes of inequality which have emerged as society has become a new condition of social inclusion. I have highlighted two such types of causes. The first type has been called process-causes and with that I mean the causes that exclude. Such causes should first of all be seen as potentials, which have to be actualised to cause an effect (chapter 3). Then, actual causes emerge, depending on the specific context, which are different from the potential ones. I have defined five potential causes of inequality, which are inherent in the societal systems and therefore can be called systemic. These five are associated with capitalism and the capitalist type of state (chapter 4). I have shown the different actualisation of them during the first post-war decades in comparison with the period since around 1980 (chapter 5). They are also actualised differently across Europe, which I show with regard to growth models in chapter 6 and welfare regimes in chapter 7.

The second type of causes are the ones that set the conditions for getting included and for that reason, I have called them condition-causes (chapter 9). Three such types of condition-causes have been defined, related to the general types of inequality. If you cannot get included, it may depend on that you do not have, do and/or mean what is required. The three correspond to the losing sides of resource, structural and cultural inequality, respectively (chapter 2).

These condition-causes, I claim, lie within the discretion of actors across the whole of Europe to combat. The five criteria of transformative social innovation support exactly that (chapter 9). Firstly, by seeing the potentials of young people, regardless of whether they are, for example, poor, have a house or lack the necessary grades, actors may transcend the condition-causes of resource inequality and make it possible for people to be socially included on other conditions than the mainstream ones, at least for a while and in a certain context. Secondly, by involving young people in knowledge alliances and taking advantage of their experience and knowledge, actors may improve their own knowledge on the causes of inequality and thereby also their discretion. Thirdly, by learning to be critical, young people can strengthen their citizenship and become empowered to influence politicians to combat both the condition- and the process-causes of inequality. Fourthly, giving priority to work organisations characterised by discretionary learning combats both condition- and excluding causes of inequality. Fifthly, the causes of inequality will never be removed without a collective empowerment at the local level of young people, but also of others who think that society has to be transformed.

BIBLIOGRAPHY

Aglietta, Michel (1987). *A Theory of Capitalist Regulation: The US Experience*. London: Verso.
Amin, Ash, Cameron, Aangus & Hudson, Ray (2002). *Placing the Social Economy*. New York: Routledge.
Anderson, Perry (2009) *The New Old World*. United States: Verso.
Andersson, Roger, Bråmå, Åsa & Hogdal, Jan (2007). *Segregationens dynamik och planeringens möjligheter: en studie av bostadsmarknad och flyttningar i Malmöregionen*. Malmö: Malmö stad, Stadskontoret.
Andreotti, A., Mingione, E. & Polizzi, E. (2012). Local Welfare Systems: A Challenge for Social Cohesion. *Urban Studies*, 49(9), 1925–1940.
Appelqvist, Örjan (2012) The Continuing Crisis of the Euro –A Weak Link in the Global Financial System?. *Ensaios FEE*, 33(2), 333–362.
Arrighi, Giovanni (2007). *Adam Smith in Beijing: Lineages of the Twenty-first Century*. London: Verso.
Arthur, Christopher J. (2007). The concept of subsumption. Available at: http://www.the seis.com/synedrio/04_a_Arthur.pdf (accessed 25 February 2018).
Atkinson, Rob & Davoudi, Simin (2000). The Concept of Social Exclusion in the European Union: Context, Development and Possibilities. *Journal of Common Market Studies* 38(3), 427–448.
Becker, Joachim & Weissenbacher, Rudy (2012). Berlin Consensus and Disintegration. Monetary Regime and Uneven Development in the EU. Paper presented at the 18th Euromemo Workshop on Alternative Economic Policy.
Becker, Joachim & Jäger, Johannes (2011). European Integration in Crisis: the Centre-Periphery Divide. Paper presented at the 17th Euromemo Workshop on Alternative Economic Policy.
Becker, Joachim, Jäger, Johannes, Leubolt, Bernhard & Weissenbacher, Rudy (2010). Peripheral Financialization and Vulnerability to Crisis: A Regulationist Perspective. *Competition and Change*, 14(3–4), 225–247.
Bhaskar, Roy (1975). Feyerabend and Bachelard: Two Philosophies of Science. *New Left Review*, 94, 31–55.

Bibliography

Bhaskar, Roy (1989). *Reclaiming Reality. A Critical Introduction to Contemporary Philosophy.* London: Verso.

Blackburn, Robin (2011). Crisis 2.0. *New Left Review*, 72, 33–62.

Boyer, Robert (2000) Is a Finance-led Growth Regime a Viable Alternative to Fordism? A Preliminary Analysis. *Economy and Society* 29(1), 111–145

Brante, Thomas (1997). Kausal realism och sociologi. *Sociologisk forskning* 34(1–2), 311–335.

Brante, Thomas (2014). *Den professionella logiken: hur vetenskap och praktik förenas i det moderna kunskapssamhället.* Stockholm: Liber.

Brante, Thomas (2015). Från teoretisk filosofi till empirisk kunskapssociologi. In G. Andersson et al. (ed.), *Det personliga är sociologiskt: 14 professorer om svensk sociologi.* Stockholm: Liber.

Byrne, David (2005). *Social Exclusion.* Glasgow: Open University Press.

Callinicos, Alex (2010). *Bonfire of Illusions: The Twin Crises of the Liberal World.* Cambridge: Polity.

Cassiers, Tim & Kesteloot, Christian (2012). Socio-spatial Inequalities and Social Cohesion in European Cities. *Urban Studies*, 49(9) 1909–1924.

Cassinari, D., Hillier, Jean, Miciukiewicz, Konrad, Novy, Andreas, Habersack, Sarah, MacCallum, Diana & Moulaert, Frank (2011). *Transdisciplinary Research in Social Polis.* Available at: http://www.socialpolis.eu/the-social-polisapproach/transdisciplinarity/ (accessed 8 July 2017)

Colletti, Lucio (1998 (1978)). Value and Dialectics in Marx. *Int. Journal of Political Economy*, 28(3), 74–83.

Daly, Mary (2001). Globalization and the Bismarckian Welfare States. In R. Sykes, B. Palier & P.M. Prior (ed.): *Globalization and European Welfare States.* New York: Palgrave.

Danermark, Berth (2002). *Explaining Society: Critical Realism in the Social Sciences.* London: Routledge

Ehrenberg, Johan & Ljunggren, Sten (2011). *Ekonomihandboken: [en bok om ekonomi, politik, vinst, lön, lögn och myt : ett försök att bryta maktlöshetssjukan].* 3, uppdaterade och utök. uppl. Stockholm: ETC förlag

Eizaguirre, S., Pradel, M., Terrones, A., Martinez-Celorrio, X. & García, M. (2012). Multilevel Governance and Social Cohesion: Bringing Back Conflict in Citizenship Practices. *Urban Studies*, 49(9), 1999–2016.

Eklund, Klas (2005). *Vår ekonomi. En introduktion till samhällsekonomin.* Stockholm: Norstedts Akademiska Förlag.

Elson, Diane (1979). The Value theory of Labour. In Diane Elson (ed.): *Value: The Representation of Labour in Capitalism.* London: CSE Books.

Esping-Andersen, Gösta (1990). *The Three Worlds of Welfare Capitalism.* Cambridge: Polity Press.

Esping-Andersen, Gösta (1999). *Social Foundations of Postindustrial Economies.* Oxford: Oxford University Press.

Eurofound (2012). *NEETs – Young people not in employment, education or training: Characteristics, costs and policy responses in Europe.* Luxembourg: Publications Office of the European Union.

Eurofound (2015), *Social inclusion of young people.* Luxembourg: Publications Office of the European Union.

EuroMemorandum (2015). *What future for the European Union – Stagnation and polarisation or new foundations?*

European Commission (2002). *Joint report on social inclusion 2002.* European Commission (Employment and social affairs). Brussels.

European Commission (2005). *Joint report on social inclusion 2004*. European Commission (Employment and social affairs). Brussels.
European Commission (2008). *Industrial relations in Europe 2008*. European Commission (Employment and social affairs). Brussels.
European Commission (2010a). *Europe 2020 – A strategy for smart, sustainable and inclusive growth*. European Commission. Brussels.
European Commission (2010b). *Fifth Report on Economic, Social and Territorial Cohesion*. European Commission (Directorate-General Regional and Urban Policy). Brussels.
European Commission (2010c). *The Social Situation in the European Union 2009*. European Commission (Employment and social affairs). Brussels.
European Commission (2012a). *EU Youth Report*. European Commission. Brussels.
European Commission (2012b). *Employment and Social Developments in Europe*. Luxembourg: Publications Office of the European Union
European Commission (2013a). *Industrial relations in Europe 2012*. European Commission (Employment and social affairs). Brussels.
European Commission (2013b) *EU Youth Report 2012*. European Commission. Brussels.
European Commission (2014). *Employment and Social Developments in Europe 2013*. Belgium: European Union.
European Commission (2016a). *EU Youth Report 2015*. Luxembourg: Publications Office of the European Union.
European Commission (2016b). *Employment and social developments in Europe 2015*. Luxembourg: Publications Office of the European Union
Evans, Trevor (2009). Money and Finance Today. In: J. Grahl (ed.): *Global Finance and Social Europe*. Cheltenham, UK: Edward Elgar.
Fairclough, Norman (2000). *New Labour, New Language?*. London: Routledge
Fairclough, Norman (2003). *Analysing Discourse: Textual Analysis for Social Research*. New York: Routledge.
Fairclough, Norman, Jessop, Bob & Sayer, Andrew (2002) Critical Realism and Semiosis. *Journal of Critical Realism*, 5(1), 2–10.
Ferge, Zsuzsa (2001). Welfare and 'Ill-Fare' Systems in Central-Eastern Europe. In: R. Sykes, B. Palier & P.M. Prior (ed.): *Globalization and European Welfare States*. New York: Palgrave.
Field, John (2008). *Social Capital*. New York: Routledge.
Fine, Ben (2001) *Social Capital Versus Social Theory: Political Economy and Social Science at the Turn of the Millennium*. London: Routledge.
Fine, Ben (2007) Eleven Hypotheses on the Conceptual History of Social Capital: A Response to James Farr. *Political Theory*, 35(1), 47–53.
Fine, Ben (2011). *Financialisation on the Rebound?* Available at: http://eprints.soas.ac.uk/12102/ (accessed 8 July 2017).
Foster, John Bellamy & Magdoff, Fred (2009). *The Great Financial Crisis: Causes and Consequences*. New York: Monthly Review Press.
Foster, John Bellamy & Yates, Michael D. (2014). Piketty and the crisis of neoclassical economics. *Monthly Review*, November 2014.
Fraisse, Laurent (2010). *Local Initiatives and Neighbourhood Development*. (Survey paper 11 from Social Polis). Available at: http://www.socialpolis.eu/fields-themes/neighbourhood-development-and-grassroots-initiatives/ (accessed 8 July 2017).
Furlong, Andy & Cartmel, Fred (2007). *Young people and social change: new perspectives*. 2. ed. Buckingham: Open University Press
Gamble, Andrew (1988). *The Free Economy and the Strong State. The Politics of Thatcherism*. Southampton: Macmillan Education Ltd.

Gamble, Andrew (2016). *Can the Welfare State Survive?* Cambridge: Polity Press
Giddens, Anthony (1984). *The Constitution of Society. Outline of the Theory of Structuration.* Cambridge: Polity Press.
Goss, Sue (1988). *Local Labour and Local Government. A Study of Changing Interests, Politics and Policy in Southwark, 1919 to 1982.* Edinburgh: Edinburgh University Press.
Gowan, Peter (2009). Crisis in the Heartland: Consequences of the New Wall Street System. *New Left Review,* 55, 5–29.
Graham, Stephen (2011). *Cities under siege: the new military urbanism.* Pbk. ed. London: Verso
Gramsci, Antonio (1971). *Selections from Prison Notebooks.* London: Lawrence and Wishart.
Guillén, Ana M. & Álvarez, Santiago (2001). Globalization and the Southern Welfare States. In: R. Sykes, B. Palier & P.M. Prior (ed.): *Globalization and European* Welfare *States.* New York: Palgrave.
Gustavsson, Bernt (2002). *Vad är kunskap? En diskussion om praktisk och teoretisk kunskap.* Kalmar: Skolverket.
Guttmann, Robert (2008). A Primer on Finance-Led Capitalism and Its Crisis. *Revue de la régulation,* 3/4. Available at URL : http://regulation.revues.org/5843 (accessed 25 February 2018)
Hall, Stuart (1988). *The Hard Road to Renewal. Thatcherism and the Crisis of the Left.* London: Verso.
Hall, Stuart (2011). The Neoliberal Revolution. *Cultural Studies,* 25(6). 705–728.
Halpern, David (2005). *Social Capital.* Cambridge: Polity.
Harvey, David (1992(1989)) *The Condition of Postmodernity.* Cambridge, MA: Blackwell.
Harvey, David (2005). *A Brief History of Neoliberalism.* Oxford: Oxford University Press.
Harvey, David (2008). The Right to the City. *New Left Review,* 53, 23–40.
Harvey, David (2010). *The Enigma of Capital: and the Crises of Capitalism.* London: Profile Books.
Harvey, David (2012) *Rebel Cities. From the Right to the City to the Urban Revolution.* New York: Verso.
Healy, Kieran (1998). Conceptualising Constraint – Mouzelis, Archer and the Concept of Social Structure. *Sociology,* 3, 509–522.
Hemerijck, Anton (2012). Two or Three Waves of Welfare State Transformation? In: Nathalie Morel, Bruno Palier, & Joakim Palme (ed.): *Towards a Social Investment Welfare State?: Ideas, Policies and Challenges.* Bristol: Policy.
Hermant-de-Callataÿ, Corinne & Svanfeldt, Christian (2011). *Cities of Tomorrow. Challenges, Visions, Ways Forward.* Luxembourg: European Commission – Directorate General for Regional Policy.
Housing Europe (2015). *The state of housing in the EU 2015.* Brussels(Housing Europe, the European Federation for Public, Cooperative and Social Housing).
Ingelstam, Lars (2006). *Ekonomi på plats.* Linköping: Centrum för kommunstrategiska studier, Linköpings universitet.
Jackson, Tim (2009). *Prosperity without growth? The transition to a sustainable economy.* Available at: http://www.sd-commission.org.uk/publications.php?id=914 (accessed 8 July 2017).
Jenson, Jane (2012). Redesigning Citizenship Regimes after Neoliberalism: Moving Towards Social Investment. In: Nathalie Morel, Bruno Palier, Joakim Palme (ed.) *Towards a Social Investment Welfare State?: Ideas, Policies and Challenges.* Bristol: Policy.
Jessop, Bob (1990). *State Theory. Putting Capitalist States in their Place.* Cambridge: Polity Press.
Jessop, Bob (2002). *The Future of the Capitalist State.* Cambridge: Polity Press.
Jessop, Bob (2003). From Thatcherism to New Labour: Neo-Liberalism, Workfarism, and Labour Market Regulation. Department of Sociology, Lancaster University. Available at:

http://www.lancaster.ac.uk/fass/resources/sociology-online-papers/papers/jessop-from-t hatcherism-to-new-labour.pdf (accessed 8 July 2017).

Jessop, Bob (2004). Critical Semiotic Analysis and Cultural Political Economy. *Critical Discourse Studies* 1(2), 159–174.

Jessop, Bob (2005). Critical Realism and the Strategic-Relational Approach. *New Formations*, 56, 40–53 .

Jessop, Bob (2006). Spatial Fixes, Temporal Fixes, and Spatio-temporal Fixes. In: N. Castree, & D. Gregory (ed.): *David Harvey: a Critical Reader*. Oxford: Blackwell, 142–166.

Jessop, Bob (2007). *State Power: A Strategic–Relational Approach*. Cambridge: Polity Press.

Jessop, Bob (2008). Promoting Good Governance, Disguising Governance Failure: Reflections on Policy Paradigms and Policy Narratives in the Field of Governance. *Public Governance* 1(2), 5–25.

Jessop, Bob (2009a). Contingent Necessity in Critical Political Economy Theorization. In: Eva Hartmann, Caren Kunze, & Ulrich Brand (ed.): *Globalisierung, Macht und Hegemonie*. Münster: Westfälisches Dampfboot.

Jessop, Bob (2009b). Cultural Political Economy and Critical Policy Studies. *Critical Policy Studies* 3(3), 336–356.

Jessop, Bob (2011). *Poulantzas's State, Power, Socialism as a Modern Classic*. Available at: https://bobjessop.org/2014/03/27/poulantzass-state-power-socialism-as-a-modern-classic/ (accessed 8 July 2017).

Jessop, Bob (2013a). Recovered Imaginaries, Imagined Recoveries: A Cultural Political Economy of Crisis Construals and Crisis-Management in the North Atlantic Financial Crisis. In: M. Benner (ed.): *Beyond the Global Economic Crisis: Economics and Politics for a Post-Crisis Settlement*. Cheltenham: Edward Elgar.

Jessop, Bob (2012a). Marxist Approaches to Power. In: E. Amenta, K. Nash & A. Scott (ed.): *The Wiley-Blackwell Companion to Political Sociology*. Oxford: Blackwell.

Jessop, Bob (2012b). Neoliberalism. In: George Ritzer (ed.): *The Wiley-Blackwell Encyclopedia of Globalization*. Chichester, West Sussex: Wiley Blackwell.

Jessop, Bob (2012c). Rethinking the Diversity of Capitalism: Varieties of Capitalism, Variegated Capitalism, and the World Market. In: G. Wood & C. Lane (ed.): *Capitalist Diversity and Diversity within Capitalism*. London: Routledge.

Jessop, Bob (2013c). The North Atlantic Financial Crisis and Varieties of Capitalism: A Minsky Moment and/or a Marx Moment? And Perhaps Weber too? In: S. Fadda & P. Tridico (ed.): *Financial Crisis, Labour Markets and Institutions*. London: Routledge.

Jessop, Bob (2013b). Revisiting the Regulation Approach: Critical Reflections on the Contradictions, Dilemmas, Fixes and Crisis Dynamics of Growth Regimes. *Capital & Class*, 37(1), 5–24.

Jessop (2015a). The Symptomatology of Crises, Reading Crises and Learning from Them: Some Critical Realist Reflections. *Journal of Critical Realism*, 14(3), 238–271.

Jessop, Bob (2015b). *The State: Past, Present, Future*. Cambridge: Polity Press

Jessop, Bob & Sum, Ngai-Ling (2006). *Beyond the Regulation Approach. Putting Capitalist Economies in their Place*. Norfolk: Edward Elgar.

Jessop, Bob, Brenner, Neil & Jones, Martin (2008) Theorizing Sociospatial Relations. Environment and Planning D. *Society and Space* , 26, 389–401.

Jones, Owen (2012). *Chavs: The Demonization of the Working Class*. Updated ed. London: Verso

Joseph, Miranda. (2014). *Debt to Society: Accounting for Life Under Capitalism*. Minneapolis: University of Minnesota Press.

Karlsson, Jan Ch. (2013). *Begreppet arbete: definitioner, ideologier och sociala former*. 2., översedda uppl. Lund: Arkiv.

Laclau, Ernesto & Mouffe, Chantal (1985). *Hegemony & Socialist Strategy. Towards a radical democratic politics*. London: Verso.
Lapavitsas, Costas (2013). *Profiting without Producing: How Finance Exploits Us All*. London: Verso.
Lapavitsas, Costas et al. (2012). *Crisis in the Eurozone*. London: Verso.
Levitas, Ruth (2005). *The Inclusive Society?: Social Exclusion and New Labour*. Basingstoke: Macmillan.
Liedman, Sven-Eric (1998). *I skuggan av framtiden. Modernitetens idéhistoria*. Stockholm: Bonnier Alba.
Liedman, Sven-Eric (1999). *Att se sig själv i andra. Om solidaritet*. Stockholm: Bonnier.
Liedman, Sven-Eric (2001). *Ett oändligt äventyr. Om människans kunskaper*. Stockholm: Albert Bonniers förlag.
Liedman, Sven-Eric (2006). *Stenarna i själen. Form och materia från antiken till i dag*. Stockholm: Albert Bonniers förlag.
Liedman, Sven-Eric (2011). *Hets! En bok om skolan*. Stockholm: Albert Bonniers förlag.
Liedman, Sven-Eric (2015) *Karl Marx: en biografi* . Stockholm: Albert Bonniers förlag
Lockwood, David (1992). *Solidarity and Schism: 'The Problem of Disorder' in Durkheimian and Marxist Sociology*. Oxford: Clarendon Press.
Lundvall, Bengt-Åke & Lorenz, Edward (2012). Social Investment in the Globalising Learning Economy: A European Perspective. In: Nathalie Morel, Bruno Palier, & Joakim Palme (ed.): *Towards a Social Investment Welfare State?: Ideas, Policies and Challenges*. Bristol: Policy.
Madanipour, Ali & Cars, Göran & Allen, Judith (2003). *Social Exclusion in European Cities*. London: Routledge.
Marmot, Michael (2015). *The Health Gap: The Challenge of an Unequal World*. London: Bloomsbury.
Martinelli, Flavia, Moulaert, Frank & Novy, Andreas (eds.) (2012). *Urban and Regional Development Trajectories in Contemporary Capitalism*. London: Routledge.
Marx, Karl (1986). Outline of the Critique of Political Economy. In: Karl Marx & Friedrich Engels *Collected Works*. Volume 28. London: Lawrence & Wishart.
Marx, Karl (1996). *Capital, vol. 1 (Collected works)*. Vol. 35). London: Lawrence & Wishart
Marx, Karl (1998). *Capital, vol. III (Collected works)*. Vol. 37), *Karl Marx: Capital, Vol. III*. London: Lawrence & Wishart
Marx, Karl & Engels, Friedrich (1979). *Collected works*. Vol. 11, *Marx and Engels: 1851–53*. London: Lawrence & Wishart.
Massey, Doreen (1984). *Spatial Divisions of Labour. Social Structures and the Geography of Production*. London: Macmillan
Massey, Doreen (2007). *World City*. Cambridge: Polity Press.
Miciukiewicz, Konrad, Moulaert, Frank, Novy, Andreas, Musterd, Sako & Hillier, Jean (2012). Introduction: Problematising Urban Social Cohesion: A Transdisciplinary Endeavour. *Urban Studies*, 49(9), 1855–1872
Mills, C.Wright (2000 [1959]). *The Sociological Imagination*. Oxford:Oxford University Press.
Morel, Nathalie, Palier, Bruno & Palme, Joakim (eds.) (2012). *Towards a Social Investment Welfare State?: Ideas, Policies and Challenges*. Bristol: Policy.
Moulaert, Frank, Jessop, Bob & Mehmood, Abid (2016) Agency, Structure, Institutions, Discourse (ASID) in Urban and Regional Development. *International Journal of Urban Sciences*, 20(2), 167–187.
Navarro, Vicente (2016). Is The Nation-State And Its Welfare State Dead? A Critique Of Varoufakis. *Social Europe*4 August.
Novy, Andreas (2011). Unequal Diversity – On the Political Economy of Social Cohesion in Vienna. *European Urban and Regional Studies*, 18(3), 239–253.

Novy, Andreas (2017). Emancipatory Economic Deglobalisation: A Polanyian Perspective. *Brazilian Journal of Urban and Regional Studies*, 19(3), 558–579.
Novy, Andreas, Coimbra Swiatek, Daniela & Moulaert, Frank (2012). Social Cohesion: A Conceptual and Political Elucidation. *Urban Studies*, 49(9), 1873–1889.
Novy, A., Habersack, S. & Schaller, B. (2013). Innovative Forms of Knowledge Production: Transdisciplinarity and Knowledge Alliances. In: F. Moulaert et al. (ed.): *The International Handbook on Social Innovation. Collective Action, Social Learning and Transdisciplinary Research*. Cheltenham: Edward Elgar.
OECD (2011). *Divided we stand – why inequality keeps rising*. OECD: OECD Publishing.
Olofsson, Gunnar (1979). *Mellan klass och stat. Om arbetarrörelse, reformism och socialdemokrati*. Lund: Arkiv.
Pettifor, Ann (2017). *The Production of Money: How to Break the Power of Bankers*. London: Verso.
Pijl, Kees van der (1984). *The Making of an Atlantic Ruling Class*. London: Verso
Piketty, Thomas (2014). *Capital in the twenty-first century*. Cambridge, Mass.: Belknap Press of Harvard University Press.
Polanyi, Karl (2001[1944]). *The Great Transformation. The Political and Economic Origins of Our Times*. Boston: Beacon Press.
Porte, Caroline de la & Jacobsson, Kerstin (2012). Social Investment or Recommodification? Assessing the Employment Policies of the EU Member States. In: Nathalie Morel, Bruno Palier & Joakim Palme (ed.): *Towards a Social Investment Welfare State?: Ideas, Policies and Challenges*. Bristol: Policy.
Poulantzas, Nicos (1978). *Political Power and Social Classes*. London: Verso
Poulantzas, Nicos (1980). *State, Power, Socialism*. London: Verso.
Power, Michael (2004). Counting, Control and Calculation: Reflections on Measuring and Management. *Human Relations*, 57(6), 765–783.
Pratschke, Jonathan & Morlicchio, Enrica (2012). Social Polarisation, the Labour Market and Economic Restructuring in Europe: An Urban Perspective. *Urban Studies*, 49(9), 1891–1907.
Pratten, Stephen (2009). Critical Realism and Causality: Tracing the Aristotelian Legacy. *Journal for the Theory of Social Behaviour* 39(2), 189–218.
Robotham, Don (2005). *Culture, Society and Economy: Bringing Production Back In*. London: SAGE
Ryner, Magnus (2013). Klasskampen och den fallande löneandelen. In: Erik Bengtsson & Ingemar Lindberg (ed.): *Den sänkta löneandelen: orsaker, konsekvenser och handlingsalternativ*. Stockholm: Premiss.
Sayer, Andrew (1992). *Method in Social Science. A Realist Approach*. Worcester: Routledge
Sayer, Andrew (2000). *Realism and Social Science*. London: SAGE.
Sayer, Andrew (2015). *Why We Can't Afford the Rich*. Bristol: Policy Press
SCB (2003). *Tid för vardagsliv*. Rapport 99.
SCB (2012). *Nu för tiden – en undersökning om svenska folkets tidsanvändning år 2010–2011*. Rapport 123.
Sen, Amartya (2013[1999]). *Development as Freedom*. Oxford: Oxford University Press.
Sennett, Richard (2007). *Den nya kapitalismens kultur*. Finland: Atlas
Skolverket (2011) *Curriculum for the Compulsory School, Preschool Class and the Recreation Centre*: https://www.skolverket.se/om-skolverket/publikationer/visa-enskild-publikation?_xurl_=http%3A%2F%2Fwww5.skolverket.se%2Fwtpub%2Fws%2Fskolbok%2Fwpubext%2Ftrycksak%2FRecord%3Fk%3D2687
Smith, Adam (2008 [1776]). *Wealth of Nations*. Oxford: Oxford University Press.
Smith, Richard (2010). Beyond Growth or Beyond Capitalism? *Real-world Economics Review*, 53, 28–42.

Social Mobility Commission (2017). *Social mobility policies between 1997 and 2017: time for change*. https://www.gov.uk/government/organisations/social-mobility-commission
Standing, Guy (2011). *The Precariat: The New Dangerous Class*. London: Bloomsbury Academic.
Stenfors, A., Clark, E., Farahani, I., Hansen, A.L., Passarella, M. (2014) The Swedish Financial System, *FESSUD Studies in Financial Systems* No 13 (October 2014).
Stigendal, Mikael (2006). *Young People – from Exclusion to Inclusion. Revitalising European Cities*. Available at: www.mikaelstigendal.se (accessed 25 February 2018).
Stigendal, Mikael (2010a). *Cities and Social Cohesion. Popularizing the Results of Social Polis*. MAPIUS6/Malmö högskolas publikationer i urbana studier. Malmö. Available at: www.mikaelstigendal.se (accessed 25 February 2018).
Stigendal, Mikael (2010b). *Kapital*. Stockholm: Liber.
Stigendal, Mikael (2014a). The Future of Capitalism Will Be Decided in the Cities. In: Włodzimierz Dymarski, Marica Frangakis & Jeremy Leaman: *The Deepening Crisis of the European Union: The Case for Radical Change*. Poznan: Poznan University of Economics Press.
Stigendal, Mikael (2016). *Samhällsgränser: ojämlikhetens orsaker och framtidsmöjligheterna i en storstad som Malmö*. Stockholm: Liber
Stigendal, Mikael & Östergren, P.-O. (2013). *Malmo's Path Towards a Sustainable Future*. Malmö: Malmö Stad.
Stiglitz, J., A. Sen, & J.-P. Fitoussi (2009). *Report by the Commission on the Measurement of Economic Performance and Social Progress*. Available at: https://en.wikipedia.org/wiki/Commission_on_the_Measurement_of_Economic_Performance_and_Social_Progress (accessed 25 February 2018)
Stockhammer, Engelbert (2013). Why have wage shares fallen? A panel analysis of the determinants of functional income distribution. *The International Labour Organisation (ILO) project "New Perspectives on Wages and Economic Growth"*. Geneva: ILO.
Streeck, Wolfgang (2011). The Crises of Democratic Capitalism. *New Left Review*, 71, 5–29.
Streeck, Wolfgang (2013). *Köpt tid: den demokratiska kapitalismens uppskjutna kris*. Göteborg: Daidalos.
Streeck, Wolfgang (2016). *How Will Capitalism End?*. London: Verso
Sum, Ngai-Ling & Jessop, Bob (2013). *Towards a Cultural Political Economy: Putting Culture in its Place in Political Economy*. Cheltenham: Edward Elgar.
Svensson, Lennart, Ellström, Per-Erik & Brulin, Göran (2007). Introduction – On Interactive Research. *International Journal of Action Research*, 3(3), 233–249.
Therborn, Göran (1981). *Klasstrukturen i Sverige 1930–1980*. Lund: Zenit.
Therborn, Göran (1983). Which Class Wins. *New Left Review*, 138, 37–55.
Therborn, Göran (2006). Meaning, Mechanisms, Patterns, and Forces: An Introduction. In: Göran Therborn (ed.): *Inequalities of the World: [New Theoretical Frameworks, Multiple Empirical Approaches]*. London: Verso.
Therborn, Göran (2011). *The World: A Beginner's Guide*. Cambridge: Polity Press.
Therborn, Göran (2013). *The Killing Fields of Inequality*. Cambridge: Polity Press.
Tridico, Pasquale (2013). *Italy: From Economic Decline to the Current Crisis. A Comparison with France and Germany*. Available at: http://www.euromemo.eu/annual_workshops/2013_london/london_workshops_papers/index.html (accessed 25 February 2018).
Turner, Graham (2008). *The Credit Crunch: Housing Bubbles, Globalisation and the Worldwide Economic Crisis*. London: Pluto Press in association with GFC Economics.
Wacquant, Loïc (2008). *Urban Outcasts. A Comparative Sociology of Advanced Marginality*. Cambridge: Polity Press.

Wilkinson, Richard & Pickett, Kate (2009). *The Spirit Level: Why More Equal Societies Almost Always Do Better*. London: Allen Lane.
Wood, Tony (2010). Good Riddance to New Labour. *New Left Review*, 62, 5–28.
World Health Organization (2008). *Closing the gap in a generation: health equity through action on the social determinants of health. Final report of the Commission on Social Determinants of Health*. Geneva: World Health Organization.
Wright, Erik Olin (2009). Understanding Class. Towards an Integrated Analytical Approach. *New Left Review*, 60, 101–116.

Citispyce (http://www.citispyce.eu/)

Athens

Avatangelou, G., Papadimitriou, P. & Pothoulaki, M. (2013). *Athens*. Report from the EU project Citispyce, funded by the Seventh Framework Programme.
Tryfona, Stella, Pothoulaki, Maria & Papadimitriou, Pyrros (2014a). *WP3 Report on "Fieldwork I" in Athens*
Tryfona, Stella, Pothoulaki, Maria & Papadimitriou, Pyrros (2014b) *WP4 Report on "Fieldwork II" in Athens*

Barcelona

Roiha, M., Jubany, O. & Güell, B. (2013). *Barcelona*. Report from the EU project Citispyce, funded by the Seventh Framework Programme.
Jubany, Olga & Güell, Berta (2014a). *WP3 Report on "Fieldwork I" in Barcelona*
Jubany, Olga, Güell, Berta & Arasanz, Juan (2014b). *WP4 Report on "Fieldwork II" in Barcelona*
Jubany, Olga & Güell, Berta (2015a). *WP7 Case Study: Innovative Practice 'Educational Demos'*
Jubany, Olga, Güell, Berta & Martínez, Arlette (2015b). *WP7 Case Study: Innovative Practice 'Forn de Teatre Pa'Tothom'*

Birmingham

Robinson, J., Hussain, A., Bains, S. & Higson, H. (2013). *Birmingham*. Report from the EU project Citispyce, funded by the Seventh Framework Programme.
Hussain, Ajmal, Higson, Helen, Robinson, Jill, Browne, Richard & Bains, Suwinder (2014a) *WP3 Report on "Fieldwork I" in Birmingham*
Hussain, Ajmal, Higson, Helen, Yasmin, Samia & Burke, Carey (2014b) *WP4 Report on "Fieldwork II" in Birmingham*
Robinson, Jill & Commane, Gemma (2015). *WP7 Case Study: Innovative Practice 'Beatfreeks'*

Brno

Sirovatka, T. & Valkova, J. (2013). *Brno*. Report from the EU project Citispyce, funded by the Seventh Framework Programme.
Sirovátka, Tomáš, Krchnava, Anna & Hora, Ondřej & Válková, Jana (2014). *WP3 Report on "Fieldwork I" in Brno*
Sirovátka, Tomáš, Válková, Jana & Hora, Ondřej (2015). *WP7 Case study: Innovative Practice 'Learning by Working'*

Hamburg

Gehrke, A.-M., Güntner, S. & Seukwa, L.H. (2013). *Hamburg*. Report from the EU project Citispyce, funded by the Seventh Framework Programme.
Gehrke, Anne-Marie, Güntner, Simon & Seukwa, Louis Henri (2014a). *WP3 Report on "Fieldwork I" in Hamburg*
Gehrke, Anne-Marie, Seukwa, Louis Henri & Güntner, Simon (2014b) *WP4 Report on "Fieldwork II" in Hamburg*
Gehrke, Anne-Marie, Seukwa, Louis Henri & Güntner, Simon (2014c). *Citispyce comparative WP3 report on "Fieldwork I"*

Krakow

Chrabąszcz, R., Frączek, M., Geodecki, T., Grodzicki, M., Kopyciński, P., Mazur, S. & Możdżeń, M. (2013). *Krakow*. Report from the EU project Citispyce, funded by the Seventh Framework Programme.
Chrabaszcz, Robert, Fraczek, Maciej, Geodecki, Tomasz, Grodzicki, Maciej, Kopycinski, Piotr, Mazur, Stanislaw & Mozdzen, Michal (2014) *Citispyce WP3 Report on Fieldwork I in Krakow*
Chrabaszcz, Robert, Fraczek, Maciej, Geodecki, Tomasz, Grodzicki, Maciej, Kopycinski, Piotr, Mazur, Stanislaw & Mozdzen, Michal (2015). *WP7 Case Study: Innovative Practice 'Free remedial tutoring for young people with learning deficits'*

Malmö

Grander, Martin (2013). *Malmö*. Report from the EU project Citispyce, funded by the Seventh Framework Programme.
Stigendal, Mikael (2013). *Citispyce comparative WP2 report*
Grander, Martin & Stigendal, Mikael (2014). *Citispyce WP3 Report on "Fieldwork I" in Malmö*
Grander, Martin & Alwall, Jonas (2014). *WP4 Report on "Fieldwork II" in Malmö*
Grander, Martin (2015). *WP7 Case Study: Innovative Practice 'Multisectoral cooperation for social sustainability'*
Alwall, Jonas & Hellberg Lannerheim, Pia (2015). *WP7 Case study: Innovative Practice 'Brightful'*

Rotterdam

Spies, H. & Tan, S. (2013). *Rotterdam*. Report from the EU project Citispyce, funded by the Seventh Framework Programme.
Tan, Suzanne & Spies, Henk (2014a). *WP3 Report on "Fieldwork I" in Rotterdam*
Tan, Suzanne & Spies, Henk (2014b). *WP4 Report on "Fieldwork II" in Rotterdam*
Davelaar, Maarten, Tan, Suzanne & Spies, Henk (2015a). *WP7 Case study: Innovative Practice 'Buzinezzclub Rotterdam'*
Davelaar, Maarten, Tan, Suzanne & Spies, Henk (2015b). *WP7 Case Study: Innovative Practice 'Challenge Sports'*

Sofia

Hajdinjak, M. & Kosseva, M. (2013). *Sofia*. Report from the EU project Citispyce, funded by the Seventh Framework Programme.
Hajdinjak, Marko, Kosseva, Maya & Zhelyazkova, Antonina (2014). *Citispyce WP3 Report on "Fieldwork I" in Sofia*

Hajdinjak, Marko (2014). *Citispyce WP4 Report on "Fieldwork II" in Sofia (Young people in Fakulteta and Hristo Botev – can innovative social practices overcome inequalities and exclusion?)*

Hajdinjak, Marko & Kosseva, Maya (2015). *WP7 Case Study: Innovative Practice 'The Health and Social Centre'*

Venice

Campomori, F., Della Puppa, F. & Ferrari, M. (2013). *Venice*. Report from the EU project Citispyce, funded by the Seventh Framework Programme.

Campomori, Francesca, Della Puppa, Francesco, Pinocchio, Irma & Baccelliere, Giannina (2014). *WP3 Report on "Fieldwork I" in Venice*

Della Puppa, Francesco & Campomori, Francesca (2014) *WP4 Report on "Fieldwork II" in Venice*

INDEX

abstraction 3, 31–34, 147
accumulation by dispossession 53, 62, 88–90, 97, 121–122
action research 8
active labour market policies 91, 94, 106, 128
actors and agency (collective and individual) 5, 42
actualisation 37, 41, 46, 147
Aglietta, M. 5, 64–66
approach: potential-oriented 1, 6, 145, 154–162; problem-oriented 1, 154
Arena 305 112, 142
Aristotle 17, 39–40

Becker, G. 40, 77
Bentham, J. 76
Bhaskar, R. 4, 41
Bourdieu, P. 77
Bulgaria 14–15, 91–92, 104–106, 108

capability approach 13
capital: commodity 52; defined as a social relation 50, 78; defined as an asset 50, 78; definition 48; finance capital 52, 72; money capital 52; productive capital 52
capitalism 151
capitalist 48
Casal dels Infants 78, 81
causality, humean notion of 37, 38, 43
cause: actorial cause 46, 165: actual cause 38, 89, 94, 147; in the aristotelian sense 39; cultural cause 43, 46; definition 37; potential cause 33, 38, 46, 62, 147; structural cause 46, 165
cities (in the Citispyce project): Athens 20, 138; Birmingham 2, 42, 139; Hamburg 87, 100; Malmö 10, 111, 143, 147; Rotterdam 88, 139; Sofia 189; Venice 108
Citispyce 2
civil society 6, 79–81, 125–128, 143–145
class: marxian definition 30; weberian definition 29
Coleman, J. 77
collective agreements 69–71, 80, 96–98, 123, 127
commodification 67–68
commodity 21, 76: as capital 52, 67; contradiction 54; definition 17; housing as 20; labour power as 18
complexity reduction 5, 43
context of meaning (see also culture) 6, 43
contradiction: between increasing societalisation and concentration of power, 58; between use-value and exchange-value of the commodity 54, 67; dialectical, 54
creativity 8, 49, 150, 155
critical realism 3–13, 37: the real, the actual and the empirical 4, 36, 154, 161
Cultural Political Economy 4, 33, 45
culture 5, 43–49, 124, 139–141, 158
Czech Republic 91, 105–106, 108

decommodification 70, 99, 102, 124
discretion 5, 40, 42, 44, 46, 59, 136, 144, 152–154, 165
discretionary learning 3, 87–88, 94–98, 127, 159
Durkheim, E. 119, 150, 161

education 18, 107
Elson, D. 22
emergence 38, 46
empiricism 37, 43
empowerment (individual and collective) 65, 112, 157, 159–163
Esping-Andersen, G. 70
EU Youth Report 1, 32–33, 150
EU Youth Strategy 1, 150
Euro and the Eurozone 3, 37, 87

Facebook 67
financial crisis in 2008 48
financialisation 3, 84, 91–95, 150
football 38
Ford, H. 65
Fordism: as a growth model 68; as a mode of regulation 69, 83; as a regime of capital accumulation 68; as a work process 65
Friedman, M. 73, 77

Germany 87, 100, 102
Glokala Folkhögskolan 79
Goldman Sachs 48
grading 19, 44
Gramsci, A. 5, 65
Greece 37, 85, 106
growth 47
growth model 68, 82: finance-driven 52, 72–73, 84, 89, 92–93, 123, 151; Fordism 69, 70; sweat-shop 64

Harvey, D. 65
Hayek, F. 73
hermeneutics 43
housing 20, 50, 105, 111
Hume, D. 37

Index of Multiple Deprivation 103
individualism 40, 60, 75, 125
industrial relations 83
inequality: as a word 13; cultural 20, 34, 62; definition 13; health 33, 54, 62; relational definition 6; resource 14, 20, 33, 51; structural 23, 26–28, 33–34, 62, 123, 127
institutions 58
integration, system and social 103

interactive research 8
Italy 85, 108

Jackson, T. 48
Jessop, B. 4–5, 41, 71–74, 93
Joint Report on Social Inclusion 118

Keynes, J. M. 66
Keynesian Welfare National State 71
knowledge: approach to 6, 61, 74; factual, interpretative, skilled and tacit 7
knowledge alliance 8, 156, 162

labour power 18, 48, 51–52, 54
labour theory of value 21
Laclau, E. 4
Levitas, R. 103, 122
Liedman, S-E. 4, 58
Lisbon Strategy 118
living conditions: exchange-value side 71, 82; use-value side 99
London 93

Malmö Commission 156
Marx, K. 21, 39, 119, 161
Massey, D. 133
means of production 53, 55, 89
mechanisms 23, 42, 91
Milanovic, B. 12
Mills, C. W. 4, 119
moments (internally related objects) 39, 122
money (what it is) 17
Mouffe, C. 4

National Curriculum 7, 72
Neighbourhoods (in the Citispyce project): Athens - Aghia Sophia 16, 140; Athens - Elefsina 16, 132; Athens - Piraeus 135, 140; Barcelona - El Raval 20; Barcelona - Trinitat Nova 131; Birmingham - Bordesley Green 42; Birmingham - Lozells & East Handsworth 129, 141; Brno - Cejl 137; Hamburg - Dulsberg 64; Krakow - Rzaka 32; Malmö - Sofielund 111, 130, 134, 139–140, 143; Rotterdam - Feyenord 140; Rotterdam - Middelland 131; Sofia - Fakulteta 15, 23, 128, 136, 138; Sofia - Hristo Botev 23; Venice - Marghera 68, 140, 141
neoclassical economics 4, 66, 76, 77
neoliberalism 2, 9, 73, 76, 80, 93, 113, 116, 122
New Public Management 74
normalisation of debt 90, 97

norms 44
Novy, A. 72

ontology 5
opportunity hoarding 29
outlook on people 45, 60–61, 77, 114, 119, 125, 157

Pettifor, A. 22
phenomenology 43
Piketty, T. 5, 12, 22, 50, 66
place 133
Poland 91
Polanyi, K. 70
policy, economic and social 71, 82
political economy 4
potential 5–6, 37
Poulantzas, N. 5, 58
power 17, 32, 40, 98
poverty 12–16, 105, 117–118, 123
Practices (in the Citispyce project):
   Barcelona-Educational Demos 154, 155, 157, 158; Barcelona-Forn de Teatre Pa'Tothom 117, 160; Birmingham-Beatfreeks 44, 159; Brno-Learning by working 44; Krakow-Free remedial tutoring 153; Malmö-Brightful 154; Malmö-Multisectoral cooperation 156; Rotterdam-Buzinezzclub 17, 74, 89, 90; Rotterdam-Challenge Sports 91; Sofia-Health and Social Centre 159
productive forces 30, 58
profit 21, 49
Putnam, R. 77

Reagan, R. 73
reference object 6, 13, 19, 36, 44, 74
referent object 6, 13, 19, 36, 44
regime of accumulation 68: dependent export-orientation and financialisation 91; dependent financialisation 84; export-orientation and financialisation 95; extensive and intensive 64; finance-dominated 84; fordist 84; superior export-orientation 87; superior financialisation 93
regulation theory 5, 66, 83
relations of production 30
retroduction 3
Ricardo, D. 4, 21
roles 39, 42, 126

Say, J-B. 66
Sayer, A. 151
scale 133, 135

Schumpeterian Workfare Post-national Regime 71
Schäuble, W. 42
segregation 129, 132
selectivity 41
semiosis 5, 43
Sen, A. 22
signified 13
signifier 13
Smith, A. 4, 21, 50
social capital 77
social economy 102, 111
social exclusion 103, 113, 116: background of term 100; condition definition 119; condition-causes of 121; definition 116; EU definition 117; moral underclass discourse (MUD) 103; process definition 117; process-causes of 121; redistributionist discourse (RED) 104, 118; system integrationist discourse (SID) 103, 118
social housing 101, 103, 106, 108
Social Impact Bond 90
social inclusion agenda 150
social innovation 149–150, 153
social structure 39
societal borders 32, 124–128, 138
societal model: conservative 125; definition of 122; neoliberal 122, 144; social democratic 127, 143
Sofielunds Folkets Hus 79, 81, 145
solidarity 161
Spain 84, 108
spatio-temporal fixes 71
stagnation 66
Standing, G. 28
state 58
Stiglitz, J. 22, 50
strategic selectivity 41
structuration 5, 43
structure and agency 39
Sum, N-L. 4–5
surplus-value 51–57, 64
Sweden 95, 110
systemic causes of inequality: individualistic outlook on people 72, 101; intellectualising approach to knowledge 72, 101; the capitalist relation of exchange 69, 97; the capitalist relation of production 69, 94, 98; the tendency of the organic composition of capital to rise 69, 97–98

territory 133
Thatcher, M. 73

Thatcherism 102
the 'right to buy' policy 102
The Brewery 80
the do-nots 24, 34, 121
The Garage 112
the have-nots 14, 17, 33, 121, 124
the mean-nots 34, 121, 124
The Netherlands 101
the sociological vision 4
Therborn, G. 22, 30, 33
TPSN (Territory, Place, Scale and Network) 133

UK (United Kingdom) 93, 102
URBAN (EU programme) 143

value: exchange-value 17–20, 79–81; labour value 21–22; use-value 17–20, 79, 81
value theory of labour 22
variegated capitalism 82

wage relation 67, 69, 80, 83
Weber, M. 29
welfare regimes 70: conservative 71, 100; familial 106; liberal 71; social democratic 71, 112
welfare state: conservative 110; familial 106; four dimensions 71; Keynesian 70; social democratic 110
work 27, 95: domestic 27; informal (grey, black) 109; paid and unpaid 27
working class 64, 67, 69, 161